Acker-Hocevar, Cruz-Janzen and Wilson have produced a remarkable book after a sustained and comprehensive piece of research. They have found seven schools that can overcome the odds, the odds of having a student group that doesn't come from the right side of the tracks and an education system that is built on hierarchy and punishment. They have likened the success of each school to a tree, a Learning Partnership Tree (LPT), with a solid trunk of core values and a substantial root system of leadership, communication and involvement that branches into what they call their Systems Alignment Model (SAM). And like a tree, they found that each school was unique in terms of how it applies the various aspects of trunk, roots and foliage to develop into a fully functioning organic system. Some are Aspen, others are Oaks, but all in their own way are beautiful. However, what also needs to be said is that these trees have grown on barren ground. The study also found that these schools were able to achieve all of this in spite of, rather than because of, the state system of education in which they found themselves. We find schools that struggle to make ends meet, where teachers and principals can be moved overnight and where schools are punished if they don't meet a narrow range of standards, regardless of how many other skills and attitudes schools might help students attain. It leaves us with the question, how much better would these trees grow, if they found some fertile soil to support them?

—**Tony Townsend,** Professor
Chair of Public Service, Educational Leadership and Management
School of Education
University of Glasgow

This book will be received as a timely and significant piece of research. It represents a balanced discussion about the meaning of educational excellence within a framework of equity and fairness, and measurement and impact. In part, the study is a critique of a high stakes testing frenzy, which unfortunately has emerged as the dominant tool for evaluating public schools, and worse, the quality of education. The authors explain convincingly that other measurable factors, like respect for culture, support for parents, involving teachers in decision-making, and other features, must be part of the equation for success at schools with any history of traditionally low-academic performance.

—**Professor James Jennings**
Tufts University
Department of Urban and Environmental Policy and Planning
Professor Jennings has held visiting appointments at Northeastern University (1988), Massachusetts Institute of Technology (1992), and Yale University (1997).

Acker-Hocevar, Cruz-Janzen, and Wilson conclude that standards-based reform approaches may be necessary but they are not sufficient to promote student success. A more humanistic framework emerges in this book that reaffirms the value of principals', teachers', and parents' shared leadership and participation in a more context-driven, additive notion of school reform.

—**Marilyn J. Taylor,** Ed.D.
Associate Professor
Institute for Teacher Education and Department of Curriculum Studies
University of Hawaii at Manoa

This wonderful book reminds us that successful schools are complex, human organizations. They exist—and persist—in spite of many policies and in the face of many challenges. They exist—and persist—because committed administrators, teachers, and staff work with families and learners to ensure that everyone is well and respected and cared for and successful. Acker-Hocevar, Cruz-Janzen, and Wilson are to be commended for providing us with rich portraits of seven marvelous schools and for helping us understand how each became a great place to work and learn.

—**Lynn G. Beck**
Dean and Professor
Gladys L. Benerd School of Education
University of the Pacific

Leadership from the Ground Up

*Effective Schooling in Traditionally
Low Performing Schools*

A volume in
Issues in the Research, Theory, Policy, and Practice of Urban Education
Denise E. Armstrong and Brenda J. McMahon, *Series Editors*

Issues in the Research, Theory, Policy, and Practice of Urban Education

Denise E. Armstrong and Brenda J. McMahon
Series Editors

—————————————————

Leadership from the Ground Up

Effective Schooling in Traditionally Low Performing Schools

Michele A. Acker-Hocevar
Washington State University

Marta I. Cruz-Janzen
Florida Atlantic University

Cynthia L. Wilson
Florida Atlantic University

INFORMATION AGE PUBLISHING, INC.
Charlotte, NC • www.infoagepub.com

Library of Congress Cataloging-in-Publication Data

Acker-Hocevar, Michele, 1948-
 Leadership from the ground up : effective schooling in traditionally low performing schools / Michele A. Acker-Hocevar, Marta I. Cruz-Janzen, Cynthia L. Wilson.
     p. cm. – (Issues in the research, theory, policy, and practice of urban education)
 Includes bibliographical references.
 ISBN 978-1-61735-650-6 (pbk.) – ISBN 978-1-61735-651-3 (hardcover) – ISBN 978-1-61735-652-0 (ebook)
1. School improvement programs–United States–Case studies. 2. Educational leadership–United States–Case studies. 3. Children with social disabilities–Education–United States–Case studies. I. Cruz-Janzen, Marta. II. Wilson, Cynthia L. III. Title.
 LB2822.82.A27 2011
 371.2'07–dc23

                                                        2011038824

Printed in the United States of America

Dedication

We dedicate this book along with our heartfelt appreciation to our husbands, Fritz Hocevar, John Janzen, and Mel Wilson, for their patience and support. We thank our children Shawn Moffitt; Kevin and Shawn Hocevar; Bryn Black; Eva Hodgens; Ashley Brooks; Amber, Andrew, and Austin Wilson; and our grandchildren Evan and Ryan Moffitt; Elsa and Jonas Hocevar; and Jude and Zack Hodgens, who have graciously sacrificed time they could have had with us had we not been working on this project. We are each grateful to our families for their love and encouragement as we pursued this work over the years.

Contents

Series Editors' Preface

Denise Armstrong and Brenda McMahon

This series focuses on contemporary issues in the theory, practice, and policy of urban education. Our primary aim is create a substantive body of research and scholarship that (a) examines how urban education is currently conceived, enacted, and transformed; and (b) provides critical and/or innovative perspectives on urban education that contribute to our understanding of the complexities inherent in urban educational contexts.

From the Ground Up: Effective Schooling in Traditionally Low Performing Schools by Michele Acker-Hocevar, Marta Cruz-Janzen, and Cynthia L. Wilson is the fifth book in IAP's *Issues in the Research, Theory, Policy and Practice of Urban Education Series.* This volume presents research findings from seven elementary schools located in low income and visible minority communities that achieved and continue to maintain high levels of academic achievement over several years. The profiles of the schools run contrary to depictions of heroic notions of leaders working in isolation at the helm of turn-around schools. The participants from each location identify themes that are specific to their site, and the authors provide an organic framework for sustainable school improvement that is applicable to all of the schools in this collection and transferable to other jurisdictions.

The overarching and interrelated factors that contribute to the success of these schools can be understood in terms of site-based decision-making, collaboration, and resourcefulness. Site-based decisions are embedded in

Leadership from the Ground Up, pages xiii–xiv
Copyright © 2012 by Information Age Publishing
All rights of reproduction in any form reserved.

high expectations and scaffolding for all students, faculty, and staff. Pedagogical approaches reflect commitments to accountability rather than standardization and include authentic and meaningful learning and teaching strategies. Passion for education and ownership of the schools as learning communities is evident from the participants in each of the case studies. Site-based decisions are found in policies and practices which embrace students' cultural and social capital, create permeable school and community boundaries, and ensure that physical plants are welcoming and well-maintained. They are also apparent as educators work proactively to anticipate and overcome obstacles that are imposed from state and district levels.

Collaborative school cultures are clearly important to the success of these schools and are enacted in multiple ways, through shared leadership, decision-making, and expertise. Administrators and teachers respect each other as professionals and share expertise in teaching, evaluations, and grant-writing endeavors. Ongoing dialogue among educators as well as with students and parents is integral to sustainable success. High student attendance and low faculty turnover rates relative to low-performing schools with similar demographics support participants' claims that students, parents, and teachers want to participate in these schools.

The cases attest to the importance of resourcefulness in the current political, social, and economic climate. Schools make strategic decisions about the use of human and fiscal capital and are able to access financial resources from governments, businesses, and communities that exceed government allocations. In addition specific schools create partnerships with high schools and universities to create mentorship programs and develop the skills of teacher candidates.

The authors provide questions at the end of each chapter which challenge school administrators, teachers, and professional preparation program faculty to examine the theories and practices which could either enhance or inhibit academic achievement for students.

Acknowledgements

We wish to thank David Walker, Perry Schoon, and Ellen Supran, who were members of our original research team. David provided expertise in the area of research methodology and statistics. Perry assisted with the fieldwork and with the graphic development of the Systems Alignment Model that is integral to this work. Both have been co-authors with us in the publication of journal articles that preceded this book. Ellen was valuable in data collection in the field and assisted in writing the field reports for some of the cases. All of their contributions are significant, and we are forever grateful. We would also like to thank our graduate assistants: Amy Brown, Pauline McLean, Jennifer Johnson, and Michael Hrabak for their indispensable assistance with many tasks associated with a research study of this magnitude. Amy Brown served as a field researcher and provided much support during the beginning stages of the study, while Pauline McLean and Jennifer Johnson conducted literature reviews and assisted with data coding and analysis at the concluding stages of the study. Michael Hrabak served as an in-house editor of the book as it approached its final stage. In addition, our research was supported by a team of field researchers whose work contributed to the individual case studies. We would be remiss if we didn't thank the principals, teachers, and parents who welcomed us into their schools. We appreciate their openness.

Finally, we wish to acknowledge the funding support of the Council for Educational Change (established by the Annenberg Foundation), which funded the initial study and provided the list of schools to be researched. The Council had access to the individual school data through the Florida

Leadership from the Ground Up, pages xv–xvi
Copyright © 2012 by Information Age Publishing

Department of Education, which was not yet accessible to the public at the time of this study. Acker-Hocevar and Cruz-Janzen also want to thank the Florida Atlantic University College of Education for the seed grant awarded them to conduct a follow-up study with several of these schools to validate the findings in the Learning Partnership Tree.

Introduction

This book presents case studies of seven high-performing elementary schools in the state of Florida, which have built strong cultures to help them respond to external accountability mandates. The seven schools serve primarily students from low socioeconomic (low SES) backgrounds, racial and ethnic minorities (students of color), and students who are English Language Learners (ELL). The case studies illustrate the different ways that the educators in these schools are able to sustain high achievement with students who are traditionally low performers. The specific rationale for this book is the finding that what sustained high performance in these schools is rooted in a learning partnership that builds a strong culture and climate for learning and working together. This culture and climate enables the educators in the schools to develop strong internal connections with each other, build upon their unique strengths, and cultivate alliances with parents and the community, including local businesses, to address the unique needs in their respective schools. Through distributed and shared leadership, additive schooling, and a strong and positive culture and climate, these cases illustrate effective schools. The book describes in detail how each of these seven distinctive schools was successful in sustaining high student achievement within the framework of learning partnerships. The variety of cases illustrates overarching themes that relate back to a distinct variable (attribute) of the learning partnership, such as resources, instruction, leadership, or decision making, etc., which helped to sustain their overall performance. As well, the variety of cases illustrate that there is no one-size-fits-all answer or set of external mandates that can lead to school

Leadership from the Ground Up, pages xvii–xviii
Copyright © 2012 by Information Age Publishing
All rights of reproduction in any form reserved.

effectiveness and high achievement, but rather what matters most is what happens at each individual school.

The knowledge base for this book draws on the literature from effective schools, standards-based reform, and successful practices with students from low-SES backgrounds, students of color, students who are ELLs, and schools that have beaten the odds by being able to sustain high achievement (see Chapter 1 for body of literature that informs this study). The literature on effective schools identifies variables such as leadership, accountability, personnel, information management, resources, instruction, culture and climate, communication, decision making, and parent and community involvement. Moreover, current literature on standards-based school reform focuses on accountability, instruction, personnel, resources, and information management, with lesser and/or unclear focus on culture and climate, communication, leadership, decision making, and parent and community involvement (see Chapter 2 for detailed discussion and supporting references for these variables).

In addition to the seven case studies, the book also includes questions for reflection at the end of each case study. These questions urge readers to engage in thoughtful reflection and discussions about these schools and how they are successful with these populations. The questions also encourage the readers to consider what they might learn from these schools that could help them in their own schools.

1

Let the Journey Begin!

We all know about schools overflowing with students who are not expected to perform well on standardized tests of academic achievement. Every state has these schools; we all know them, they are the ones that have lots of students from poor homes and communities (low SES), lots of racial and ethnic minorities (students of color), and lots of students who are English Language Learners (ELLs), the students whom most everyone expects to fail and bring the school achievement levels down. But what if there are schools with those same demographics beating the odds? Wouldn't it be fascinating to tell their stories? Wouldn't everyone want to know about their success; their beliefs, attitudes, and practices that have enabled them to be successful?

These are the stories we went searching for when we began this journey. Who are we? We are interdisciplinary education faculty researchers interested in finding these schools so that we could tell their unique stories, knowing that they may offer suggestions for schools that experience continuing underperformance patterns of many student populations and schools across the nation. As a scholarly research team, we have extensive individual and collective educational and professional backgrounds, and we are able to view schools through the multifaceted lenses of school and district administration, classroom instruction of diverse learners including students from low SES backgrounds, students of color, students who are ELLs and students with disabilities, urban and rural school districts, state-level school support and accountability, as well as principal and teacher preparation programs.

Dr. Michele A. Acker-Hocevar has a varied and rich education and corporate background spanning over 35 years. She has national and international education experiences. Her undergraduate psychology degree, combined with her personal history, led quite naturally to her seeking an interdisciplinary PhD in organizational studies and school leadership, along with her MEd in administration and supervision. Dr. Acker-Hocevar has designed and taught such courses as action learning and action research to practicing school leaders. She is currently a faculty member in the Educational Leadership and Counseling Psychology Department at Washington State University (WSU), after 21 years of working in Florida as a teacher, school administrator, research assistant, and faculty member, with 4 years in Alabama as a faculty member. Throughout Dr. Acker-Hocevar's career, she has been interested in power relationships that exist between and among role groups, especially in regard to the voice within organizations regarding informal and formal power, the scarce allocation of resources (i.e., access and opportunity to education changes and learning), and how members within an organization relate to and learn from one another. Dr. Acker-Hocevar is on the editorial board of the *International Journal of Educational Leadership* and the co-principal investigator for a national study of principal and superintendents' voices sponsored through the University Council for Educational Administration (UCEA). She was recently named the co-editor of the *Journal of Research on Leadership Education.*

Dr. Marta I. Cruz-Janzen has over 30 years experience in the field of education, from elementary school through postsecondary education. She also has extensive background in private industry. Dr. Cruz-Janzen holds an MA and an MEd in human development and guidance, and a PhD in curriculum and instruction, with a focus on the impact of school curricula on the self-identify, self-concept, and the educational achievement of students of color and particularly, students who are biracial and biethnic. Her background encompasses elementary bilingual/ESOL classroom teaching in New York City and Denver, Bilingual/ESOL curriculum and staff development, race and gender equity, technical support to urban and rural school districts with the Colorado Department of Education, elementary principal-ship, and teacher preparation with the Department of Secondary Education of Metropolitan State College of Denver. Currently, Dr. Cruz-Janzen teaches Developmental and Educational Psychology, TESOL/ESOL, and Multicultural Education classes at Florida Atlantic University (FAU). Throughout her career, Dr. Cruz-Janzen has also been involved with gender equity and women's studies. Currently, she serves as Faculty Associate with the FAU Center for Women, Gender, and Sexuality Studies. Her research centers on (a) the role of teachers, schools, and society in schools' curricula and the subsequent impact on student achievement, particularly students from low SES backgrounds, students of color, and students who are ELLs; (b) educational policy and reform; teacher and principal preparation programs; (c) effective/high-performing schools with high populations of students from low SES backgrounds, students of color, and students who are ELLs; and (4) multicultural education program reform.

Dr. Cynthia L. Wilson has been a special educator for 30 years in the State of Florida. She holds a BS, MS and PhD in special education. Her background includes experience as an elementary classroom teacher of students with disabilities, program specialist of teacher grants at the Florida Department of Education (FDOE) in the Bureau of Education for Exceptional Students, and faculty member of special education at the University of Miami. Dr. Wilson is currently a professor in the Department of Exceptional Student Education at FAU, where she has also served as the department chair. She currently teaches Inclusive Education for General Educators, Overview of Programs Serving Students with Varying Exceptionalities, Behavior Management, Grant Writing, and Cultural and Linguistic Diversity: Policy Issues and Implications in Special Education. Additionally, Dr. Wilson serves as a consultant with local school districts, where she provides professional staff development. She also has significant experience in grant writing and has served as the principal or co-principal investigator of several research and personnel preparation grants. Her primary research focus emphasizes the preparation of teachers to implement research-based, effective teaching practices in an effort to improve educational opportunities for children with mild to moderate disabilities and children who are at risk for academic failure, including students from low SES backgrounds, students of color, and students who are ELLs.

Originally, we came together because we were approached by our college administrators responding to a grant proposal from a funding agency interested in research that would examine schools demonstrating sustained academic success; the keyword being *sustained*. The coming together, however, revealed that each of us had concerns about particular student groups labeled at-risk for academic failure. This book shares our journey and examines seven elementary schools that have sustained progress with students from low SES backgrounds, students of color, and students who are ELLs. Since it is atypical for schools that serve disproportionate numbers of these students to sustain academic progress (Acker-Hocevar & Touchton, 2002; Chenoweth, 2007; Darling-Hammond, 1995; Kozol, 1992; Yan, 1999), we thought that adding their stories to the educational literature was extremely crucial and timely. Additionally, the dearth of scholarly research on schools attaining high performance with similar student demographics, which typically underperform schools with more affluent, White, and native English-speaking students in the United States (Valdés, 1996), encouraged us to examine these atypical high-performing schools to get to know them better, learn about their practices, and identify the variables that contributed to their sustained academic progress with the kinds of students who are far too often not expected to meet the requirements of high-stakes academic-achievement testing.

Given the politics of high-stakes testing and the fact that few educators (e.g., Carter, 2000; Charles A. Dana Center, 1999; Scheurich, 1998) have been able to assist their students from low SES backgrounds, students of color, and students who are ELLs to meet the challenges of sustaining successful performance on high-stakes tests, it is critical to understand how some schools are better able to address the external mandates for reform such as those required under the No Child Left Behind Act (2001). Within these high-performing schools, little is known about their internal cultures; the beliefs, attitudes, and practices that have led to their sustained performance; and what may be learned about sustainable school improvement from these schools.

Inconsistent improvement patterns have raised concerns among parents and policymakers about why some schools with similar demographics are doing better than others. Furthermore, it becomes increasingly important to understand the experiences of schools with similar student demographics that have demonstrated and sustained school improvement over time. The research on classroom practices that explains teacher effects dominated the discourse on student learning in the 90s (see studies by the University of Tennessee with Sanders and Horn, 1995). However, in the last 5 to 7 years, the conversation has shifted to focus more on the role that principals play in creating and sustaining school cultures that support teaching and learning within the school and enhance student achievement (Davis, Darling-Hammond, LaPointe, & Meyerson, 2005; Leithwood, Seashore-Louis, Anderson, & Wahlstrom, 2004; Southern Regional Educational Board, 2007; Waters, Marzano, & McNulty, 2003).

Each school case study provides descriptions of the internal organizational values and practices that have helped to sustain these schools' reform efforts, and each case study offers a description of how these efforts work synergistically in a model that can be used by other educators. Further, the case studies provide more detail about the individual schools than was possible in the journal articles (Acker-Hocevar, Cruz-Janzen, Wilson, Schoon, & Walker, 2005/2006; Wilson, Walker, Cruz-Janzen, Acker-Hocevar, & Schoon, 2005/2006) that preceded this book's publication.

To our amazement, only nine elementary schools in the State of Florida were identified originally as meeting the initial criteria of sustaining high performance across a 2-year period while serving student populations with whom other schools across the state were unsuccessful. With the passing of NCLB in 2001, schools were required to publicly report their accountability data (high-stakes achievement test results, progress toward Adequate Yearly Progress (AYP), school grades) beginning with the academic year 2002–2003, which is the year our research team began to visit the schools; therefore, this was the first year the research team was able to access the data and track the schools on an annual basis. Careful and continued scrutiny of these schools' academic data over subsequent years led to eliminating two schools because they were unable to sustain the required high-achievement criteria. With annual data across nine academic years (2000–2009), the data demonstrates that these seven remaining schools have, indeed, developed an internal culture that definitely can sustain high achievement levels across multiple years. Additionally, the data demonstrates that a couple of years of data can present only a snapshot rather than provide evidence of sustained achievement. We aim to share the stories of these accomplished schools so we can learn from them the valuable lessons they hold. It is essential to examine how each school's story shares elements in common across all the schools. The differences are in the ways that each school has built on their unique strengths that represent signatures for their culture and school development.

To examine the practices within these schools and determine which variables contributed to their success, we developed the Systems Alignment Model (SAM). The SAM, which is fully described in Chapter 2, provides a graphic display of the conceptual framework and literature that was used to ground our initial study. Based on the standards-based reform literature, we included the variables of accountability, information management, instruction, personnel, and resources in the SAM and called them standards-based reform variables. However, we knew from our own experiences as teachers, principals, parents, and educational researchers that there were other contributing factors that led to school effectiveness. Thus, we also included the variables of leadership, decision making, communication, parent and community involvement, and culture and climate in the SAM and called them embedded variables.

We went to the schools trying to apply the SAM. Yet, analysis of each school's data revealed that while the SAM's standards-based reform variables and embedded variables were present in each of the schools, the presence of each variable and the relationship between them led to a different operating model; a model that was more fluid, interconnected, and interdependent as well as more internal and unique to each school and its community. Rather than being driven by external requirements and mandates through the standards-based reform variables, each school appeared to be more strongly grounded through its own internal culture and climate working with the remaining embedded variables, jointly serving to orchestrate the relationship among all the variables (standards-based reform and embedded). Essentially, the picture that emerged for each school pulled the embedded variables to the forefront of their school effectiveness.

Each school's culture and climate shaped leadership through collaboration as shared leadership that further empowered everyone as a leader, collectively accountable for the school's achievement. Significantly, a school culture that viewed everyone in the organization, from administrators and teachers, students and parents, secretaries and custodians, and all personnel, as having talents and resources that can be pooled to add to areas that are lacking (including funding) and enrich the school, unfolded a pervasive additive schooling perspective. The converse, subtractive schooling, is driven by well-established notions of assimilationism and practices designed to divest minority students of their cultures and languages. Subtractive schooling views students, parents, and communities from a deficit paradigm as lacking the resources and skills needed to succeed in today's schools and society. Through additive schooling, parents and community, including local businesses, become integral to the learning partnership, not only contributing their human assets and resources but also seeing the school as an asset to them. Similarly, additive schooling frames the school organization within a humanistic philosophy that values the integrity and well-being of each member as reciprocally vested within the integrity and well-being of the organization as a whole.

Lack of resources, mostly described by each school through a deficit funding paradigm, charged all school leaders with the task of becoming more resourceful and entrepreneurial in securing what was needed to keep the school afloat and functioning. Instruction became the incremental and complementary collective pooling of expertise; everyone in the organization was a valued expert at something and therefore was responsible for enhancing each other's expertise and success. Personnel were carefully selected to support and promote the school's culture of shared leadership and pooled expertise. Information, such as test results, was used to improve instruction, select appropriate materials and programs, and engage in collaborative self-assessment and self-monitoring.

When we analyzed the data and pulled the major themes together, we found humanistic philosophy, additive schooling, entrepreneurship and resourcefulness, high professionalism and efficacy, creative ways to overcome obstacles, and a principal at the helm with shared leadership and accountability, etc. Each school's story lets us see that what matters most is what happens in each school; that what drives the success of each school was their own ability to determine what works for them. We found that there was no one-size-fits-all formula for school effectiveness, but rather what works for one school, may or may not work for another.

In Chapter 2, we explain the theoretical basis for the book and provide the research methodology that was used to investigate the schools. The titles of each of the case studies that follow in chapters 3–9 reflect the overarching theme that captured the essence of each school as described to us by the administrators, teachers, and parents. Chapter 10 presents the Learning Partnership Tree (LPT), which emerged from the data and demonstrates that rather than high performance based on a federal- and state-mandated model, what creates and sustains high achievement stems from a much different model grounded in systems theory, partnership power, and additive schooling. The entire school community becomes a learning organization, supporting the notion that what matters most is what happens at the schools, building on their collective expertise, and the needs of the students. These schools were successful because they created highly developed internal cultures that were grounded in sharing, collaboration, and consensus building within the school and between the schools and their respective communities.

Chapter 11 describes how a new framework, the Sustainable School Improvement (SSI) theory-in-practice, emerged from the lessons we learned. This emergent framework brings the school culture and climate into focus through the themes that come together to support school effectiveness at the core: additive schooling, humanistic philosophy, resourcefulness, and shared leadership and accountability that promote organizational efficacy. The model helps to explain how the high-performing schools gained increased autonomy from external domination and beat the odds pitted against them. Jointly, the LPT and the SSI theory-in-practice help us better understand how these schools have successfully created highly developed internal cultures that are enabling and capacity building. Overall, this book has the potential for revisiting the internal human work structures and connections within schools.

Finally, Chapter 12 describes what was learned in follow-up visits made to a subsample of the schools to find out what uniquely made them successful. It presents the findings of these last visits to the schools, which suggest an apparent mismatch among external, federal, state, and district expectations and demands, and the daily realities of schools. Furthermore, the findings suggest a significant disconnect between preparation programs and subject matter that principals and teachers at these schools identified as integral to their effective school and organizational development. As well, this book also has potential for promoting the reform of principal and teacher preparation programs statewide and nationwide, particularly for educators in schools with high populations of students from low SES backgrounds, students of color, and students who are ELLs.

2[1]

The Conceptual Framework and Research Methodology

Developing the Systems Alignment Model (SAM)

One of our first endeavors as we thought about this project was to conceptualize the framework and literature that would guide and ground our study. Our thoughts were directed toward what we knew collectively about school improvement, standards-based reform, and school effectiveness. Thus, we began the development of a model grounded in the literature that would allow us to examine school practices. This model, which we named the Systems Alignment Model (SAM, see Figure 2.1), was organized around 10 theoretical variables. Five variables were explicit within the standards-based school reform literature: accountability, instruction, personnel, resources, and information management; as such, they were termed standards-based reform variables and described as the outer ring of the SAM.

The remaining five variables were embedded within the standards-based reform variables and thus, termed embedded variables: leadership,

Leadership from the Ground Up, pages 9–23

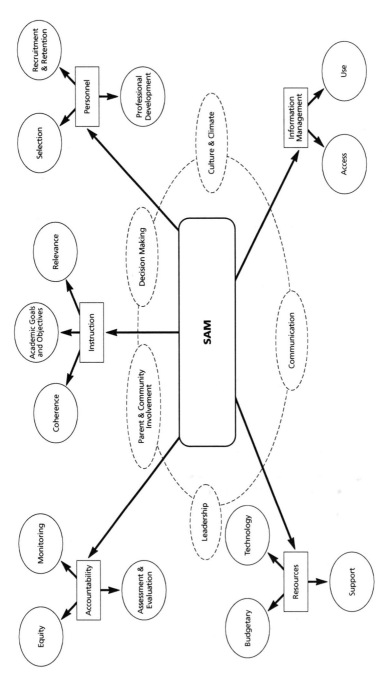

Figure 2.1 Systems Alignment Model (SAM). This is the conceptual framework that was used to ground our initial study and examine the practices within the schools to determine which variables contributed to their success. Based on the standards-based reform literature, we included the variables of accountability, information management, instruction, personnel, and resources. However, we knew that there were other factors that led to school effectiveness, and thus, we included the variables of leadership, decision making, communication, parent and community involvement, and culture and climate.

parent and community involvement, decision making, culture and climate, and communication. Several assumptions undergirded the model. First, it assumes that within a standards-based environment, there is systems alignment of standards-based reform variables among different levels (e.g., district, school, and classroom). Second, since students from low SES backgrounds, students of color, and students who are ELLs have systematically underperformed in comparison with students who are more affluent, White, and English-speaking, the model assumes there is evidence in these schools of successful practices for these students, with information management that helps educators disaggregate student data and assess instructional practices. Third, there is an assumption that the model is a system mediated by different contextual relationships where the local site becomes the place for interpretation and enactment of school accountability. The model's standards-based reform variables and embedded variables are described in this chapter. Since this model is grounded in systems theory and standards-based reform literature, it purports to show the relationship among variables emphasized in standards-based reform, while simultaneously making connections to other variables that might assist in supporting equity and excellence for students from low SES backgrounds, students of color, and students who are ELLs.

Standards-Based Reform Variables

Accountability. The standards-based reform variables are accountability, instruction, personnel, resources, and information management. The variable of accountability is paramount to the current standards-based reform efforts. Accountability within the SAM addresses three areas: assessment and evaluation, monitoring of instruction, and equity (meaning all students have fair and reasonable access to equal opportunities to be successful learners, regardless of SES, race, ethnicity, and English-language proficiency). Weiss, Knapp, Hollwag, and Burrell (2001) identified three channels of influence through which classroom practices for school improvement can be affected. These areas are changes to the curriculum, teacher development, and assessment and accountability practices. The corollary to accountability in the educational reform movement is standards-based curriculum coupled with tightly linked assessment criteria. What is less apparent, however, is how differently states choose to enact standards-based reform and accountability (Swanson & Stevenson, 2002).

A comparison of two states, for example, provides a stark contrast to how standards-based curriculum and accountability reforms were enacted. In one state, Florida, school accountability was built around state standards and a plan that grades schools and impacts the allocation of resources, with sanctions for failing grades and rewards for high grades on school improvement measures. In the other state, Connecticut, all improvement efforts were tied to a commitment to teacher quality to increase accountability. While the demographics of both states have changed considerably over the last 10 years, with students from low SES backgrounds, students of color, and students who are ELLs on the increase, the state committed to teacher quality continues to show achievement growth and outperforms other states on national assessments (Wilson, Darling-Hammond, & Berry, 2001).

Unmistakably, principals play an important role in improving pedagogical quality (Marks & Printy, 2003). Principals make numerous decisions every day, and these choices weave the "cultural tapestry" that defines the culture, priorities, and way of life at the school (Supovitz & Poglinco, 2001). Often, principals have to choose between instructional, political, and managerial responsibilities (Reyes-Guerra, 2009; Yukl & Lepsinger, 1991). In an extensive interview conducted with a group of effective principals, findings revealed that they felt instructional leadership, even if it meant restructuring their job, had to be their top priority (Marks & Printy, 2003). While these principals acknowledged that an accountability system must be in place, they noted spending more time in classrooms, talking with students, and examining students' work as a way of monitoring student achievement. It appears that principals that provided teachers with the opportunity to build a professional culture around instructional improvement viewed monitoring instruction as a collective endeavor, involving teachers in the process. Specifically, Supovitz and Poglinco found principals who became more skilled at discerning quality instruction, facilitated teachers' acquisition of additional knowledge and expertise, and promoted a culture of teaching and learning.

Standards' policies in the United States bare directly on how "well-educated" students are defined, what is taught, and ultimately, on the purpose of schooling. Meier (2002) questioned whether it is desirable to have a single definition of a well-educated person and demand that all schools be held to that solitary definition. Scheurich and Skrla (2003) argued that the present reform movement of standards-based assessment holds schools accountable in unprecedented ways for the achievement of students from low SES backgrounds, students of color, and students who are ELLs. Having the same standards for all students, without considering the social and cultural capital students bring to school, may work against students from low SES backgrounds, students of color, and students who are ELLs unless specific instructional practices are put in place that build on students' prior knowledge (Acker-Hocevar & Touchton, 2002; Scheurich & Skrla, 2003).

Instruction. Instruction within the SAM addresses three areas: academic goals and objectives, relevance, and coherence. Instructional goals and objectives are the most critical components for guiding aspects of curriculum development and implementation. Effective teaching must begin with clearly defined goals, followed by clear objectives and outcomes, and ending with equally defined assessments of students' learning that simultaneously establish instructional effectiveness (Posner, 1998). Objectives may be stated regarding what teachers and/or students must know and be able to do. They may be short or long term but, ultimately, must demonstrate how the goal will be attained. They must provide the guide for instructional revision or forward movement. Assessments must be developed jointly with objectives, but it is imperative that goals and objectives drive the curriculum rather than vice versa. Once a clear destination for teaching and learning is established, and performance evaluations identified, educational experiences can be organized to ensure alignment with desired outcomes. Teachers are then better prepared to select instructional content, materials, and strategies.

The historical and persistent underachievement of students from low SES backgrounds, students of color, and students who are ELLs in the United States, along with rapidly changing demographics, has signaled national alarm to find educational solutions that work. It is well-known that effective teaching is more relevant for students who underachieve. It is also well-known that the poorest children are more adversely impacted by having the least experienced, and often least effective, teachers (Brunner, 1977; Darling-Hammond, 2000). There has been a call for a standardization of curriculum in the United States; that is, national common knowledge across the content areas and demonstrated levels of competencies in those areas. This call has been driven by desired improved national performance across all grade levels. However, currently, schools are required to align curricula and instruction to external state mandates, including state content standards and standardized assessments, to ensure successful outcomes on such standardized tests. Test results are used to evaluate students, teachers, and schools, even compare states to each other. While there is much debate surrounding the appropriateness, effectiveness, and/or equity of such expectations, the national lens has shifted and is now focusing on what seems to work across schools, districts, and states and how schools can begin to share this expertise at meeting the educational needs of diverse students.

Assessment of curricular and instructional effectiveness calls for structured analyses of formal curriculum, including examination of instruction, how academic goals and objectives are aligned to research-based resources, programs and the district mission, and whether the academic goals and objectives are prioritized in school improvement plans. It analyzes the overall link of district goals and school improvement plans to classroom instruction and communications to parents. Included is how instructional teams determine desired student outcomes and actions taken if schools, teachers, and students do not reach expected performance goals and objectives.

Instruction involves coherence or systems in place that look at how curriculum extends beyond standardized tests and academic goals and objectives, and whether organizational structures facilitate grade-level, academic, and vertical teams to meet and revise curriculum. Coherence also confirms whether there is a system in place for development of a curricular scope and sequence matched by relevant selection of instructional materials and methods. Furthermore, coherence reviews how personnel use proven effective instructional arrangements to achieve academic goals and objectives, make adjustments to instruction based on student performance, and link classroom management to student learning. Instruction also involves relevance between student learning and the following: standardized tests, content standards, academic goals and objectives, professional development, data-based decision making, personnel selection, personnel retention, mission, school improvement plans, and districtwide strategic plans. Additionally, relevance examines the linkages between asset allocation and student needs, community involvement, and technology integration.

Personnel. Any attempt to examine the success of schools must consider the variable of personnel as essential. Research on effective schools identifies several personnel-related attributes as common among schools, including (a) strong leadership, (b) shared principal and teacher understanding about students, (c) shared involvement in decision making, and (d) a collaborative and team-oriented approach to reform (Coyle & Witcher, 1992; Edmonds, 1979; Glidden, 1999; Thacker & McInerney, 1992). Further, complimentary research on organizational reform in the business sector asserts that because schools and industry share certain common characteristics, including recruitment and management of personnel, many facets of industry could be fruitfully related to education (Van Der Linde, 2000). For example, the Total Quality Management approach directed at producing quality organizations can also be applied in education. Advocates suggest that Total Quality Management must embrace the concept of dignity, respect, and value of all human potential. Thus, the personnel variable includes the subvariables of recruitment, retention, and professional development. To that end, the SAM also considers these personnel-related subvariables. There is an abundance of literature in education emphasizing the importance of effective recruitment, retention, and professional development of personnel (e.g., Holloway, 2003; Sargent, 2003; Travis, 2001); it highlights the importance of creating an organization that hires high-quality personnel and includes supportive structures and systems for its personnel.

Resources. The resources variable within the SAM addresses three areas: budget, technology, and support. While most schools in the nation are provided a so-called operating budget, which is characterized by hierarchically mandated allocations, procedures, and operations, there has been more recent demand for a "flexible, user-friendly, response-driven support and provision system known as school-based management" (Siegel, 2003). In a financially demanding era, with increasing pressures from mandated standards-based reform, schools are struggling. Increased emphasis on high-stakes testing, benchmarks, and performance standards have school board members, district staff, school administrators, and teachers seeking ways to link budgeting to efforts to improve student and school improvement.

Technology can be a useful tool for education, especially in relationship to standards-based education, where the goal is for management of every individual's learning progress. As standards-based reform becomes ubiquitous, teachers increasingly find themselves accountable for delivering what is measured on standardized tests. If the curriculum has actually been changed to reflect new content standards, teachers will need technology to help deliver it. Similarly, if tests are aligned to revised curriculum, technology— if teachers are able to access and use it—can help students perform much better on tests. Computers and other technologies are increasingly essential to the validity of any systems-alignment model that provides educators with a road map for school development, and therefore, technology is an element of the resources variable in the SAM.

On paper, budgets appear the same across schools, but when individual schools are examined, differences become quite apparent. Many schools depend on volunteers (as a source of support) to supplement insufficient and diminishing staffing, assist teachers in classrooms, and tutor students who are identified as low-achieving. Schools vary widely in their ability to secure external funds to maintain and/or upgrade their technology and provide needed instructional materials and programs. Securing volunteers and external funds is closely tied to the skills and connections of leadership team members. Some educational leaders become adept at grant writing and/or hold personal connections to external funding sources. Consequently, the support that individual schools have does influence student achievement.

Information Management. As educational institutions attempt to restructure and redesign the school and its culture, a means of unobtrusively, continuously, and automatically gathering information and making it available for various decision makers has become a critical need. Informational data, such as records of attendance, schedules, curriculums, assessments, resources, grades, and performance evaluations, are generated as a result of daily, monthly, and annual operations. The importance of the information generated, how it integrates with information originated by others, and the available access to and use of the information broadens the dimensions of the learning environment. Thus, the variables, information management, and its subvariables, access and use, are integral to the SAM.

All school districts face the ever-increasing challenge of preparing students for the future. Increased emphasis on high-stakes testing, benchmarks, and performance standards have school board members, district staff, school administrators, and teachers seeking ways to improve student performance, develop better lesson plans, and create more meaningful classroom assessments. However, the adaptation of goals, standards, and benchmarks do not, in and of themselves, ensure improved instruction. To improve learning, schools must make sure that standards are aligned with the curriculum. Information management is critical to the alignment of curriculum objectives, outcomes, and standards with instruction and assessment if both the curriculum and instruction are to be evaluated (Carter, 1999). Coupled with the alignment should be the ability to track individual student performance and outcomes as they relate directly to the curriculum being taught. Curriculum alignment must occur if the use of standards and high-stakes testing are to bring about improved student performance.

Embedded Variables

Leadership. The embedded variables are leadership, parent and community involvement, decision making, culture and climate, and communication. Of these, the leadership variable disproportionately affects the other embedded variables within the inner circle of the SAM. Although there is a plethora of leadership theories, several contemporary ones capture the essence of the intent of school leadership within the SAM, thus affecting the relationship between the school and community to build a more tightly coupled and aligned system, and to develop the capacity and collective agency of all personnel to address ongoing school improvement. From a systems perspective, then, the leadership variable is an adhesive variable, bonding together the school staff and community to address school improvement (Sergiovanni, 1994) and to create tightly coupled systems that focus on teaching and learning (Weick, 1982).

Specifically, three leadership theories emerge to provide the most plausible linkages to the SAM, furthering student-learning outcomes, sustaining school improvement patterns, and engendering tight linkages with instruction. These are systems leadership (Snyder, Acker-Hocevar, & Snyder, 2000), distributed leadership (Spillane, Halverson, & Diamond, 2001), and instructional leadership (Glickman, 2002; Scheurich & Skrla, 2003). The first, systems leadership, is couched within complexity and chaos theories of systems thinking and fosters strong partnerships and connections across school staff and their constituents to support ongoing growth and development. Systems leaders make decisions about how best to allocate time and resources (amidst ambiguous and often conflicting messages), specifically, teacher time for interaction and collaboration by teams and across teams. What's more, these principals seek to benchmark changes (using a comparison group or standard) and work on continuous school improvement around the shared vision, values, and beliefs for all students to be successful. Necessarily, systems leadership takes into account how resource-dependent the school is with its outer environment and encourages and supports stakeholders to seek additional resources actively (Snyder et al., 2000).

The second leadership theory is that of distributed leadership. This theory, in concert with systems leadership, might help explain why principals today must seek to build pools of expertise with the needed organizational capacity to solve schoolwide problems, increase teacher leadership, and promote organizationwide efficacy. Distributed leadership theory supports the wider sharing of leadership among all professionals to participate actively in the school's knowledge construction, decisions, and ongoing critique and examination of the school improvement process (Spillane et al., 2001).

Finally, instructional leadership theory (Glickman, 2002; Scheurich & Skrla, 2003) suggests that the leader's role is to develop professional communities of practice that make better pedagogical decisions about teaching and learning for students (e.g., equity and excellence), create a clear accountability process to monitor instruction and learning over time, tie standards to specific learning goals and objectives that are assessed and monitored regularly, and support more authentic and real-world opportunities for student learning (Newmann, Secada, & Wehlage, 1995). Viewed together, these three leadership theories support sustainable school improvement over time, build school capacity, foster shared decision making, and promote a tighter coupling of work systems.

Parent and community involvement. A collective variable of parent and community involvement in schools should be considered an integral part of a systems-alignment model. The concept of parent and community involvement in schools is a very expansive variable. Research (Elmore, 2000; Steinberg, 1996) has indicated that improving student achievement is related to shared contributions of skills and experiences from stakeholders involved in students' education (i.e., parents and community). In fact, community involvement in the area of social support plays a prominent role in student achievement. Research has established a strong relationship between high student achievement and social support via community involvement in students' K–12 experiences (Coleman, 1990). Parental involvement, incorporating both formal and informal activities, has been found to have a strong, positive relationship with increased student achievement, particularly in the area of reading (Bali, Demo, & Wedman, 1998; Scribner, Young, & Pedroza, 1999).

Decision making. The previously mentioned variable of parent and community involvement, seen as an outside influence, is also an element of decision making and student achievement. This variable has been found to be a primary factor in producing increased student achievement. As noted by Roderick, Jacob, and Bryk (2002), "Student achievement ultimately depends on the daily decisions made by teachers and principals" (p. 338).

As such, decision making includes the idea of strong school leadership between administrators, teachers, and parents, manifested through the importance of promoting student learning. This variable is realized through continuous curricular planning, budgetary alignment with priorities, instructional effectiveness, professional development, and organizational characteristics such as school size (Northwest Regional Educational Laboratory, 2003).

Culture and climate. Research establishes a clear positive correlation between school culture and student achievement (Snyder et al., 2000; Tyler, 1949; Valenzuela, 1999). An inviting and collaborative learning environment for students and parents helps to foster attendance and academic achievement. The positive impact of parent involvement on student motivation, engagement, and achievement has been well-documented. When students and parents feel welcomed, respected, and valued by the schools, they will participate more readily. Learning takes place through the learner's experiences; that is, through reaction to the learning environment in which one is placed (Tyler, 1949; Valenzuela, 1999). Education must, therefore, provide opportunities for students to "enter actively" with experiences of interest and relevance to their lives and needs, and reflective of their cultures, backgrounds, and experiences.

The work environment, shaped by leadership style, decision-making processes, communication, and parent and community involvement, contributes to the work culture and climate. A strong and positive work culture, grounded in distributed leadership, is fueled by collaboration. The principal cannot be the only one responsible for actuating and sustaining change. All members of the organization, including parents, staff, and community, must be participants in the decision-making and improvement process. In order to accomplish this, lines of communication must be open, fluid, extensive, and interconnected.

Communication. An important factor of the work involved in the functioning of partnerships is the effective use of communication. Thus, any systems-alignment model, and any examination of schools as organizations, must include an examination of the communication systems in those schools. Effective communication has been emphasized in schools by many national organizations for leaders such as the National Associations of Elementary and Secondary School Principals, the American Association of School Administrators, and the National Commission on Excellence in Educational Administration (Wentz, 1998). These organizations have stressed that effective communication is essential in schools to promote better relationships with their constituents. An understanding of the communication that happens in schools is significant to understanding the success of schools (Wentz, 1998). Effective school communication extends well beyond the walls of school sites. It reaches into the heart of the community itself and has far-reaching implications (Peterson, 1996). Mutually beneficial partnerships between business, education, parents, and schools can be the result of effective communication, but are not likely to occur without effective systems alignment with the other embedded variables.

In summation, the SAM provides a way to examine why some schools with large populations of students from low SES backgrounds, students of color, and students who are ELLs are considered successful in terms of student achievement. In the SAM, the standards-based reform variables address the social and technical systems that enable schools to make necessary adjustments to align their practices to the needs of students and community. Within this alignment process of accountability, instruction, personnel, resources, and information management are the embedded variables of leadership, parent and community involvement, decision making, culture and climate, and communication. Recent literature has focused almost exclusively on the standards-based reform variables. What is less clear is how these variables work in concert with the embedded variables in the SAM. Importantly, the SAM model brings together both standards-based reform and embedded variables.

Research Methodology

Selection of Schools

Our research team systematically examined the research literature and data on high-performing schools to ground the research. We focused on elementary schools in the state of Florida with certain demographic profiles. The seven schools featured in this text meet the following criteria: (a) sustained achievement in reading or math for 2 consecutive years (i.e., 65% or greater students scored at Level 3, which is considered to be at grade level, or higher on the reading or math section of the Florida Comprehensive Assessment Test (FCAT); (b) competence in both of these disciplines for 2 consecutive years (i.e., 50% or greater students scored at Level 3 or above on both the reading and the math sections); (c) 50% or greater students from low SES backgrounds as defined by Title I (i.e., free or reduced-price lunch); and (d) 10% or greater students who are ELLs as defined by Title VII and the Multicultural Education Training Advocacy (META) agreement. Students who are ELLs receiving English for Speakers of Other Languages (ESOL) services for 2 years or less were not part of the reported scores. Sustained achievement that correlates with school letter grades as determined by the state report card on schools is depicted in Table 2.1. Although the state's criteria have changed every year, making comparisons impractical, trends can be noted.

Design-Based Research

A design-based paradigm was implemented to advance the research for the study of these schools (Design-Based Research Collective, 2003). In this method, quantitative data, derived from an interview instrument, were used as a supplement to a theory-driven design, afforded for systems alignment. Since prediction and studying the effect of a specific intervention was not the goal of this inquiry, the design-based research for this project attempted to connect with the outcomes of the study, the theoretical framework of the context and politics of educational reform, systems theory, and power structures found in schools with large percentages of students of color, students from low SES backgrounds, and students who are ELLs. It was felt that this link may yield plausible answers to context-bound questions of why some schools with large percentages of these students were successful and others were found to be unsuccessful in terms of student achievement. The

TABLE 2.1   Summary of High-Performing School Grades by Year and School

School	2008–09	2007–08	2006–07	2005–06	2004–05	2003–04	2002–03	2001–02	2000–01	1999–00	1998–99
X1	A	A	A	A	A	A	A	B	A	C	A
X2	A	A	A	A	A	A	A	A	A	B	C
X3	A	A	A	A	A	A	A	A	B	A	C
X4	A	A	A	A	A	B	A	A	A	A	C
X5	B	A	A	A	A	A	A	A	A	B	C
X6	A	A	A	A	A	A	B	A	A	A	B
X7	A	A	A	A	A	A	A	A	A	C	C

Note: Source of information in table is from No Child Left Behind Public School Accountability Reports.

essential element for this paradigm was to procure a model that provided approximate and reasonable answers to this question, and other queries, within authentic elementary school settings, which could add to practitioner knowledge at the school and classroom levels and also augment established and developing theories concerning systems alignment, educational reform, and power systems. As the Design-Based Research Collective notes, "The intention of design-based research in education is to inquire more broadly into the nature of learning in complex systems... models, rather than particular artifacts or programs are the goal..." (p. 7).

Instrument

As part of the research design for this study, evidence of best practices from two levels—school and classroom—needed to be collected and analyzed. In the pilot phase of the research, principals, teachers, and district-level personnel were asked to identify common evidences that researchers should be able to obtain from each of the two levels to denote best practices toward educational achievement. To prompt field researchers, an interview instrument with probing questions (see Appendices A & B) and rubrics was developed by the research team. The instrument was used to assist researchers in determining how effective each of the rubric levels were in exhibiting student achievement; wherein 1 = none, 2 = below average, 3 = average, 4 = above average, and 5 = excellent (linked to an A through F scale). For the instrument, the research team identified 10 variables linked to student achievement and grounded in school effectiveness literature (Edmonds, 1979; Purkey & Smith, 1993; Spillane & Seashore-Louis, 2002; Teddlie & Reynolds, 2000; Wiggins & McTighe, 1998). Each question was applied to the two levels of school and classroom.

Pilot Study

An initial pilot test was conducted on the instrument. The concept of reliability refers to scores and not a test or instrument, and provides an account of the data under study. Reliability is sensitive in terms of changing with sample composition and score variability. Therefore, the reliability of scores is coupled directly to a specific instrument and is related to particular person(s) within a certain time and context. A reliability measure used with data derived from the instrument's Likert-type scale was Cronbach's alpha (α). For a Cronbach's alpha score, a range of .70 to 1.00 is considered sufficient for measuring internal consistency and proper variable validity. The reliability for the instrument's scores was very high, which meant that this instrument was effective in measuring what it was intended to measure. For the classroom scale, $\alpha = .9150$ with

90% confidence intervals (.8396, .9686) and accounts for 83.72% of the variance. For the school scale, $\alpha = .9253$ with 90% CI (.8591, .9724) and accounts for 85.62% of the variance. In light of this reliability analysis, a revision of the instrument for parsimonious purposes called for the deletion of 13 questions, all of which added virtually no new information. The instrument decreased in number from 161 questions to 148. The final instrument, however, was further reduced to 81 questions after it was field-tested for use with teachers and principals (see Appendix A), and further modified for use with parents (see Appendix B).

Inter-Rater Reliability

For the seven schools that performed well on the state achievement test over the required 2-year period, the researchers' ratings from the classroom section yielded interclass correlation coefficient (ICC) scores ranging from .5504 to .9408. The ICC scores from the school portion were from .6081 to .9547. These ICC scores seem reasonable and were for the most part within the good to excellent range, regardless of the specific portion of the instrument being analyzed. Researcher bias on the instrument, such as observation or confidence, appears to be limited. The seven schools deemed successful were found by the field researchers to exhibit between average (3) to excellent (5) evidence on the instrument. This indicated that the researchers found some form of tangible evidence related to these schools' performance within their classrooms and school pertinent to the various variables identified in the scholarly literature that appear to promote and sustain a system aligned to attaining student achievement.

Site Visits

Site visits were conducted in the fall of 2002 and the spring of 2003. During the 2-day site visits, interview participants for each school were grouped as follows: principals and assistant principals, teachers, and parents (see Table 2.2 for number of interview participants in each school). All interviews were recorded and transcribed, with each transcript read and coded by two researchers independently. A preliminary list of codes emerged, which researchers shared with one another. Researchers then agreed on the working codes and began to develop categories to examine practices within and across schools (Merriam, 2001; Patton, 1990). Eventually, these categories were clustered together under themes and led to the development of the framework to situate the findings. This emerging framework became a lens to examine findings, along with the SAM.

TABLE 2.2 Number of Interview Participants

School	Principals	Assistant Principals	Teachers	Parents
X1	1	0	6	6
X2	1	0	3	3
X3	1	2	9	8
X4	1	0	6	4
X5	1	0	3	3
X6	1	1	5	4
X7	1	1	3	3
Total	7	4	35	31

Research Questions

Edmonds (1979) demonstrated that schools can attain high academic achievement with high populations of students from low SES backgrounds, students of color, and students who are ELLs, laying a foundation for other scholars to further identify practices affecting student achievement positively. As researchers, we sought to answer three questions:

1. What theories-in-practice seem to sustain school progress over time?
2. What practices lend credibility to the initial conceptual lenses for this study?
3. Do practices in high-performing schools confirm or reject the SAM?

Note

1. This chapter was adapted from Wilson et al. (2005/2006).

3

Show Me the Money

If you get a reputation of knowing how to spend the dollars, they will give it to you. I have found in our district if you need resources, there are ways to get additional dollars. Philosophically, whatever the teachers want, we say tell us what you want, we will purchase what you need, and we have so many resources that we go to. (Principal)

He [the principal] is a very good budget, moneyman. He uses it wisely. He is very generous with what he has. He goes out to find money. It is wonderful. Because of that, we have all the resources we do. (Teacher)

Introduction

As illustrated by the two quotes that introduce this school, the principal and teachers are extremely proud of their ability to find additional resources beyond state and district allocations. These additional resources have assisted this school in their school improvement initiatives such as reducing class size, improving staff development, implementing a family literacy program, and the other varied efforts that have sustained the high performance of its students. This school is labeled X7, and annual grades from 2000–2001 through the 2008–2009 school year can be found in Table 3.1, "School X7

Leadership from the Ground Up, pages 25–41
Copyright © 2012 by Information Age Publishing
All rights of reproduction in any form reserved.

Indicators of High Performance," located at the end of the chapter. The five major themes distinguish this school from other school cases presented in the book. These practices have helped to establish and sustain high-performance levels with a student population that other schools across the state and nation are not succeeding with at such high levels. The themes are entrepreneur funding, internal accountability and expertise, shared leadership, universal school, and overcoming external obstacles. Entrepreneur funding is the hallmark of this school that is well-known and admired as a master in resource funding for their ability to secure large external grants and other funds. Internal accountability and expertise represents the commitment school personnel have to accountability for the achievement of goals and objectives, which is accomplished through frequent monitoring of student work. Accountability is internally driven by developed and shared expertise. This school represents a cohesive community of experts who pull together for everyone's success, especially the students. The principal understands that while the district holds the lead administrator responsible for running the school and making all final decisions, one person cannot really totally run a school. Through shared expertise, the principal has also established a school culture and climate of collegiality, professionalism, and shared leadership. In fact, the principal often extolled the fact that his presence was often not needed in many decisions made by teachers and staff. This school is further united through a common vision and mission that it takes a whole community to educate a child, and that community must be local, state, national, global, and universal; thus, the school theme is "A Universal School for the Individual Child." The final theme, overcoming external obstacles, acknowledges obstacles, often externally imposed, that must be overcome in order to meet the needs of increasingly diverse and high-needs student populations.

Description of the School

At the time of our visit in fall 2002, this school was on its 7th year of operation. It was located in a rapidly growing area of the county, considered middle and lower income. The campus was approximately 10 acres and consisted of four classroom buildings, one of which housed the cafeteria/auditorium. A fifth building housed the media center and yet another, the physical education facilities. There was one portable classroom. The school had a strong commitment to technology, having spent in excess of $130,000 on technology during the 2001–2002 school year. Every classroom had a minimum of two computers. The school also had a 15–station computer lab, a computer graphics lab in the art room, and a specialized music lab. All the classrooms and offices were networked with the Internet. It also had a wireless network utilized by most classrooms. As a result of a federal $1.1 million bilingual education grant, the school planned for all students to have access to 165 laptop computers over a 5-year time frame, up from 75 at the time.

This community school enrolled 1,116 students in grades P/K–5, including 93.3% Hispanic/Latino, 5.4% non-Hispanic White/Caucasian, 0.7% Black/African American, 0.4% Asian American, and 0.3% multiracial. Students on free and reduced-price lunch accounted for 55.5% of the total school population. The mobility rate was approximately 19%, mostly due to a continuous influx of immigrants. Some 14% of the students were classified as students who were gifted, 10% students with disabilities, and 30.7% students who were ELLs. Most of the students who were ELLs were in the lower grades, decreasing with grade level and minimal participation in the upper grades. Average class size was 26.8 students. Many students came from single-parent homes, with many parents also working more than one job and having limited English communication skills. A sizeable number of students were new to the country and consequently, experienced adjustment and communication difficulties.

The school employed 69 full-time teachers and another 75–100 hourly and part-time employees. A project director was funded through the federal bilingual education grant to coordinate both the Bilingual Program and an Extended Foreign Language Program. At the time, most of the teachers were relatively new to the school and the profession with less than 10 years of teaching experience. The principal was a non-Hispanic White/Caucasian male with a master's degree and 20 years of experience as an administrator, 15 of those as a principal at the middle and elementary levels. He had been at the school since its inception. Three different assistant principals had been assigned during the school's 7 years. The assistant principal at the time of our visit was in her 2nd year in the position. The research team's interview with the school administrators included both the principal and assistant principal.

Entrepreneur Funding

As illustrated at the opening to this chapter, the culture at this school is strongly poised to seek external funds. The school has developed a strong, positive energy, capacity-building culture, driven with astuteness, creativity, and initiative. Challenges are met with systematically analyzed risk taking. This contributes to their success in being able to address the diverse needs of their school population. Countering the limitations of federal, state, and district funding, both teachers and administrators actively seek external funds to use these resources for such things as programmatic improvements, upgrading technology, and creating bilingual programs that build upon the student's primary language and enhance student learning.

The principal plays a supportive role in creating pathways for teachers to work together in order to garner the needed skills to seek external funding. For example, the principal utilizes the district's professional development department to assist teachers in grant writing: "Our district has been very successful in extensive grant writing. We have huge grants that provided tons of the training we've done over the years." Even with the training the district avails itself of, the principal acknowledges that there is a science to grant writing: "Certain teachers have a better grasp of this than others." These teachers become a valuable resource for the school and for other teachers to learn the ins and outs of grant writing from those with the most knowledge and expertise.

It is important to point out that external funding is a rich source of extra resources for this school, not only for what the resources currently provide, but for the future grant writing potential and opportunities that are created: supplementary personnel provide important resources to the school in terms of grant expertise, which is also supported by additional personnel, who can free up teachers to pursue grant writing opportunities; they can help with other areas that need to be attended to by the school. Some of the grants the school has been awarded include a 5-year bilingual grant of approximately $1 million and a 2-year family literacy grant, which is $75,000 per year. Thus, the supplementary personnel hired by the school because of these grant funds include a teacher who is the Project Coordinator in charge of bilingual programs; 15 paraprofessionals paid by the bilingual grant; and teachers on staff who get paid additional monies to design, deliver, and conduct parent workshops after hours. The Project Coordinator, additionally, provides inservice training and support for teachers, and this person organizes informative meetings and workshops for parents on the objectives of the grant to develop students who were bilingual and biliterate.

External funding is also sought through more traditional partnerships and venues with the community and Parent–Teacher Association (PTA). The principal is proud of the fact that the "PTA supports key initiatives; they give us lots of money for our special purpose, and we are able to do things" (e.g., like buy more computers for each classroom). A teacher comments, "Right now, we are very big on technology, especially when we got that one million dollar grant that the school was given through one of the teachers that wrote a grant." Clearly, the combination of the PTA, community, and grant support has created a powerful synergy for this school to address its resource priorities.

The culture of entrepreneurship of this school suggests that teachers feel the principal has listened when they express a need for more computers and/or resources in general: "I asked for more computers. I had five in my room within a week" (Teacher). Thus, besides the hardware, teachers also have a computer technician available to assist them with their technology questions and implementation. As a result, the school not only provides the tools, but the personnel to assist teachers with using computers and the expertise to work in a bilingual program.

Teachers generally feel the principal will get them what they need. To illustrate, one teacher said, "If there is something you need in order to get the teaching done, you got it. You don't have to beg. You need this and you get it." Sometimes, however, there are situations in education where resources have not been used wisely. This is not the case at this school. Teachers and the principal are acutely aware of using resources wisely. The principal highlights the reputation the school has developed as spenders and for the skills required for getting additional monies related to budget with this statement:

> I think it's one of our strengths [meaning knowing how to get resources] because of the way we use the budget. We are able to utilize our resources to the max. Our class size is probably amongst the lowest in the entire county, and we start out with the budget process with the most important thing—we are going to put as few kids in every class as we possibly can, then everything else will be supported on top of that. . . . Yesterday we got $10,000 more in [federal] funds. We didn't even ask for them. In all honesty, there are schools that don't know how to spend money. They [the district and other funders] will call schools and say we will give you this money, so spend it by Friday; they don't know how to do it; they know that they will get a reputation of not knowing how to spend the dollars. If you know how to spend, they [district and funders] will give it to you.

The entrepreneurial spirit of this school has gained it a reputation for knowing how to respond quickly to funding opportunities; success has bred success. Teachers feel supported by the principal; additional personnel assist educators with lowered class sizes and bilingual support; there are workshops for parents and extra tutorials for students. And after-school programs create a rich environment for extended learning with things like dance, chorus, and videography.

The infrastructure for technology, built into this school's resource plan, can sustain a viable platform for maintaining up-to-date technology.

More $ = smaller class sizes, doesn't wear out small class sizes so is it happiness? I just don't understand stress-achievement why? research how do I understand why? this translation

The principal has strategically focused on technology for the past 7 years. Thus, the school's resource priorities are clearly focused and have built the basic infrastructure for continued technology and bilingual support that has the seeds of sustainability. This means the school is able to update and upgrade its technology on a regular basis, with a reduced capital outlay; it also recognizes that bilingual education is a priority and that additional funding is needed to support it.

There is no doubt that this school's success with students is supported by their entrepreneurial attitude and procurement of additional resources, the skills of the principal and the teachers, and the ability of the principal and teachers to prioritize and use resources wisely. Importantly, the school principal has built the necessary support structures to enable information about grants to be disseminated widely, quickly, and response-"ably." Support structures for getting grants, initiating writing projects, improving grant writing skills, and supporting teachers with release time is built into the culture. Moreover, teachers sustain this culture by gaining, acquiring, and developing the necessary skills to obtain external funding. Similarly, teachers can see the benefits of obtaining these additional resources. As one teacher says, "Not only do we have materials galore in the sense of everything from tutoring to [reading materials for] decoding in sixth grade, but this has nothing to do with the state achievement test." The focus within this school appears, therefore, to be placed on values that relate to creating a successful environment for teaching and learning; this means that the focus on doing what is best for students is not merely instrumental for raising scores. Educators at this school know that federal, state, and district funding are inadequate for this school to address the needs of its students.

Overcoming External Obstacles

> There [are] a lot of obstacles in the way of becoming a school that does things really well, and unfortunately, it's the state, for the most part, and to a lesser extent the district, that merely creates the problems that don't allow the schools to do what they need to do. I think you have to have an administration that is persistent, intelligent, and creative; that's not going to quit and can figure out a way to knock down those roadblocks or go around them in order to do the right thing by your [students]. (Principal)

Too often, success does not come easy. This principal's words clearly illustrate the alarming reality of many schools struggling with very needy student populations. The reality is that many schools must learn how to block external interference. This school has done so and in turn, enhanced its internal ability to effectively meet the educational needs of its students. That "doesn't mean we should not have district initiatives and school board goals and things of that nature," but rather that "schools need to have more freedom to do what is right for that particular school." The principal adds, "If we didn't have to deal with the state achievement test, we would be able to do wonderful things, much better than we are doing now in terms of educating our children." This principal further expresses great concern about high-stakes tests: "It's what they do with the test that's bad," even though the actual examination is good because it gets students to think and write down the answers. Another concern is that the state school recognition program does not fairly evaluate school progress or reward schools adequately. The principal describes this school's feeling about the recognition problem by saying,

> We...really wish that the governor would take a very strong look at the school recognition program, because we feel that the program doesn't adequately reward certain schools and certain staffs who work very hard and diligently and may not necessarily make those kinds of gains. We found it to be very distasteful the way in which the money is allocated to the schools; and then you ask our school communities to divvy up dollars, and that's always a very unpleasant experience.

The principal further elaborates,

> Rather than uniting the school, the reward money created dissentions and divisions within a previously unified community. From teachers to clerical to custodians to security to our parents to our kids and business members; and it was really embarrassing; this year we have a wonderful faculty, but we were embarrassed with the way this thing played out because there were groups in the school who felt seriously slighted, and everybody was allocated something, but obviously it wasn't to the level that they felt they were worth, and you will never make everybody happy.

Another key area where educators in effective schools have had to learn how to get around external demands and expectations from the district and/or state levels is in actual personnel selection:

> We deal with the district on a larger basis with surplus issues and things of that nature every year. Sometimes we win and sometimes we lose. But more often than not we win, and I think the reason we win is we have a passion for bringing in the right people. I think that is such an important thing, and unfortunately, I think that what [Y county] does is just horrible. (Principal)

In this district, as in many others across the state and nation, the process is that every year the district has to place surplus personnel, and if there is an opening at the school, they have to first find a place for the surplus personnel.

> They don't necessarily match up the person to the strengths of that particular school. Their primary mission is to clear the decks... and there are a million different problems with that whole situation because now [X county] is losing qualified applicants to [Z county]. We also have the issue of people being hired as permanent subs instead of regular teachers, which is another real problem as well. (Principal)

Contrary to what many districts proclaim, principals lack autonomy to make crucial personnel selection decisions directly linked to their effectiveness. This principal states, "I don't think any principal in our district has total control to hire anyone, do you?" This is followed by much laughter. Too often, personnel decisions vary with the region, the principal, "even the day of the week," but mostly with how well the principal can negotiate. In other words, how personally connected the principal is with the personnel director and others in central administration. Fortunately for this school, personnel turnover is small—the high morale and mentoring provided for newly hired personnel make the school a desirable place to work. The school is relatively new, and many of the teachers started when the school opened. As such, the entire school culture has evolved over the years. Many teachers are former student teachers and paraprofessionals. New teachers are mentored carefully. Paraprofessionals are a valued and nurtured instructional resource. Highly trained paraprofessionals work with students and teachers in preparing and conducting activities, including preparing lessons, organizing materials, and tutoring students.

Another area closely linked to school effectiveness is budgetary spending. With shrinking state and district allocations, and less and less funding going to the actual classroom and teaching, this principal complains,

> They [the district] make us spend all this money on things that we don't even really need. You have to buy these social studies books. A lot of good teachers don't even want to use them to teach social studies. They are preventing us from being the kinds of educators that we want to become, so we do a lot of it anyways, and it's really a crime... to have to spend money on books that we don't really need—at 50 bucks each.

It doesn't end there. School funding to support classroom instruction continues to diminish; for example, the principal explains budget cuts related to staff. The "paraprofessional budget was cut this year. Sometimes you look at principals, and I feel for them because they have been cut seriously with their paraprofessionals." The principal and teachers feel that even the school improvement process needs revisiting. "I wish the school improvement process was more relevant to the schools. Sometimes we get [to do it] in order to complete it, you know." This statement from the principal is confirmed by the teachers who add, "I really don't know that the way we are functioning today, that we really need to have school improvement plans in the way we have established them years ago."

The staff at this school has learned that one way to overcome all the obstacles placed in their way is to be "proactive" in anticipating the future. They do not stand around waiting to be told what to do or how to do it. They survey staff, students, and community for concerns and needs. They collaboratively agree on a course of action, including where to find resources and/or training. Then they follow their goals with passion. Teachers attend numerous workshops and bring back that information, whether one-on-one or in the weekly grade-level meetings.

Internal Shared Leadership

The school has developed internal shared leadership, with collaborative and distributive leadership at its heart. This model of leadership recognizes teacher, community, and staff expertise. The culture of transparency invites people who work at the school to feel safe in applying and developing their knowledge, skills, and expertise in areas that are priorities within the school. The principal is clear that "my leadership is collaborative." This leadership orientation takes into account that if others are involved in decision making, they have a "vested interest in seeing that something is successful." The principal also couples collaborative leadership with a belief in leading by example. "I never ask anybody to get dirty without me getting dirty myself."

The principal recognizes the expertise within the faculty and staff: "Our counselor is a strong leader in this school, and so is the secretary." Not uncommon, grade-level chairs are seen as strong leaders in the school as well. The principal trusts these leaders: "I don't even need to be here anymore. We have a really great staff." The principal talks about the faculty and staff thusly:

> My assistant principal—I have to say administration—I think a lot comes from administration and great teachers, and you know what it is, we have a professional environment in this school. I have four or five secretaries who

are all so proficient in their jobs; you can never minimize their importance. I have a head custodian who is amazing; he contributes greatly to what happens in this school. We have a cafeteria manager who does everything along with the mission of this school. We have leaders on our faculty without whom we probably couldn't get off of square one. They are willing to do it. They are willing to go that extra mile; they believe in what we are trying to accomplish. They are the heart and soul to this school. We have surrounded ourselves with the most high-quality human beings and the nicest people, that you would do anything as administrators because you just know they are doing the right thing by the children. Everybody in this building is an incredibly special person.

Teachers see the administration, teachers, and all the staff as making up the leadership of the school: "Everybody is a team. It is not one individual person because everybody here works very close together." Teachers feel comfortable asking one another for help. They are also encouraged to attend conferences and share what they have learned with other teachers. There is an active learning culture that supports asking questions and engaging in discussions about practice. One teacher comments, "When we sit at [a] grade-level meeting, [we ask], is there anyone you know that has expertise in certain areas for improvement? What can we do to help?" The faculty see the school leadership as very supportive. A teacher states, "I think we're fantastic, because we have great support from administration. And we have great parents that are involved, and it's just a very, very united effort." The principal is always asking the teachers what more they need to learn. Staff development is tailored to the needs of the school.

Universal School

This is the theme selected by the school to describe them and represent the school mission statement: "A Universal School for the Individual Child." The mission statement includes the following:

> Our "Universal School," composed of students, school staff, family members, and business leaders, is committed to the process of educating creative and successful future citizens in an ever evolving multi-faceted community. Each child's unique intellectual and affective needs are addressed through innovative, dynamic, and relevant approaches to teaching and learning.
>
> [X7] is a school in which every adult who works with students has the highest expectations for the students and the belief that each and every child can and will realize his or her potential. Staff members will endeavor to make each child feel safe, secure, and special by providing the most nurturing

environment possible. The end result will be that at [X7], no child will be left behind.

Everyone in the school believes that their mission is to build a community of learners. This mission is reflected in the entire school culture. An atmosphere of friendliness and hospitality permeates throughout the school. Both the administrators and parents treat teachers like professionals. New teachers are assigned mentors, and new students are assigned "buddies" to learn the school culture; a culture based on mutual respect and a positive work environment. School rules, including those dealing with discipline, are all grounded in kindness and respect. As such, the school does not have any serious discipline problems. Everyone's effort, including students, is recognized and rewarded through "many awards, many accolades."

A key component of the school culture and climate is the conviction that everyone, from every school staff member—instructional and non-instructional—to students and parents, has assets that contribute to the school success. Assets do not need to be fiscal, but cultural, community networks, volunteerism, etc. This is the glue that binds the school, together with high levels of trust and connections within and beyond the school walls. At this school, it is reflected through extensive parent and school communication, collaboration, and services that meet the needs of students and their community.

> The new kids are basically treated with kindness and everything when they come into this school, and the parents are welcome and invited to become part of the school culture as well. We don't run parents off the campus. You can walk outside and you can see parents. They will be sitting on the benches. We encourage them to come have lunch with their kids, as long as they don't eat lunch per se in the cafeteria. A lot of parents come here to check the school out, but we do offer them tours, and we do show them our different facilities; everything we have available to offer their child. (Principal)

Teachers echo the principal in saying, "We work well with our community. That makes a difference. We always have their support." This school has an open-door policy. Repeatedly, teachers expressed that administrators are available to them at all times. Administrators listen to teachers' needs, concerns, and suggestions. Administrators are open in the assessment of teachers and keep them informed of their progress regularly. As such, teachers state that they know "just how they are doing." Additionally, administrators constantly ask teachers for their input on schoolwide matters, including budget, and matters impacting their instruction; what they need and what they are lacking in the classroom.

Parents state that teachers are also readily available to them. Communication with parents is ongoing and timely, often daily. "We converse with them a lot" (Principal). Everything is communicated to parents bilingually. As such, parents have a clear sense of belonging. Extensive communication and abundant meetings let everyone feel that they have a part in what goes on at the school. Parents are warmly invited and welcomed to the school. The presence of parents throughout the campus is evident, whether visiting or volunteering, parents sitting on benches conversing, helping in the office and classrooms, reading to and with children, monitoring the halls and cafeteria, etc. "The teachers are wonderful in communicating with parents. Even though it's time-consuming, the rewards are outrageous. Because of that, we have a lot of parent support" (Teacher).

Parents do much more than just "sell candy"; they are legitimately involved in decision making and the learning process. Throughout the year, numerous conferences are held with parents, individually as well as in groups, in addition to many parent nights hosted by grade levels. Coverage is always provided for teachers to attend conferences with parents. Parents actually discuss, agree, and sign a document delineating both parent and school responsibilities. As well, parents are involved in the learning and teaching process. Teachers teach them strategies to reinforce school learning at home.

> Also, our parents can come in here and they can use our Internet. We are open until six every night. We have somebody in the library every night until six, and we encourage parents to come in. We like to see them on the Internet helping their children. (Principal)

A variety of parent workshops are offered on a regular basis, including educating parents on how the school and district function, where they can find information and resources, and how they can participate. Parents have access to intergenerational reading literacy, adult ESOL, adult computer skills, as well as parenting classes. When needed, childcare is provided so parents can attend these classes. It is recognized that these skills empower parents in supporting their children's learning at home.

Communication is multidirectional, multilateral, and multifaceted. It is open and transparent, formal and informal; keeping everyone apprised of significant issues and needs on a regular and timely basis. This leads to a high level of trust: administrators and teachers trust each other's professionalism and expertise. They, in turn, trust parents' willingness and capacity to support them and their children. Parents trust everyone at the school; teachers trust each other, etc. Collegiality is evidenced by the collaborative work of all staff members.

We're some of the best teachers there are. I think so... yeah. The teachers are fantastic, and I think we're fantastic because we have such great support from administration. And we have great parents that are involved, and we have great kids, and it's just a very, very united effort. Whatever you need to make your teaching better, you'll... get it. One way or another, you'll get it. And it's not like the teachers are limited to what he or she can do, but there's always that extra, that "whatever it is" throughout. (Teacher)

There is dedication and passion. Teachers are very involved: "We have teachers that come here morning, noon, and night." In addition to a very large after-school care program, the school holds early-bird and Saturday classes for students. Early-bird classes take place 1 hour before the regular school day begins. These programs offer dance, chorus, cheerleading, and videography. Academic tutoring with certified teachers and paraprofessionals, for students needing the extra help, is available before, during, and after school, including Saturdays. Over 400 students participate in these programs.

We do an assessment of different subjects and then go ahead and speak to the people in charge of the programs and say this student would benefit from this kind of tutoring, this student maybe needs this, and this student would benefit from that. Then we are making sure that in the room their needs are being met through the different programs that we offer here at this school. (Teacher)

Students with disabilities and who are ELLs are included in everything the school does; they are encouraged to participate, and every opportunity is made to ensure their inclusion right along all other "standard-curriculum kids." Thus, tutoring classes are available for everyone, including these special populations. Language arts instruction is offered in both English and Spanish. Two self-contained classes at each grade level are designated Dual Bilingual Developmental. There, students who are ELLs learn English while continuing to use and develop their native language. They are matched with English-dominant children learning the native language of the students who are ELLs. Additionally, the school offers an Extended Foreign Language Program for English-monolingual students, who are not in bilingual classrooms. Science is also offered in Spanish. The goal is to develop students who are bilingual and biliterate in both English and Spanish.

The school has a multicultural committee that runs all the co-curricular activities. Although the student population is predominantly Hispanic/Latino, the principal emphasized, "You won't come into this school and find just a Hispanic heritage program. You will find a multicultural program." Everyone agrees that all different cultures must be incorporated into the classroom. Cultural diversity is celebrated throughout the entire school year, not just for the students but for the faculty as well. It is agreed that students must be given the opportunity to share their heritage. According to the principal, emphasis is placed on letting students develop pride in their culture: "We stress that, and our extended language program goes a long way toward making that a reality." This helps students feel comfortable and valued, and fosters an environment of cultural affirmation so essential in the development of high and positive self-perceptions and academic achievement for students.

Internal Accountability and Expertise

"We fight like cats and dogs to get the personnel we want in this school, and it's important to us. We are obsessed with it. . . . we have a passion for bringing in the right people." In other words, accountability is internally driven and begins with the personnel within the school (as illustrated by this quote from the principal). Astute and knowledgeable about budgeting and with the assistance of grant funds, the principal of this school has been able to hire needed personnel, including 75–100 hourly or part-time staff to assist the students and staff. Teacher recruitment and selection is so intense, that it may mean

> We bring people back ten times sometimes before we would offer them a position, literally. We interviewed over a hundred people for, like, four positions; when we narrowed our pool, we brought them back three, four, and five meetings, some of them ten times. (Principal)

There is a professional environment in this school that appreciates the individual expertise of the faculty and staff. Personnel are held accountable for achievement of goals and objectives through frequent monitoring of student work. During common planning meetings, data on students are discussed, and students needing additional help are identified. Instructional decisions are data based. Continuous assessment and monitoring is integral to the emphasis placed on internal accountability. It includes monitoring through the use of benchmark testing, district-made pre- and progress tests for the standardized state achievement test, and informal teacher-made tests. Within the classroom, students are assessed daily and/or weekly. Assessments developed at the school are tailored to students' needs, for example, in math, science, and reading. Benchmarking and assessments are also used to establish student achievement in Spanish. An external evaluator helps monitor both the Bilingual Program and the Extended Foreign Language Program. The Developmental Reading Assessment instrument is used as well as the Accelerated Reader Program.

The school has access to online data in a multitude of areas, including student data (e.g., demographic, health, report card grades, test scores, psychological data, attendance, discipline referrals). In addition, a wealth of information, for both the school and the community, is available through the district's Web site. Detailed state achievement test results, Educational Excellence School Advisory Council (EESAC) information (including minutes of meetings, roster, and bylaws), and overcrowding and safety issues are some of the obtainable information. All parents have access to the school improvement plan, which is online. Parents are encouraged to use the school's computers and checkout of laptops is permitted and encouraged. These efforts help to keep the school accountable to the school administrators, teachers, and parents. This internal accountability is seen as key to the success of this high-performing school. High expectations and teacher expertise are other indicators of internal accountability in this school. As a result, the principal confirms, "The students are making growth and they are growing each year, you can see that clearly." A teacher agrees:

> We set very high expectations for our students. So therefore, we expect the most from these students. They do perform that way. That is evident in our scores, and that is pretty much how we have gotten to where we are, because we expect so much from them. We expect more of them than just good scores on the state achievement test. It is not easy teaching here; there is a lot of pressure that the people put on themselves from within. We don't even have to do it.

This school "took on" the very real reality that the funding schools get from federal, state, and district resources are often not sufficient to meet the needs of the school. Rather than just accepting this as an obstacle that can't be overcome, both the teachers and administrators actively seek external funds resulting in a strong culture of entrepreneurship and capacity building. The principal plays a supportive role in creating pathways for teachers to work together to garner the needed skills to seek external funding. External resources have been sought and used to provide professional development for teachers and parents, upgrade technology, reduce class size, and create bilingual programming that builds on the primary language of the large population of students who are ELLs. In addition, numerous partnerships have been established with local businesses and organizations.

The School in 2009–2010

According to the 2009–2010 School improvement Plan, the school enrolled 650 students, including 90% Hispanic/Latino, 8% non-Hispanic White/Caucasian, less than 1% Black/African American, and 2% Asian American and multiracial combined. Students with disabilities were 14%, and students who were gifted represented 10.5% of the student population. The student stability rate was 98%, while the rate for the state was 94%. Students absent more than 21 days was 3%, while the rate for the state was 7%. The average class size for primary grades (P/K–2) was 15.17 and upper grades (3–5) were 17.21. These numbers are typical for ESOL classrooms. The school now has self-contained bilingual classes in the primary grades and "push-in" transitional classes in the upper grades. With 38% of students identified as ELLs and 61% who received free or reduced-price lunch, this school would be perceived as less likely to sustain high performance. To the contrary, for the previous consecutive 9 years, this school received a grade of "A." Other indicators of high performance for this school include 70% or more students scored Level 3 or above on the reading and math FCAT for the previous 8 years and 60% or more students made learning gains in reading and math. The school also had the distinction of meeting the federal requirement of making Academic Yearly Progress (AYP) for 4 of the previous 5 years (see Table 3.1).

TABLE 3.1   School X7 Indicators of High Performance

Academic year	Adequate yearly progress met	School grade	Students scoring Level 3 & above on FCAT		Students making learning gains	
			Reading	Math	Reading	Math
2008–09	No[a]	A	88%	78%	68%	57%
2007–08	Yes	A	88%	84%	70%	63%
2006–07	Yes	A	86%	81%	78%	61%
2005–06	Yes	A	88%	82%	75%	67%
2004–05	Yes	A	83%	79%	69%	71%
2003–04	No[b]	A	82%	76%	75%	73%
2002–03	No[c]	A	73%	73%	72%	66%
2001–02	NR	A	78%	74%	72%	91%
2000–01	NR	A	79+%	54+%	NR	NR
1999–00	NR	C	58+%	45%	NR	NR
1998–99	NR	C	NR	NR	NR	NR

Note: NR = Data not reported.
Source: No Child Left Behind School Public Accountability Report.
[a] 97% of AYP criteria met. ELLs did not meet math proficiency requirement.
[b] 97% of AYP criteria met. Students with disabilities did not meet math proficiency requirement.
[c] Percentage of AYP criteria met was not reported. ELLs did not meet reading proficiency requirement. Students with disabilities did not meet math proficiency requirement.

The school had a new principal assigned for the 2009–2010 school year. The principal, a Hispanic/Latino female, held a bachelor's degree and 6 years of administrative experience, including a previous elementary school principalship. The assistant principal held a bachelor's degree and had been at the school for 3 years, with 8 years of experience as an administrator. The school had 49 instructional staff, including a reading instruction coach and math instruction coach. There were no teachers teaching out-of-field. There were no 1st-year teachers, and 32.7% of the teachers had over 15 years of experience. Teachers with advanced degrees were 36.7%, while 18.4% were certified by the National Board for Professional Teaching Standard, and 77.6% were ESOL endorsed.

Questions for Discussion

1. How can schools overcome the many obstacles, both internally and externally imposed, that prevent them from developing cultures that are more responsive to the needs of today's student populations?
2. How are budget and resource-allocation decisions made at your school? How can these processes at your school be improved?
3. How can schools build their capacity for fundraising beyond the allocated school budget? What knowledge and skills are required? How can schools support external fundraising efforts by all members of the faculty?
4. What systems, structures, and processes are in place at your school that are reflective of the cultures of the community it serves? What systems, structures, and processes are there to support students' cultural backgrounds?

4

Whatever Works

Roll Up Your Sleeves and Get It Done Happily and Lovingly!

We plan together, we work together, and we accept ideas from different people—whatever works. If you want to teach in a tree and that works, you can teach in a tree.... I know the teachers are frustrated, but they [parents] don't want to hear it from the teachers. They still need to teach, happily. They come in and that is my style. That communication with the parents on an individual basis pays off. For me, it pays off a lot. I hold the parents responsible. The teachers have to teach happy, and the parents have to do something. That combination made the school an "A." (Principal A)

Introduction

As clearly stated by the quote opening this chapter, Principal A sets the tone and stays directly on top of the entire school's pulse at all times. It seems as if this principal sees, hears, and knows everything related to the school and is directly involved in all areas of the school's functioning. Her approach is very hands-on, personal, and informal. This approach is viewed as crucial to this school's continued progress and success. Labeled X2, this school has been rated "A" consistently since the 2000–2001 academic year. Grades for the school, from the 2000–2001 through the 2008–2009 school years, can be found in Table 4.1, "School X2 Indicators of High Performance," located at the end of the chapter. This chapter discusses the major themes propelling this very low-income school to high performance: culture and climate of access and inclusion, principal at the helm, building internal accountability and shared expertise, and deficit funding: scarce fiscal resources-wealth of human resources. A profound overarching theme at this school is culture and climate, which is characterized as very open and creating opportunities for all students through access and inclusion. As exemplified by the opening quote, two major subthemes within the school's culture and climate are teamwork and planning together.

The current principal has been assigned to this school since the fall of 2001. To distinguish between the current and previous principal, this chapter will address the current principal as "Principal A" and the previous as "Principal B." Principal A maintains that teachers are professionals, who can make decisions about what might work better, are accountable for student learning, and can be happy in their school environment. In this school, leadership and accountability are inseparable, and high internal accountability goes hand-in-hand with the principal at the helm. Teachers and parents trust the principal's navigational skills to pull everyone together as an empowered cohesive organizational system. In her 2nd year at this school, during the research team's spring 2003 visit, Principal A had already played a vital role in the development of the school and its transition. Rather than rest on the laurels of stepping into an already "A" rated school by continuing the operating status quo established by the previous principal (B), Principal A decided to build internal accountability by creating a more effective learning partnership, where everyone in the organization is an accountable leader and team player ready to contribute to the success formula. Deficit funding is a constant reality at this school; resources are notorious for their deficiency; yet the prevailing readiness of everyone, including Principal A, to roll up their sleeves and do whatever needs to get done and compensate for shortcomings, have turned fiscal poverty into a wealth of human capital.

Description of the School

During the initial site visit, this was a community school serving P/K–5 and located in a suburban, although highly developed, area of a major city and county. The surrounding neighborhood had mostly one-story, single-family homes. The school was surrounded by commercial areas with a few shopping centers and several fast-food restaurants. It consisted of nine buildings, housing 37 classrooms, a media center, music center, and cafeteria/auditorium (cafetorium), along with six portables. The school also had an ESOL technology lab. At the time of our initial visit in January 2003, this 41-year-old school was retrowired to provide Internet and intranet access to 86% of the classrooms. The media center had just been remodeled and housed a state-of-the-art closed-circuit classroom.

Although the school was aged, the corridors and public areas were very well-maintained and attractive. The school was very open and airy, with classrooms opening to the outdoors. The main office was small, yet welcoming. A few chairs divided the staff's work area from the waiting area. Both the waiting area and the principal's private office opened to the outdoors. There always appeared to be a buzzing of activity with teachers, students, and parents coming and going in the main office. The office staff spoke in English to some children and parents and in Spanish to others. The staff also used both languages comfortably among themselves.

During the 2001–2002 year, the school enrolled approximately 861 students. The majority of the students were Hispanic/Latino (90.6%). The percentage of non-Hispanic White/Caucasian students was 6.4%, Black/African American 0.7%, and 2% Asian American and multiracial combined. Students on free and reduced-price lunch were 52.9% of the population. The student mobility rate was 21%. Students who were ELLs were 31%, students classified as gifted were 14.6%, and 4% were students with disabilities. The school had established an in-house program for students who were gifted. Average class size (K–5) was 25.2 students. The school employed a principal and an assistant principal. The principal was a Hispanic/Latino female with a master's degree. At the time of our visit in January 2003, Principal A had over 20 years of experience in education, including 11 as a classroom teacher, 3 as a guidance counselor, almost 5 as assistant principal, and 5 as principal at another school. She had completed a PhD in Organizational Leadership and Curriculum Development, and had additional extensive coursework in human development and counseling. The school employed 66 full-time and 25 part-time staff; 2 administrators, 29 classroom teachers, and 8 special education teachers, 3 of which taught students who were gifted. There were 24 new teachers. The average years of experience for teachers was 12, and 24 had advanced degrees. There was one guidance counselor, six paraprofessionals, four clerks, seven cafeteria workers, and five custodians.

Culture and Climate of Access and Inclusion

The school culture and climate that permeates throughout this entire organization seems key to the orchestration of all the other components. This school stands out for its open and welcoming atmosphere that creates opportunities for all teachers and parents to excel and combine their collective human capital. The school is very supportive and welcoming of students and the local community. Communication is very regular, open, and most often casual. The school adheres to an open-door policy that welcomes parents whenever they can come. The doors to the main office, including one of the principal's doors exit to the school courtyard, and remain open, especially in the morning and at the end of the school day, when teachers, children, and parents are coming and going. This allows the principal to be aware of things going on in the main office and outdoors. It creates opportunities for all students to have access and feel the invitation to be included. The school's open-door policy is very much appreciated by everyone. Teachers, students, and parents often peek their heads in to greet the principal and share quick comments and/or request appointments. Principal A takes advantage of these informal times to speak with parents and teachers, particularly to remind teachers of tasks to be completed related to instruction and student progress:

> [To Spanish teachers]—You are teaching main idea. Are you teaching geometry in Spanish? [To art teacher]—Are you teaching...? You better! [laughter]...I just spoke with [teacher] on his way out about three-thirty—Are you sure you are finished teaching geometry? Because I see by the charts this week that geometry is low.

Principal A acknowledges that communication skills must be carefully learned and honed. She has taken communication courses and recommends that all educators do so as well. She has come to the realization that much communication is nonverbal and often requires more listening than talking. Skilled communication recognizes the importance of having an open atmosphere where everyone can express their feelings. This becomes crucial in working with students. "They [parents] might be going through a divorce. Sometimes they will come in and tell you that you might be noticing this or that [about their child]" (Teacher).

Access and inclusion are integral parts of the school culture and climate. "When I do my schedule, I make sure that everybody has equal access to all the programs at the school" (Principal A). Besides holding a lot of meetings, the school sends information to parents in various languages. Parents' cultures, languages, and family/communal networks are considered assets—human capital—to be valued and integrated into the school's resources year round and, thus, a successful formula. "We plan our activities all around the year. Activities for Hispanics, like history, holiday celebra-

So what is the explanation for other who do the same thing and don't succeed?

tions around the world. We incorporate that into the curriculum, and we have special activities all year round" (Principal A).

The school further recognizes and values the humanity in everyone. Principal A recognizes that when teachers have problems, even personal ones, their classroom effectiveness may become compromised. As a leader, she has created a work environment whereby teachers, and all staff members, feel unthreatened sharing when issues may interfere with their work. In turn, the principal is willing to step in, even cover classes, to allow individuals time to regroup and get back on track. The principal may even allow teachers to take noninstructional time to resolve personal problems. She openly recognizes that when strapped by rigid and constraining mandates, individuals may be forced to find ways to circumvent rules and/or exploit unguarded avenues. Instead, this principal prefers that staff communicate and do things openly.

Principal A also understands that when staff socializes together, they also develop cohesive work teams. During a subsequent visit by research team members in 2005, the principal explained how, during a planning day, a group of teachers went out together to have lunch and shop. They even invited her to join them and asked if she needed them to bring her something back. When they returned, they brought t-shirts for the other teachers. "So maybe on a Wednesday, they want time to go to [a department store].... let's face it, I'm not around to see who leaves early, but now they tell me, we're going to [a department store]. But at the same time, when those teachers go to [a fast-food restaurant] and they buy a hamburger for each child, they don't ask me for the money (Principal A).

Principal A has a strong educational background in human developmental psychology and motivation. Although the district's expectation is for principals to be "tough" on teachers, she has learned that treating persons with humanity and dignity goes further in creating a work environment of true team cohesiveness and collaboration. "I don't force people, because I don't want, especially dealing with children, I do not like teachers or any staff dealing with children in the school to do it in a nonpositive way. If you do not want to do it in a positive way, don't do it" (Principal A). She has learned that intimidation and inhumanity "do not get the job done" and recounts her own experiences as a teacher:

> I had various principals...when the principals told me in a bad way what to do, I didn't do it. Can you imagine? I feel ashamed. But there was a particular principal that...I was eating a sandwich, and he said, "No, you can't eat here. You have to go to the cafeteria." And I said, "Sir, but I'm pregnant, I can hardly walk now, let me..." "NO!" Then, one time, he asked me, "Oh, I

need this to pass, the faculty to vote on." Of course, he had to realize I was a leader in that school. When he wouldn't let me eat that sandwich there and I cried, ... then at the faculty meeting when he needed that vote—you know! I feel ashamed that I did it. That's what I don't want teachers to do. That's how I interpret it here, in a nice way.

As a teacher, I saw that when a principal asked me to do nine-week lesson plans in advance, they were not my own, and I did not build them with my coworkers, it didn't mean anything—I never even went back to read those. I went just through the motions of opening the book and putting in the nine-week lesson plans. So I think that whatever I saw work as a teacher, for those teachers, is what I implement. (Principal A)

There is a strong sense of empathy toward parents and students shared by the principal and the teachers. They agree that parents are truly interested in their children's education and well-being and are doing the very best they can within their daily obligations. Everyone at the school is realistic concerning the parents' daily lives and their desires and their inability to participate more fully in the school. According to the principal, the parents "are very good." The principal says,

Involvement—they don't do much. I don't have a big PTA. They don't make any money. This is a working community. If you are in a working community, you don't have time to come to school. They are working, so they don't have time to come in. But I make myself available. I have meetings all the time. I have one-to-one meetings, and they come in. I am open here until seven, so I make appointments. They are very good, very good. They come in all the time. (Principal A)

Further, the principal and teachers openly state that the state-mandated standardized tests are unrealistic in measuring student progress at their school with their unique student population. There is also the sense that the state-mandated standardized test punishes students unfairly, students who are working very hard. The principal remembers one student in particular:

I am hoping he [student] will improve. He is very nice; he is very good and tries his very best. I have about twenty students like that. [Student] and [student] that are Level One. Thank God they are not in third grade. [Student] says, "I'm doing good," and I say, "[Student], you are doing good, honey." He comes to Saturday school and after school and he does his very best. He was already assessed in ESE and he did not qualify. He is borderline. He is going to suffer later on when they retain him because he is trying his best. (Principal A)

The following statement describes a frequent experience for ELL students:

> They take it [state-mandated standardized test]. The poor kids. I don't believe in that....they come from different countries. They can't read. They tell me I don't understand. I accommodate small groups, flexible time.... If they have been here less than two years—they don't count. A lot of schools don't have the students take it. I do.... I feel bad. Maybe they don't know the answers, but at least they saw the test and know what it is. (Principal A)

Principal A is also very self-reflective, recognizing and overcoming her own shortcomings for the benefit of everyone at the school:

> I am not too sociable. However, in the mornings I am always available. That is how I socialize on a daily basis. I don't make a special effort. I am there every morning, and I make sure I greet them every morning and in the afternoon again. New students to the school, I escort them to the class, and I meet the parents. New students to the school have to meet me. Usually in the morning they are informal, like you saw me in the back [private office].

Significantly, this principal is a recognized motivator:

> Administration has been choosing one teacher and gives them a little award, and they try to celebrate everybody's birthday every month...We have Teacher of the Year...We have the Student of the Month. We also do a little on our own. She also recognizes the students who have perfect attendance. She does something for them. Gives them an ice cream party...They have to fill out a calendar, and at the end of the month she will call every single student that was here every day of the month and give them something— bag of chips, candy or toy—anything. She goes out and purchases on her own. (Teacher)

Principal A is also a candid risk taker, regularly finding many ways to publicize and celebrate both their victories and defeats: "Two weeks ago I had 'Honk if you like reading.' Nobody honked. The secretaries were making fun. A lot of laughter about honking." That does not deter them, and they move on with the next plan.

Building Internal Shared Leadership and Accountability

Principal A is described as having the strongest role in leadership, accountability, and decision making. "Teachers expressed a shift from the previous administrator's practices of more involvement" (Acker-Hocevar et al., 2005/2006, p. 261). Her style is perceived as having moved the school from one where the previous principal (Principal B) was described as collaborative, to one picturing the entire school as acquiescing to the new principal's dominating power. Parents are not very involved and/or knowledgeable of the school's decisions and daily operations. They perceive the principal as the "main thing": "If she is not on top of the employees like she is, nothing gets done." The study team was puzzled by the lack of coherence between this school and the others in the study sample in terms of internal power relationships. "These parents were the most ignorant of school leadership processes, decisions, and the school mission and improvement plan. They expressed that their involvement in decision-making was minimal and limited to a small group of parents" (Acker-Hocevar et al., 2005/2006, p. 261).

This chapter also examines the way in which Principal A moved quickly upon assuming the school's leadership to build shared leadership inextricably linked to accountability. Her initial goals were very strategic, first, to develop "expert leaders...on something that I don't know." This would foster a collaborative team bond between the principal and the school staff, something that seemed to have been lacking with the previous principal. Next, her goals included development of expertise in areas crucial to school effectiveness, "to become leaders in subject areas, critical thinking, standards" and finally, her goal was to develop a cohesive pool of experts working together in unison to move the school community forward. Her encouragement of teachers is evidenced by the following statement:

> Three teachers that have been here about seven or eight years never had their master's. So I provided them to do their master's at [university]. I forced them. They are very happy, happy to do that. They are a bit overwhelmed. (Principal A)

Teachers are encouraged to attend leadership development workshops, and they agree that the principal encourages "a lot of the teachers [who] want to be involved [in leadership]." Principal A adds, "Going back to developing leaders, now we have an ethics staff development. Veteran teachers were recommended to go to ethics training. I want to train everyone in the school...custodians, everyone, to [have] good moral values, teach ethics."

Principal A admits that technology is one of her weaknesses, thus, she relies on teachers as experts to assist her. "I am not too technology oriented, so they do the graphs, they come up with the ideas [development and evaluation of assessments]." The district provides very detailed data.

She supports teachers in becoming technology savvy and learning how to interpret data as a way to make effective instructional decisions. With computers and Internet access in each classroom, everyone is involved in assessment of student performance data, whether district or classroom/teacher generated. When a new child arrives at the school, data from the previous school is quickly obtained and evaluated in order to provide appropriate placement and instruction immediately. Although the school does not use electronic grade books, together, by grade-level teams and/or across teams, the entire staff charts and reviews student progress. Similarly, they track how individual teachers do with their students across content areas. Data is shared as students move up the grades and used to identify strengths and weaknesses of both teachers and students. As such, instruction is data driven. The principal emphasizes the importance of examining the data: "We study it and make decisions from there; what we need to teach, by semester, weekly...Because I see by the charts this week that geometry is low. With data, we can assess, and we know what to teach" (Principal A).

Principal A has also been key in hiring a significant percentage of the school teaching and support staff, and being carefully selective of the staff brought on board to support her vision and goals for the school. Ultimately, Principal A expects everyone to get on board as a team player: "I interview and hire whomever I feel can do the job. If they have surplus, I understand. They come in and I hire them. They [the district] send them to me and I have no choice on that. But they still need to teach, happily. They come in and that is my style. With a principal, the style is everything." Teachers are expected to do a lot of mentoring of new teachers as well as veteran teachers new to their school. As a result, although expectations were very demanding and workloads heavy, soon there was a much improved staff, higher teacher satisfaction, and high morale with decreasing faculty turnover. Teachers share resources and expertise and go into each other's classrooms to model teaching strategies while the classroom teacher is there. Plus, they engage in peer evaluation. During faculty meetings, each grade has to share materials and present lessons representative of "best practices" within the school. Teacher visits across grade levels are expected and supported. "They do visit four times a year the other classroom, and the teacher stays to watch. The articulation between middle school, the ESOL teachers, ESE teachers meet, everybody meets" (Principal A).

Principal A also saw the need to integrate parents more into the school community. At the beginning of each year, the school provides parents with strategies. The principal does this when meeting with individual parents, especially with parents of students who receive D and F grades. These parents are required to pick up the first report card directly from the principal. A teacher describes the substantial effort they make to assist parents:

> We also do a lot of parental workshops. We even offer free English classes to parents who don't speak English from a grant that we got from [university]. She [principal] holds a workshop every month. We as teachers hold workshops two or three times a year. Besides open house, we teach the parents what they need to do with the homework. I think that opens up their eyes. You know, what to do with the reading and the writing, and they know a lot about the [state-mandated standardized] test. So the parents can help the kids. We got a lot of feedback when we told the parents about the new law. They weren't aware of it. They were in shock. We try to let them be aware of it because we don't want any surprises. We do need their help. We can only do so much. Like the math teacher of the fourth grade was telling me today, "I can teach them until I am blue in the face, and then they go home and they don't study. They come back and they forgot everything."

Principal at the Helm: Role Model, Teacher, Motivator, and Leader

Principal A draws on her strengths as an experienced, knowledgeable, and skilled classroom teacher, who fully understands what effective instructional practice must be, and demonstrates her role as an educator and team player. She is a role model, teacher, motivator, as well as developer of collaborative teams and leaders.

> I lead by being a role model. That's about it. I do my teaching myself... the teachers see me teaching... In the beginning, when I first came here, there were no meetings with parents at night, so I held the workshops. I didn't need teachers, because I am a teacher. So the next month, the teachers came to me and said, "We can do that too." So I lead by being a role model. (Principal A)

As such, Principal A has gained the teachers' trust in her nonthreatening capacity to lead them toward success:

> During school, if I see a teacher that needs some changes or a teacher that is too strict or too hard, ... for example, there was a teacher who was a second grade teacher teaching kindergarten. I said, very positively, you loved kindergarten. You should be teaching second grade, not singing and playing. In a very positive way, I assess needs.

Internal accountability is ongoing, with Principal A setting high expectations for teachers about their work and student learning, along with regular monitoring of instruction and student achievement. This is supported through her visibility all around the school and very friendly, flexible, reasonable, and informal approach, and is demonstrated by her verbal commitment; everyone at the school works together and is responsible for student achievement. Along with teachers, Principal A monitors student profiles for early detection and remediation of problems, even from the previous years. The entire staff reviews and tracks students' progress charts, within and between the different grade levels. A significant aspect of this principal's accountability is talking to students and parents about what students are doing. The principal meets with parents, individually, to explain their children's progress. She also holds everyone accountable, including parents. The parents talk to each other and then come back and tell the principal, "You know, they are not teaching main idea . . . Informal assessing is good." The principal then goes back to the teacher.

Principal A goes into the classrooms and checks random lesson plans on a daily basis. Regularly, she reviews teachers' long-range goals, observes classroom activities, and personally monitors student performance profiles. Apart from everyday assessment, on any given day and at any hour, the principal calls a student from each class to bring a work folder and explain what they are doing in class: "I call them in and witness their progress. I call it show-and-tell." As such, she knows the students: "Who in the first grade can't read, who in the second grade can't read. I know. I can tell you students' names and their scores, and how they are doing." Parents know this and often ask her how their children are doing. Even students are aware of their individual progress and report on classroom instruction. Principal A states, "They [students] tell me 'My teacher didn't do anything today.'" The principal walks into classrooms and asks to see the work of individual students: "I have received teachers that are surplus from other schools. In the beginning, it was hard for them to adjust to a new principal that goes in and asks, "What are you doing, let me see your work"—not just boys and girls. This is the second year and they are already used to me." Additionally, the principal brainstorms and plans together with teachers: "That's the way I make sure that we are growing, and we have a high level of standards." The principal quips,

> I nag them [teachers] (laughter). I'm in there every day. I'm accountable and they are accountable. I don't just sit back, and they know that those kids have to perform; they have been there all year. The [state-mandated standardized test] results I highlight, I sit with all the Level One and Two.

Whoever receives a Level One and Two, I explain to the parents. I hold them accountable. I tell them to go back to the teacher and ask why your son is not reading. Everybody is accountable!

More formally, everything is documented. "We document everything every nine weeks. I collect all the data...they [teachers] have to keep a log. I collect all that every nine weeks" (Principal A). Everyone at the school is expected to be on the same page with the state standards, requiring ongoing collaboration within and between grade levels. Together they record and track all the strategies, align them to the standards, and document them in the annual School improvement Plan. A teachers concurs: "As a grade level, we have to come up with proof of what we are doing."

Yet the school is not test driven. They do not focus on standardized testing, particularly the state-mandated standardized test. They develop and administer instruction-driven, teacher-made tests that are administered each Friday. They also use book tests, writing prompts, "a little bit of everything," including student projects, to assess progress and learning.

> They do projects, especially in science and social studies...doing a narrative...with science and with activities. It is very relevant, hands-on. In the third grade, I see a lot of hands-on activities. Fourth grade, fifth grade, the math teacher does a lot with geometry. Hands-on with experiments with measuring how to measure the room. They have to bring in a map of a room.... How to measure a room, very relevant to their daily lives. (Principal A)

Teachers particularly use assessments (pretests and progress tests) to track student progress in math, reading, and writing. Principal A used to require weekly testing but realized, "They can't be testing all the time. They need to teach. I don't overwhelm them with this. I do this myself and just share information. I don't want them to have too much paperwork. Then they won't have time to teach" (Principal A). She also realizes that if they teach the standards, students will pass the state-mandated standardized tests. She states,

> People think we teach to the test, but we don't. We still teach like when I was growing up. We were not given everything, we had to find it. We had to go back to the book and underline. Find the page. That is the same that we are doing now. So we cannot teach to that test. We can only teach the skills that are going to help them, not now but later. Our job is making them go to college and be successful. That is our goal. We strive for that, we want everyone to go to college.

Instruction also focuses on everyday skills relevant to students' lives that will enhance their success both inside and outside of school. Because state-mandated standardized test results tend to come late in the school year, the data is used to guide instruction the following year. They start planning in April for the following academic year. To facilitate instruction, Principal A sees as critical the key role of increased collaboration, and thus planning, between and across grade-level teams and the entire school.

> They have work planning every week. They didn't have that before. They had a hard time, but I made a schedule when I first came in and provided them all with work planning. So they have to meet, and I made it so they have to plan here. Once a month they [also] have to plan here. So I know who has problems, who is complaining, who didn't want to do it. They can complain as long as they are teaching happily. (Principal A)

The school focuses on a seamless "spiral curriculum," which articulates learning goals from kindergarten to all higher grades, aligning the instruction to the state standards. A spiral curriculum allows for review of previously taught skills while simultaneously building on these skills to ensure students fully understand and can apply them at increasingly higher levels of application. Teachers have much instructional flexibility, as long as they follow long-range plans and teach the standards.

> At the beginning, when I first came, it was not like that. Everybody could teach their own thing. Not anymore. I need to see what everybody is teaching. You could teach your own way, but the standards have to be the same. So if you go to the fourth grade, everybody is teaching the same thing. Third grade, everybody is teaching the same standard. You can teach main idea, Little Red Riding Hood, and you can have the Three Bears, but the skill has to be the same. Teachers did not buy into that in the beginning, but they do now. (Principal A)

Teachers are considered curriculum experts and assigned significant decision-making power in those areas: "It [district math program] was frustrating us. It worked but it was very, very difficult. We told her we didn't like it and we didn't use it" (Teacher). Grade-level teacher teams study content-area curricula to decide what is relevant to their success: "We looked at the science book when we first got it and said there is a whole part right here that we shouldn't be teaching" (Teacher). Several times a year, each grade level is responsible for going to the grade level before, and they must teach a subject with the teacher and students so teachers know what will be expected of students the following year. The principal and teachers meet with the feeder middle school to articulate and plan with them too.

As a way to expand professional expertise, all teachers are supported in becoming "specialized" or "experts" in particular subjects: "We are sort of specialized in subjects. For example, he plans for language arts; I plan for math, for the whole third grade. So in essence, we are focusing on one subject and can better plan and prepare for it. We are using the tools that we have and everything that we can come up with that makes it easier" (Teacher). Simultaneously, Principal A models lifelong learning by improving her knowledge and skills, and staying current: "I read everything. I want to know what teachers are doing....It is a constant learning...I read all instructional magazines. That is how I learn. That is where I get my ideas. Sometimes they work, sometimes they don't work."

With an increasingly developing organization, the principal can see herself as a team player and facilitator of organizational effectiveness: "The teachers [who are involved in leadership], they are the ones who tell me what to do. Every month we have a faculty meeting. I am just a facilitator here." Without a doubt, there are areas where the principal remains as the main decision maker. One such area deals with the budget. While seeking input and feedback from teachers and parents, along with the EESAC composed of all school members, including teachers, clerical and other support staff, even janitorial and cafeteria staff, and students, and the Parents/Teachers Association (PTA), Principal A is the ultimate decision maker. Everyone in the organization, while admitting that they are not as involved in final budget decisions, agrees that the process is most transparent. Significantly, a teacher further stated, "However, she is involving teachers more in the decision making and developing the staff." Because most parents work and hold 9:00–5:00 work hours, parent involvement in decision making remains minimal.

Deficit Funding: Scarce Fiscal Resources—Wealth of Human Resources

Fiscal resources, external and internal, are very lacking at this school. It is not a Title I school because it misses the free and reduced-price lunch qualification by a few percentage points. Principal A describes the parents as the "working poor." The school is not able to get many donations from businesses and has had little success with grants. This is, unequivocally, a school with a deficient district-allocated budget and few outside resources. The principal states,

> I have no other money. I wanted to be a Title 1 school....That is federal money that comes in. We are poor, but we are not poor...we have one or

two grants but nothing else. This is not a poor-poor school, so we didn't qualify for that. I told the council to go around to the businesses, but they are sometimes in deficit themselves. [business X] said, "No, we are a business." But [business Y] is a day partner that is good. [business Z] used to give sample perfumes, but not anymore. (Principal A)

The school appears too concerned with the many other challenges to be stopped by the lack of fiscal resources. As such, resources do not drive the decisions of the school but rather, decision-making processes maximize scarce resources. Principal A and most teachers work well above and beyond what is "required." The principal leads by modeling commitment, perseverance, and noticeably, sacrifice. The principal explains, "I am here from seven-thirty to seven, every day, and on Saturdays from eight to twelve. I have a Saturday group that comes in. There is no money for teachers to get paid. No, they don't come in on the weekend because then you will have them burn out. They need to be happy to come in to work."

A teacher agrees: "She [Principal A] pretty much tries to make everyone happy." The principal purchases her own teacher-recognition awards.

I recognize them anyway, but not much with the school money. The PTA helps me sometimes, with a luncheon for the teachers or donations for the students. I call [a business] and they donate a small cake and we celebrate—mostly donations. I wish I could give more incentives to the students. For rewards, we give them parties for the students; for the New Year, donuts and coffee for the teachers. During [state-mandated standardized test] I buy donuts and coffee, breakfast every morning for those testing days. You know it is out of my pocket. (Principal A)

Principal A states the school's fiscal depravation succinctly: "Allocation—it all boils down to the budget. We didn't get a teacher for students who are gifted because we didn't have the money. For instance, we have thirty-seven or thirty-eight in the third grade. A grade that should have twenty-something, but we didn't have the money so we couldn't get the teacher. Or because of budget, we get less money and we have to lose someone."

With a working-poor community, the school's EESAC and PTA fundraising abilities are limited. Beyond federal and state (district) budget allocations, the major sources of funding for the school are from the EESAC and PTA and a few small external grants. Yet most of the funds raised by the EESAC and the PTA go to pay for paraprofessionals and offer a few rewards for teachers and students: "In September there were concerns about the paraprofessionals being laid off. We had EESAC money, so they said let's keep them on until June with the EESAC money" (Principal A). There is no money to pay teachers to tutor, so the principal herself runs many of the tutoring sessions, especially on Saturdays, with the help of volunteer high school students. She describes it this way: "We don't have any money. I cannot force you to stay with a small group. Some principals say it is mandatory. If you tell the teachers it is mandatory, they will call the union, and they are not doing it happily.... If you don't want to do it, it is fine. I don't want anybody to be forced to do something they don't want to. Then you don't do it lovingly." During the day, as time allows, she also "accommodates small groups for extra help." She states, "I pull the ones that are not doing well, and small group tutoring is based on the data." Few "extra" programs are provided by the district for extra instructional assistance, such as before- and/or after-school programs. Some offer enrichment, including co-curricular activities, including a chess club for students. Although teachers are often required to attend professional development offered by the district, funds for substitute teachers are not always sufficient. Principal A explains, "Now they are asking for some teachers to attend [professional development], which is not funded. Some workshops they do not give us allocation for, very little." Sometimes, if they are lucky, the sponsoring organization offering the workshop provides for substitutes.

The majority of the state-mandated standardized test reward funds for being an "A" school are used to reward the faculty and staff, including cafeteria workers, janitors, etc. The remaining amount is used to recognize students. The school has received some small grants, which mostly go to develop and reward teachers, retain paraprofessionals, and keep up with instructional demands. A small grant went for portable classrooms to relieve overcrowding and to provide classrooms with Internet access. School computers must be purchased, maintained, and upgraded primarily through grants. "The computers we have now have been from grants. I know the district is replacing our old computers, little by little, seventy percent of whatever we have. We wanted PrintShop for our classes and the PTA went ahead and provided that, and provided networking...we couldn't purchase through regular funds. Through the PTA we got that and we got the portables wired" (Principal A).

The School in 2009–2010

The school population remained stable across the years, with a total enrollment of approximately 1,000 students in 2009–2010. The percentage of Latino/Hispanic students was 94%. The percentage of students classified as non-Hispanic White/Caucasian was 4%, Black/African American 0.5%, and 1.2% Asian American, Native American, and multiracial combined.

Students classified as ELLs were 20.8%, students classified as gifted were 14.4%, and 11.8% were students with disabilities. The mobility rate of the school had been decreasing. Some 56% of the student population qualified for free and reduced-price lunch. Average class size for the P/K–3 grades was 20, and 23 for upper grades. Primary grades ESOL classes averaged 18 students. The school maintained two self-contained classrooms for students with disabilities who were served in a varying exceptionalities program, which averaged eight students per teacher, with an aide. The school became a Title I school for the 2009–2010 school year with funding used for a full-time reading coach. Principal A had been at the school for 9 consecutive years. The assistant principal had been at the school for 1 year and had a bachelor's degree and 3 years experience as an administrator. The school employed 77 teachers. It had to release a teacher due to budget cuts and decreased enrollment, even though enrollment had been increasing in kindergarten as a result of new family growth. There were no 1st-year teachers, 29.87% of the teachers had over 15 years of experience, 67.5% were ESOL endorsed, 31.2% had advanced degrees, and 6.5% were endorsed by the National Board for Professional Teaching Standards. The school continued to offer a Saturday intensive remediation program as well as after school tutoring, physical education, and small-group instruction.

The researchers conclude that improvement at the school and sustained high achievement are attributed to an effectively developed and implemented "total schoolwide" achievement plan. Indicators of high performance for this school include achieving and sustaining a school grade of "A" for the past 9 years, 70% or more students scoring Level 3 or above on the reading and math FCAT for the past 8 years, 70% or more students making learning gains in reading and math for the past 8 years, and the school also has the distinction of meeting the federal requirement of making AYP for the past 5 years (see Table 4.1).

In summary, this school was already successful when Principal A was appointed. Authentic shared leadership became increasingly established by the new principal's (A) willingness to get "her hands dirty;" thus demonstrating expertise while modeling direct involvement and teamwork. Principal A wants people to be happy at the school and maintains the fact that teachers are professionals who can make decisions that might improve educational excellence while being accountable for student learning. Teachers and parents have come to respect that the principal will do "whatever I can do" to support them and their students. Over time, Principal A has skillfully gained the organization's trust and willingness to ally in steering the school's direction. To keep her focus on the entire organization, Principal A regularly joins the various planning groups: "That way I listen to the

TABLE 4.1 School X2 Indicators of High Performance

Academic year	Adequate yearly progress met	School grade	Students scoring Level 3 & above on FCAT		Students making learning gains	
			Reading	Math	Reading	Math
2008–09	Yes	A	93%	94%	78%	77%
2007–08	Yes	A	90%	92%	70%	71%
2006–07	Yes	A	87%	90%	76%	64%
2005–06	Yes	A	89%	90%	76%	74%
2004–05	Yes	A	86%	89%	79%	72%
2003–04	No[a]	A	77%	83%	72%	88%
2002–03	No[b]	A	72%	78%	73%	72%
2001–02	NR	A	74%	71%	78%	86%
2000–01	NR	A	65%	65+%	NR	NR
1999–00	NR	B	NR	NR	NR	NR
1998–99	NR	C	NR	NR	NR	NR

Note: NR = Data not reported.
Source: No Child Left Behind School Public Accountability Report.
[a] 97% of AYP criteria met. Students with disabilities did not meet math proficiency requirement.
[b] Percentage of AYP criteria met was not reported. ELLs did not meet reading or math proficiency requirement. Students with disabilities did not meet math proficiency requirement.

planning and know what is going on." She has assumed strong leadership in creating a school environment where teachers are happy, thus ensuring that students, parents, and everyone within the school is happy as well. In an example of her commitment to having happy teachers, the principal recalled the following events:

> Those last days at Christmas, I came to school dressed as Santa. I was out and about dressed as Santa. This is not an office job. You have to come to school happy. Some days you could have a headache, have PMS, or whatever you have sitting in an office, but when you are sitting in front of thirty children, you cannot have any of those. At least I don't want anyone that has those here, so I make sure I go in and out. Making sure they are happy. I make them happy. I give them presents with my own money, every Monday. Usually people are not Monday people. I am a Monday person. I hate Fridays. Fridays I am already too tired. Monday is my best day. So every Monday, I put a little present in each teachers mailbox. Socks, things that I got on sale. I try to make them happy. I am not too strict, but they do have to teach. When I go into your class, you have to be teaching. You can't be sitting down—you

have to be teaching. I don't care how you do it. You don't have to follow anything. But you better be instructing, and happy. (Principal A)

When members of the original research team revisited the school in summer 2005, the school encountered was noticeably different. Over time, Principal A developed a synergetic, capacity-building, self-empowered unit where the principal is the captain but everyone adds to organizational expertise and resourcefulness while participating in collaborative decision making to propel the ship forward. Principal A moved away from filling in the shoes left by the previous principal (B) where, it was learned, Principal B was actually more controlling than originally reported. Teachers and parents had very little real decision-making power. While appearing to solicit teacher and parent input, the former principal (B) in fact relied little on their knowledge and expertise, making and enacting decisions almost singlehandedly. Ironically, teachers did not realize this until the new principal (A) began to change the school culture. In 2005, a teacher said,

> Everyone's opinion counts. It is not just one, like we had before. You couldn't say a word. Whatever [the former principal] said worked. Now the principal basically lets the teachers decide on a lot of things. I think that is why we have become more effective than in the past, because we feel more comfortable with an open-door policy. If we have a situation, we bring the child in. We know what is being taken care of. There is support from the administration on the teachers' part. If you learn something at a workshop, you can come in and tell the administration. They let us try new things. We tried something new this year, it didn't work, and they let it slide.

With the previous administrator, teachers and parents actually did as they were told and had, in fact, become somewhat complacent in their lack of involvement and reliance on the principal to carry the load. Complacency also appears to have been assumed because of the relative success the administrator attained in moving the school from an average "C" rating to an excellent "A" rating. Principal A inherited this school's culture and climate and began realizing that the principal cannot be it all and do it all. She understood that establishing ongoing, sustainable success could only be done through true teamwork and collaboration. Over time, Principal A worked to establish a collaborative atmosphere through modeling. Initial resistance was countered. She, however, demonstrated that she was patient, persistent, and willing to do whatever needed to be done. She recounts the following experience:

> I learned that from the beginning, but when I saw so much resistance I said, you know, I can't give up—I used to do the workshops myself. For example, we are one of the school sites that are preregistering for Pre–K, and we are

registering for the whole county. The clerical personnel had to come in two Saturdays, but they said no, we have plans, we aren't coming in. So I learned how to register and I said, "Don't worry, I will register the students myself. You don't have to come in." And sure enough, I came in on Saturday. I had other volunteers. I was able to do it myself. Two hours passed and the clerical personnel came in to help me out. I said, "You don't have to. We have already registered twenty parents." They said, "No, no, we'll help."

When I came in [as principal of this school] I wanted to have a workshop. I was disappointed—I had five days—and none of the parents showed up. So I wasn't going to just quit. I listened to the teachers. When they said, "We can't come tonight." I did it myself. Another principal would have said, "No, you are mandated to come in to give this workshop." It's a different style. I'm not going to mandate [anyone] to come to open house, because I know I'm going to lose, because you are really mandated to come only twice a year.

By 2005, the school began to emerge as a collective organization with a culture of true shared leadership and accountability deeply grounded in pooled knowledge and expertise. It was, therefore, realized that this was a school in transition. More about this transition will be discussed in Chapter 10 with an exploration of how a new principal can be a key catalyst in building an empowering culture and climate with organizational values of mutual care, confidence, competence, respect, professionalism, freedom (to share and experiment), honesty, openness, transparency, trust, and many other core values identified in similar schools leading to sustainable high performance.

Today, both the principal and teachers make themselves available to hold workshops and meet with parents, even with their busy and irregular schedules. They continue to push for parental involvement by offering a volunteer program dealing with parenting skills, parent literacy and tutoring, sports programs, and community beautification projects. Principal A says, "I get them [parents] in the morning." Teachers also have an open-door policy welcoming parents at all times. "Parents can come in and see what is going on. If they are involved in the classroom, they see what is going on. They hear and they go home." As well, teachers send a lot of personal notes, especially thanking parents for their participation or to remind them of upcoming meetings and events. Through the EESAC and PTA, or individually by classrooms, they all ensure that each parent and community member is aware of what is going on at the school and is involved in the best way they can. Although parent involvement is still low, parents are now more involved in other ways that support the school. Parents are now more encouraged to offer their opinions on school matters. Over time, teachers at this school have become increasingly affirming of each other's strengths and weaknesses as a way to pull together to enhance the total human capital, or human assets, of the school:

> We know what each of our deficiencies and strengths are. For example, my strength is math, my weakness is reading. Not that I teach it bad. I need courses to make me feel more comfortable with that, and that is what we have been doing. [A teacher] came up to ask us, what are you doing in your grade level? Who needs help? Who wants help? Who wants to go to a reading workshop? . . . [Who] will decide [who] needs it more than . . . ? I need to go more than you do. (Teacher)

Changes in school principals—particularly when accompanied with significant changes in leadership style—are often associated with initial transitional turmoil and decreased school performance. This school demonstrates that the culture and climate of a school can be transformed while maintaining high performance. This school further demonstrates that this transformation can occur while simultaneously enabling every member, from instructional and noninstructional staff to parents and community members—every person directly and/or indirectly involved with student achievement—to become empowered through self-awareness of the human capital they each possess and how to use their collective assets to further empower everyone as a cohesive unit. This principal's beliefs and values about shared leadership, teacher professionalism and accountability for student learning, and her determination to create a happy work environment, in addition to her readiness to be a role model who takes risks and rolls up her sleeves to get things done, served as catalysts to propel this school to greater unity, teamwork, and effectiveness.

Questions for Discussion

1. What can be learned from this principal and this school about developing the culture and climate over time through authentic leadership?
2. How do schools shift from two very different administrative styles and maintain excellence in student achievement and still create a positive working environment of genuine collaboration and teamwork?
3. How can school leaders ensure that they are supporting staff development in meaningful ways to prevent teacher burnout and turnover? Similarly, how can principals prevent their own burnout?
4. What processes can schools engage to identify and pool everyone's human capital to augment their resources? How does look-

ing at human capital as an important resource—perhaps the most important resource—compensate for lacking, even deficient, fiscal resources in this school?

5

We Are Family

We are family. We have our Christmas party, we have our principal's house, but we have our groups, and you can find us shopping together, and our numbers are in each other's cell phones. We have friendships outside of working relationships. That's really nice. People come and go, and all of us are here, and we are not perfect, but the fact that we can deal with our problems and acknowledge them is very comforting. (Teacher)

[At] this school, we say "we" because we do not say "I"; we work together. (Teacher)

The teachers can't do it alone; they need the parents' help. And so far at this school we have been very helpful. (Parent)

Introduction

The principal, teachers, parents, and students are all deeply connected to one another within this school and community. These connections are based on a genuine fondness for one another and a shared agreement about their common and agreed-upon purpose and understanding of working together for the common good that far outweighs favoring individual preferences that may work against the goals of the whole community. This

Leadership from the Ground Up, pages 65–82
Copyright © 2012 by Information Age Publishing
All rights of reproduction in any form reserved.

is especially apparent when these educators make decisions that impact re-source allocations and influence future resource prioritizations that can affect the whole school community versus favoring a few select individuals. This is not to say, however, that the faculty in this school would be reluc-tant to consider seriously a colleague's request for resources to be allocated for students with special needs. Rather, the consideration of the individual request and the subsequent decision would be based on a shared agree-ment of working together toward a common good, with an explicit under-standing that through consensus, everyone can support goals that everyone commits to attaining in various ways. The collective goals identified by this school community parallel their belief system that unlocks the mystery of what it means to say, "We Are Family" at this school. The family ties envelop a shared understanding of caring for others and working to come to agree-ment on decisions made together. The belief that everyone has something unique to contribute to this school community—"everyone matters"—is evident in many ways within this school and its practices. Thus, the Comer school philosophy of collaboration, consensus, communication, and no fault adopted in 1994 and the school's own philosophy have become one; inseparable from the school's identity and mission. This Comer Philosophy is the bedrock of the school's culture and is the invisible connection that members share in this school community. The school is labeled X1, and its annual grades from 2000–2001 through the 2009–2010 school years are found in Table 5.1, "School X1 Indicators of High Performance," located at the end of the chapter.

This chapter highlights four major themes that illustrate why this school's practices are different from other school cases presented in this book and what contributes to this school's success. Themes for this chapter are build-ing a sense of belonging and community, access to data and information pro-motes democratic decision making and fosters shared leadership, pooling resources, and the evolution of a strong professional culture builds capacity. These four themes work in concert with one another to support and promote an overall culture for the betterment of the common good, the attainment of mutual goals, and the achievement of collective actions that fuel collabora-tion, commitment, and cooperation across and within role groups to build expertise. The first theme discusses how relationships across role groups en-gender stronger connections within a culture of belonging and community. Consequently, the first theme, building a sense of belonging and community, emphasizes the belief that each person can contribute something in their own unique way to this community—there is a place for everyone to feel valued. This theme illustrates how the school welcomes its newest parent and student members and acculturates them to feel at home and secure—establishing connections early. The second theme, access to data and information, promotes democratic decision making and fosters shared leadership. This second theme discusses how data shapes an information-rich culture to guide democratic decision making that in turn fosters shared leadership for everyone's voice to be heard and valued. The third theme shows how pooling resources is the collective work of joining both human and fiscal resources together to achieve the common goals of the school. This creates a strong energy system within the school culture that fortifies the fourth theme, the evolution of a strong professional culture that builds capacity. This last theme depicts how a strong professional culture results because the nutrients from the other three themes are nourishment for the work these educators and their community engage to solve problems and draw upon their collective expertise to explore solutions.

Description of the School

At the time of the site visit, this urban school was 16 years old. It had been recently painted by parent and teacher volunteers who did much of the painting and minor maintenance at this school. Lush tropical landscaping adorned the campus, which included a student-planted butterfly garden. You could see the school's mission statement and goals embodied everywhere you looked. The campus provided a warm and friendly atmosphere, with benches and picnic tables throughout the gardens and common areas. The school was very clean and orderly. The school had a Children's Psychiatric Center, Community School and Parent Outreach Center, which was on-site and provided various programming for parents, which was helpful for the many parents who utilized its various services. Additionally, parents were provided with information on 25 different clubs and special activities designed to get all students involved in the school.

This school was graded an "A" by the state in 2000–2001. It was also a Five Star Award recipient and a Little Red Schoolhouse award winner. Based on data from the 2001–2002 school accountability report, the school enrolled approximately 1,300 students in kindergarten through fifth grades. The school served a 75.2% free and reduced-price lunch population. Hispanic/Latinos made up 90% of the students, 7% non-Hispanic White/Caucasian, 0.8% Black/African American, 1% Asian American, 0.1% Native American, and 0.8% multiracial. Some 9% of the students had a disability, 4.7% of the students were identified as gifted, and 44.9% of the students were classified as ELLs. Although many of the students were Hispanic/Latinos, they arrived in the United States from many different Central and South American countries and the Caribbean. A parent noted, "The majority is Hispanic, from South America, Cuba. . . . You have maybe two percent Black, White, I don't know exactly. The majority is Hispanic, and not just from one country, from different countries all over South America and Cuba."

The average class size was 25.9 students in kindergarten through fifth grade. In 2001–2002, the school had a 91.7% stability rate, which means that the majority of students that were enrolled in October were also enrolled in February. Student absences were considerably lower than the district averages, and the interviews with the teachers revealed why that may be so, since improving attendance was a schoolwide goal that had paid off as the school had exceeded district and regional averages for daily school student attendance. A parent said, "We were rated best attendance for the district for the screening period, so we're number one in the district, and we are number six in the region."

The faculty consisted of 81 members listed as instructional staff members, and three school-based administrators. Five new teachers were hired during the year we conducted the study. The teachers averaged 15.2 years of teaching experience. The principal had been at this school for 6 years. She had 25 years in education, 15 of which were as a principal, and held a doctorate. Before arriving at the school, she worked in the Professional Standards Department at the District Office. She described the school culture as "knowing and understanding that we are all here for the child, whatever it takes to make them successful."

As you become acquainted with this school, you will see that whatever it undertakes, it is committed to achieving a successful outcome. The themes all work together to show how this success occurs. The first of the four themes, building a sense of belonging and community, portrays how parents, students, and teachers at this school come together and are acculturated into the family—even before the first day of school. This theme illustrates how connections are built and sustained to make this school a vibrant family and desirable place to work and have students enrolled.

Building a Sense of Belonging and Community

When I came here from Colombia, I only spoke a little English, and I had my little daughter. They give you the English class here, so through the Flash program, I speak a little English, because I came here to the English class. At night, Monday and Wednesday, I'm here. They have childcare, so I can bring my children here, and they help me with the homework, because sometimes I get a little stuck. We are immigrants, and we don't know what kind of programs are there, and they tell us about different programs in the daytime that are available to people who came to this country, and that kind of program is here at [X1]. They help me with immigration, with computer classes. I want to go to college, and this is the way, through this information. (Parent)

The interviews with parents, teachers, and the principal demonstrate an overriding sense of belonging that is felt across role groups. Just as parents are made to feel welcome and learn how to negotiate their way from the school in this new place, the parent who spoke was invited to learn and use the school as a resource, a place where she could make sense of her new environment, and a place where she could begin to feel connected. This sense of connection helps engender a sense of belonging that builds on the family metaphor to bring members together within this school community to help each other. The Comer Philosophy professes values and beliefs of collaboration, consensus, communication, and no fault that extends well beyond the school walls to serving parents and the community in authentic ways. Parents help other parents and learn how to help their children. The first message a new parent hears, even before the school year starts, is a welcoming invitation by other parents to learn about the school. The active parent organization inducts all new parents into the school family at a meeting explicitly for new parents. A veteran parent said,

> Before the school year begins, we have "Get Acquainted Day," in which we invite all the new parents to come to the school, and the PTA and people who have been here for a long time meet with them, along with the administration and the teachers, and we talk to them.... [New parents] are acculturated into what the school is all about and what we do here.

These relationships between school administrators and teachers, parents, and community members with school personnel and students portray and symbolize the practices this school values. This community-of-practice values its relationships with each other within a highly interdependent and integrated community. Although the Comer Philosophy is identified as the glue that binds this community together, it is the beliefs and values within this philosophy that support the agreed-upon purpose of various groups working together to interpret what it means to be a member of this school community.

The principal makes a concerted effort to know new parents and greet newcomers to the school by attending workshops sponsored through the Community School and Parent Outreach Center. Of significance, a new parent relates her surprise when the principal introduces herself and says she had not met her (the parent) before. The parent acknowledges that the principal's greeting is "a big welcome" for her. Through this simple gesture, the principal makes the parent feel that her office is open to her at any time and that as the principal, she knows her community and recognizes when a parent is new to the community. A parent sums up nicely the sentiments expressed over and over again by a number of parents that were interviewed:

> This is an open-door policy that the principal is always there; the teachers are always on top of the children. At the other schools, we have to make an appointment, and we don't see the teacher or principal until a few months later. Over here, any time, day or night. My son started here, but my son was in another school for two months. I missed it, because the difference is, here, there are so many people who help. The parents, the teachers, everyone. When you have a problem, you come here and in the library, any place, if they can't find the answer, they will help you find it. It's a very open school—not only for the parents, but for the community around here.

Noticeably, parents display a genuine sense of pride in regard to being a part of this school family and community. The parents are highly respectful of the teachers and the job they do for their children and believe that both the principal and the teachers are there to support them and their children. The fact that the principal and the teachers are accessible and available to parents at any time was echoed over and over again. This feeling of being welcome by educators adds to the sense of belonging parents feel. This is also true for students.

Students new to this school are welcomed similarly by their peers as parents are welcomed by other parents and the principal. New students are assigned a peer to assist them with their acculturation into the school. The student guides show the new students the physical surroundings, answers their questions, and help them learn what resources are available to them. A peer reaching out to another peer creates a powerful sense of belonging and inclusion in the new school community. As one parent suggested, she believes that children love this school. She said, "I think children love coming here. They learn about so many different cultures. You have the Hispanic heritage; I remember in their art class, it was Hispanic heritage month, and she was learning something about the Mexican sun. She was learning about others' heritage, so I think that's very good for her."

This sense of belonging is also part of how people from different cultures and backgrounds learn to collectively value each other's cultures. This appears to result in a distinctive culture where others value the uniqueness of each person and students feel valued for who they are and where they come from. Teachers also have built strong bonds with each other at this school. A teacher explains,

I've been working here for sixteen years, and I don't want to leave. When I come here every day, I come to caring people, people I like to work with. All of my problems are resolved at [X1], personal or anything. If I have a problem, it's not my problem, it becomes everyone's problem. I always get help in everything around here, so it's a very warm environment and it's wonderful.

The culture of family caring at this school enables the teachers, administrators, and parents to work together to solve problems and to continuously seek innovative and new ways to make improvements together. The teachers told us that teacher turnover at the school is very low because no one wants to leave. The teacher who said "At [X1], all our problems are solved" illustrates the closeness to other teachers as friends and trusted colleagues. Teachers share "family" and teamwork as something their other professional friends would desire to have at their respective workplaces. Teachers report that their other teacher friends call them on a regular basis and ask if there are any openings at this school. Their teacher colleagues said that they would like to work at a school that is so caring and supportive.

This supporting and caring philosophy extends to relationships between the administration and the union representative, a relationship often portrayed as adversarial in other schools. Clearly, this is not the case at this school. Relationships have been influenced by the sense of belonging and shared community values and beliefs that members hold together. The focus on doing what is best for students far outweighs teacher interests. Divisiveness between teachers and administration is not an issue, as one teacher notes:

> The union rep here has been always part of our decision-making process. It does not have to be union against administrators or administrators against union; we have been family. We consider the total child, since we are a Comer school where we have the child in mind. If the union comes up with an idea and presents it to the union members, saying you have to be careful, this may affect our student body, then we work together as part of the staff that we are. Our past union rep just retired, and we have our new union rep. She sits at all our EESAC meetings. She's part of us as a family and represents the union as part of our family.

This sense of connection unites this family around a shared purpose of schooling that encompasses the Comer Philosophy. Belonging to this community matters because people feel valued and cared for as a person. This sense of community enables teachers, parents, and administrators to work together productively toward what they define as the common good for its students and community. This sense of connection unites this family around a shared purpose of addressing the needs of students and parents that work for the betterment of the students and the community.

Access to Data and Information Promotes Democratic Decision Making and Fosters Shared Leadership

Teachers have access to their students' data on the first day of school because the principal believes teachers should have these data on hand to make important decisions to assist them with their proper planning and placement of each student and to monitor student progress throughout the year. Because data regularly identify and address students' needs, the use of data empowers teachers to be successful with students, to make decisions, and to share leadership about how to use data for school improvement decisions. The principal describes how data are made available to teachers:

> At the beginning of the school year, or as soon as we get the FCAT and all data, we have class profiles. We give the teachers all the data that we have on the children that they're going to be teaching that year. Then the teacher prepares a profile so that they will be able to tell from day one what level the child is reading at, what math level the child is performing at, how the child does in the SRI, FCAT standardized testing, and school-designed tests. So from day one they have all the initial data. As the year progresses and they keep assessing the performance of the children, they keep adding to that profile. That's one of the unique things here—the teacher doesn't have to wait to administer placement or screening tests. They have all the data they need from day one.

Access and use of data goes well beyond assessing compliance to achieving state standards. Data are used to ensure decisions benefit individual students, alter programs and services, and change direction of things not working well. The principal is very clear about this. She says,

> Decisions on what programs to continue; what programs to end or modify. For example, our [school improvement plan] used to have tons of strategies. We now narrowed them down to five, because these are the five that we really do, and why should we do twenty when we really do five? We have plans, like our attendance plan, that were developed looking at data. Our plan of testing was developed out of looking at data. Our faculty meetings and the things that happen at our faculty meetings [arise from our use of data]; we survey [at] every faculty meeting about what needs to be changed. Then that information is used to modify [what needs to be modified].

Teachers with expertise and parents with expertise feel that they can step up and take a leadership role within the school and school community. According to one teacher, "At this school, everybody is a leader, everyone communicates; everybody is in the same stage." Teachers, parents, and school administrators use data to promote involvement in democratic decision-making practices. Data are translated into meaningful information and shared to engage students, teachers, parents, and the community in collaboration, dialogue, and the interpretation of what the data mean in regard to the school goals and making decisions together around the Comer Philosophy for school improvement. The decision-making process ensures everyone is heard and everyone has the opportunity for involvement and giving voice regarding their opinions and interpretations of the data.

Data are disaggregated routinely within this school and discussed to assess individual, group, and school progress. Data are also used to monitor and evaluate programs and services for ongoing school improvement decisions. Faculty flex their collective knowledge and expertise muscles often to identify and solve problems together. Data are information for this community-of-practice to take action and make democratic decisions together. It is important to note that this school recognizes that in order to participate in meaningful ways, parents can be involved in decision making only if they have access to information and knowledge. Parents attend workshops through the Community School and Parent Outreach Center in Spanish and English and at different hours, sometimes in the morning or at night. A teacher relates, "We hold workshops to get the parents involved. We will have one for kindergarten, tell the parents what the kids are learning, then of course you would have one for first, second, third, fourth, and fifth grade. She has one for FCAT [state-mandated test], so that the parents know what the kids are learning." Parents know they can share suggestions with the school because of its open-door policy. They provide their input informally at any time; as one parent put it, they "constantly talk with the administration and teachers in our PTA meeting about what is best." Parents report that, through the school governance structure, they agree on everything through consensus and give input on various matters. For example, one parent states, "Another suggestion from a parent that changed things is when the Accelerated Reader program came out, but at the time there was no funding. She [the principal] opened a room that was a teacher's room so that the books and computers are now available [to parents and their students]."

The principal related an example of how teacher input was used as data to influence a better schoolwide decision-making process about their successful adoption of a technology-based program. According to the principal,

> When they [teachers] initially offered, I asked who would like to do it and, through the school governance and the instructional committee, we asked for recommendations. We asked the teachers, because we said if the teacher wants to do something, it would be more successful. At the beginning, teachers were a little reluctant, because they didn't feel that they had a lot of technology skills, and the program was highly technological, but today they are pleased that they participated because we see from about five years ago when they began the program until now, so much has grown. Now they are masters.

Sharing information and using data to create a culture wherein the principal gives leadership to everyone in the school is an artifact of democratic and shared decision making. The principal gives ownership; she allows teachers and parents to engage in creative and innovative work. A teacher shares this perspective: "If we come up with a great program or good idea, she allows us to go forth." In this school, decision making is not only democratic, but demonstrates listening leadership that fosters innovation and problem solving. One teacher explains, "I think we have a voice. I didn't have a voice at the previous four schools; this is my fifth school. I was a teacher, I did my job, but it wasn't until I got here that I got a voice. Everybody has a voice, and I think that when you work in a place where at least somebody hears you, it gives you a sense of achievement right there and then." Having a voice is important. The principal also ensures that the school committees have representatives from different groups in the school. The principal described their efforts for balanced representation as follows: "We try demographically, again, most of the staff and students are Hispanic, and so we try to balance it as much as possible. But as far as representing the areas and the grade, we make sure that every committee, as much as possible, has representation from all the groups that you heard." What is readily apparent from this principal is her belief in including representatives from all the stakeholder groups on committees. This sense of inclusion underpins the decision-making process at this school and results in a governance process that encourages and fosters shared leadership.

Data also provide members with an understanding of key issues to be discussed in committees. Test scores are posted publicly, and teachers are constantly striving for improvement. There is a commitment to "raising the bar" on achievement and eliminating practices and strategies that don't move the school forward to achieving its goals. The school is dedicated to a comprehensive reading plan, and every 9 weeks every grade does benchmarking on how the grade is achieving its goals. Data on comprehension and oral reading are analyzed weekly, biweekly, and monthly. These data are shared with families to encourage their support of their child's progress. This ongoing two-way communication process is not meant to be one-way. Instead, the communication process provides parents with information as a basis for ongoing review, parent follow-up, and continued dialogue. A parent says that the teacher will take time to let her know how her daughter is doing daily when she picks up her daughter after school. If there is not enough time, the teacher will make time to communicate with the parent that day or the next.

The teachers quit using commercially produced materials and began using materials they developed to focus on higher-order thinking skills. They used instructional strategies such as probing students for analytical thinking, engaging students in drawing inferences, incorporating more hands-on activities, and involving students in think-alouds. These various pedagogical approaches provide data daily on students' responses in regard to their degree of progress. Moreover, these observational data serve to guide teachers' decision making about their instructional practices and students' performance and learning. Data and information are also shared as teachers at this school plan together as a total school, by grade level, and across special areas. During this planning time, teachers establish benchmarks and objectives as a team. Teachers demonstrate to the principal how they are making progress and achieving their goals for their class. These data are public and discussed openly among colleagues. The principal's philosophy is to teach every child in ways that make learning accessible to that child. Students are taught for mastery and application of information and also for application of learning through the use of higher-order thinking skills. The school staff firmly believes that good teaching eliminates behavior problems.

Although the above practices might be expected in today's increasing school accountability environment, what is unusual in this school is that data are collected in a number of different ways and authentically support learning together, promoting democratic decision making, and fostering shared leadership. Data are used to make the school better and to respond to the needs of students. The principal says it well:

> We look at and identify their [students] needs... by talking to the parents when they're first enrolled, we assess the language, and as time progresses, we keep assessing data, formal, through testing, or informal, through observation with the children, or observations of the parents. We do that to provide the best programs that are suited to the children. Beyond that, any-

thing that we have here at the school is available to all children, regardless of their abilities.

Pooling Resources

This school, like many of the schools in this study, pools its fiscal and human resources to create a strong synergy between the two. The ability to use resources wisely and combine individual strengths with an enterprising philosophy attracts new resources and builds on common and shared beliefs. The principal relates, "We are like activists, looking around to see what is out there and who has what that can contribute to the school and to the children. Parents, paraprofessionals, businesses, teachers, administrators, identify what everybody's good at, and they're believers in those areas, and they contribute."

A teacher shares that, as professionals, the teachers in this school work hard, and she explains why they work so hard:

> I know that if I divide my salary, the hours I spend at [X1], it would be like a dollar an hour. It is all about dedication, commitment, and administration delegates a lot, but they know what is going on. . . . [In this school] the principal has enabled everyone to be active in their ongoing learning and to share their learning with others in the school. What benefits one person has the potential to benefit each and every person.

Staff is encouraged by administration to attend as much training as possible, and they are expected to share their learning with other colleagues. After attending training, teachers report back at faculty meetings on the value of the training and its applicability to their ongoing programs. Decisions are then made by the faculty as to the training's value and applicability for the entire staff. If it is agreed-upon that the training would be of value to the entire staff, or a segment of the staff, the principal sees that the training is provided. This is a strategic use of human capital as a learning resource to identify areas that might benefit the entire school organization. A teacher points out, "We are encouraged to go to as many workshops as we can find. We have professional development from the very beginning of the year, and then as workshops and activities related to those come around, we are told that this is something we can go to. If we find it on our own, we can go to anything that will make us a better teacher."

The school involves others and builds on their strengths. A teacher relates how the school utilizes parents as a resource: "We have done a great job of involving parents at our school. We involve their heritage in our programs, in our teaching, and we make sure they feel their contributions are needed." In turn, this use of parents as a resource has been noted by the district. Parents at this school train other parents to become more involved at their local schools. In this school, students are also seen as resources; for example, students who are identified as gifted are paired with other students that they mentor. Again, the identification of ways that students can make contributions is evident and part of the overall philosophy of encouraging members to make contributions for the greater good of others. The tutoring of students, the Parent Outreach Center, and parent workshops all add to the human resource capital of this school and what it can provide to its students and parents because of these pooled resources.

In terms of fiscal resources, the principal relates that "Parents and teachers are involved in the school's budgetary process through the EESAC." Both the school PTA and partners (businesses) are generous in providing additional resources including "people, time, money, and materials." The school aggressively pursues and receives a wide range of grants to supplement their ongoing activities. Disbursement of these additional resources is a shared decision with EESAC and staff, with input from the principal. The principal feels she is very creative in the ways that she puts moneys together to "maximize development." For example, she hires four custodians at hourly rates instead of paying two at full pay. She states, "People offer resources to us because of the success that we've had, and they want to invest money in a successful place."

Administrators and teachers alike pool their knowledge about resources available to them through a variety of means such as word-of-mouth, Internet, parents, and the district business partners. The fact that the school receives grants and other monies has enabled it to continually update its technology. The principal boasts that the school is "wireless," and summarizes efforts to find additional resources:

> They are identified in many ways: by administration, by teachers, by parents. We have business communities around here, and we just salute their participation. We have a person assigned, a counselor, with the district partners. Those are resources that we identify to work with us. Also, the public education has resources through the Annenberg grant. . . . We are constantly looking at new trends, what is out there, research through the Internet, and what works from our own experience.

The school pools resources with other professional networks in the area to hire the best and most qualified new teachers. They work collaboratively with the university on the training of existing staff. The principal states that her leadership philosophy is "from the bottom up...it has to be based on the needs that are identified at the school level, student achievement, and student needs." This is how resources are prioritized and pooled to address legitimate and identified needs at this school. A teacher relates that the needs also determine budget decisions made by the whole school. For example, she says, "The manager of after school comes to me and says the kindergarten students have a need. They need construction paper, whatever. I need five thousand dollars to buy the materials on the list, for the whole school, that's how we plan our budget."

Need trumps formulaic decisions about the dissemination of funds. Resources are pooled and shared for the common good. The human and fiscal resources work together to create opportunities for student success.

Evolution of a Strong Professional Culture Builds Capacity

This last theme brings together the other themes by showing how the evolution of a strong professional culture has sustained school improvement over time and across different administrators. "I think that our first principal set the pace at [X1]. Her doors were open to handpick the faculty that wanted to be here and had a commitment to [X1]. She sets the pace" (Teacher). This emerging culture, put into place early, created the blueprint for a sense of openness and shared dialogue among members of this educational community. This openness and communication has been sustained. The result is a professional culture that has evolved over time at this school, enabling educators to respond to the needs of the students, parents, and community in meaningful ways. Another teacher says, "We've been through four administrations...we don't notice a difference between these people who have been here for four or five years, among the people who have been here sixteen, because they get acculturated immediately." Yet another teacher explains that being at X1, she does not need to be an administrator at another school because her needs for leadership are met with the many opportunities she is afforded for leadership at this school. Finally, a fourth teacher sums up the strong professional culture at the school this way:

> I think that [X1] is successful because of the culture that we have in the school. The culture is understanding and knowing that we are here for the children; that whatever it takes to meet the needs of that individual child, we are going to do it. There are no restrictions; there is nothing that we will not do to really teach individual children and try to the best of our ability to make sure that they are successful. It's having a school without walls, in

which you look at all the resources and use everything that you can get your hands on, whether it's money, people, resources. Creating that environment that will entice people to do it. I think that's our value, the fact that every single individual here, from the person that cleans the school to the administration, everybody is willing to go way beyond the call of duty for the children. We're not here for the money, and it doesn't matter how hard it is. If it brings success to the children and the school, we're going to do it. You create it one day at a time. And it's a lot of work.

Teachers in this professional culture "keep assessing the students' performance, we keep upgrading teachers' skills, and we keep looking at research and what's new in education. We continue to look at and reassess what we are doing in this school, and to see if this is working toward continuous growth" (Teacher).

This school divides the school into six groups, which are called Web sites. Each group is found on the Internet. The Web sites are set up by grade levels from kindergarten to fifth grade. Teachers who teach in special areas (i.e., music, art, and physical education) and paraprofessionals are involved by grade level. All Web sites work cooperatively with each other to plan and implement nine-week themes, including culminating activities for each site.

Parents are considered as partners in this professional culture. They are informed of the school's mission statement and goals by the principal and the teachers through meetings, fliers, bulletin boards, and one-on-one communication. The school advises each parent of the expectations for their child and what they can do personally to assist their son or daughter in becoming successful at school. Repeatedly, parents told us how welcome they were at the school and how accessible everyone was to them. Parents and teachers are involved in decision making, and decisions about resources are based on legitimate needs. New-hires know they have to be willing to give extra. A teacher claims, "Nobody here wears one hat. So, if you're a person who's going to be blindfolded to, 'I just do reading and I don't do anything else but reading,' and there are several applicants, we might look at someone else that may look at the total picture, because that's the way we function."

Students are included in all activities in which they wish to participate. The school culture openly welcomes, supports, recognizes, and celebrates all students for their accomplishments. This too contributes to the sense of a strong professional culture that builds on its successes. The school esprit d'corps is evident in what the school calls, "Spotlighting Success." This planned activity recognizes students for a variety of successful achievements. These include academics, sports, and music, or community service. The parents, teachers, and principal support a culture that acknowledges what is "good and positive." It is an appreciative culture that acknowledges that good work extends beyond the classroom. And so it seems that as we look back at where we began this case study, we see that the Comer Philosophy of collaboration, consensus, communication, and no fault has served this school well in building a strong professional culture that values, respects, and cares for its members. Being family at this school comes with certain responsibilities and the understanding that each person has something to contribute to the family that works for the common good. This has built capacity within the school over time for this school to be successful. A parent concludes,

> I think it's a success also because with a lot of the parents, you'll find that they volunteer, and now they are part of the school. You get more than one hundred percent, not just part-time; they stay all day... when teachers come here for workshops, they are amazed at how many things are done at [X1], and they wonder, where do we find the time? How are the teachers able to keep up with everything? We have [a business partnership], the new language program, the volunteers, so many things going on in the school.

The School in 2009–2010

According to the 2009–2010 School improvement Plan, this school enrolled 1,112 students, including 97% Hispanic/Latino, 2% non-Hispanic White/Caucasian, 0% Black/African American, and 1% other. Students classified as ELLs represented 40% of the school population, 10% were students with disabilities, and students classified as gifted also represented 10% of the population. Some 71% of students received free or reduced-price lunch. The attendance rate over the previous 3 years averaged 97%, though there was a student mobility rate of 22%, which could be attributed to students living in a predominantly rental community, resulting in a more transient student body. Class size was reduced to allow for greater differentiated instruction and to reduce discipline problems. The average class size for primary grades (K–3) was 18 and for upper grades (4–5) was 22. The principal of this school was a Hispanic/Latino female who had a master's degree and 11 years experience as an administrator, 2 of them as principal at this school. The assistant principal was a non-Hispanic White/Caucasian female with 8 years of experience as an assistant principal, all of them at this school. There were 84 instructional staff employed at the school, 48% had advanced degrees, and 72% were ESOL endorsed. More than half had 15 years of experience and fifteen were National Board certified. There was also one reading coach. Evidence of this school's high performance included a grade of "A" for the previous 7 years, 70% of students scored Level 3 or above on the reading and math FCAT, and the school also had the distinction of meeting the federal requirement of making AYP for the previous 5 years (see Table 5.1).

This school built a professional culture around a sense of belonging, involvement of others in decision making, support for shared leadership, and use of human and fiscal resources to sustain learning and growth. School leaders viewed their roles as inviting others with expertise and talents to exercise leadership, risk innnovation, and apply their creativity to solve problems together. This school valued and respected others and openly engaged their community in discussions to improve student progress. Collective energy supported student achievement. It was evident in teacher learning, sharing of ideas, and ongoing review of data and assessments of the school's overall effectiveness that educators in this school were deeply committed to the school purpose around the Comer Philosophy. The educators in this school not only addressed day-to-day issues but were poised

TABLE 5.1 School X1 Indicator of High Performance

Academic year	Adequate yearly progress met	School grade	Students scoring Level 3 & above on FCAT		Students making learning gains	
			Reading	Math	Reading	Math
2008–09	Yes	A	82%	81%	72%	62%
2007–08	Yes	A	80%	85%	66%	64%
2006–07	Yes	A	78%	83%	76%	66%
2005–06	Yes	A	79%	81%	66%	69%
2004–05	Yes	A	79%	81%	72%	75%
2003–04	No[a]	A	75%	75%	66%	81%
2002–03	No[b]	A	70%	75%	74%	77%
2001–02	NR	B	66%	74%	66%	85%
2000–01	NR	A	65%	71+%	NR	NR
1999–00	NR	C	53+%	66+%	NR	NR
1998–99	NR	A	NR	NR	NR	NR

Note: NR = Data not reported.
Source: No Child Left Behind School Public Accountability Report.
[a] 97% of AYP criteria met. Students with disabilities did not meet reading proficiency requirement.
[b] Percentage of AYP criteria met was not reported. ELLs did not meet reading proficiency requirement. Students with disabilities did not meet reading or math proficiency requirement.

for the future; they had their ears to the ground, listening for new trends and jumped on opportunties that may arise for them to benefit. In this sense, they were opportunists, but also they were not surprised by what was coming down the pike. This was a school where eveyone's strenghts were celebrated. Commitments and collaborations fueled this professional community to use their human resources to tackle tough problems. Their work together has built capacity over time for them to sustain high performance. These educators believed they can make a difference and they are!

Questions for Discussion

1. How does leadership impact the involvement of parents and teachers in this school?
2. What does it mean in this school to be part of the school family? How is the family metaphor overused in some school settings? What are the implications of this metaphor? Should another one be applied for this school? If so, what would it be?
3. What does it mean to have a professional culture in a school? Why is this an important antecedent for school improvement to be successful?
4. What are your feelings about the willingness of many of these professionals to give beyond what they were paid to do? Is this type of commitment sustainable? And if so, what evidence is there in the case study as to why this may be so?

Disc(u)

6

Everyone Has a Gift

When I dreamed of opening a new school, one of the things that I did with the group—the usual planning group—was to look at what we could do instead of doing what everyone else was doing. (Principal)

Mrs. [Principal] decided to write a proposal to the school [board] and with it she had to come up with a creative, innovative idea on how she would run the school, which was basically based on local intelligence. (Teacher)

Introduction

This school, labeled X3 has been rated "A" consistently since the 2000–2001 academic year. Grades for the school, from the 2000–2001 through the 2008–2009 school years, can be found in Table 6.1, "School X3 Indicators of High Performance," located at the end of the chapter. The overarching themes that make this school a success become apparent from the moment one steps onto the school grounds. The themes are vision of local intelligence; authentic, exploratory and experiential learning; cascading democratic leadership; high expectations for all; exemplary professionalism and commitment to success; and calculated risk taking. The school is grounded in the conviction that everyone—teachers, parents, students, and staff—involved with the school has gifts that contribute to the overall success of the school. This conviction is the basis for the theme, vision of local intelligence. Recognizing that most learning for the elementary school child must be grounded in concrete, hands-on experiences, the school promotes tactile teaching that "anchors" learning in the students' minds, allowing them to move on to abstract thinking and authentic, exploratory, and experiential learning. The paramount driving belief of this school, cascading democratic leadership, is grounded in the notion that everyone in a society or organization is/can be a leader in some area, everyone has the power and right to direct their destiny and decide what is in their best interest, and members of a group are collectively interdependent. First and foremost, high expectations for all are apparent for instructional and noninstructional staff as well as students. Exemplary professionalism and commitment to success is promoted by an administrative team that genuinely believes that teachers are professionals with knowledge, skills, and expertise to perform exemplarily and effectively in their profession. "My teachers are professionals "is proudly acclaimed by this school's principal. Carefully considered options serve as the force for calculated risk taking, which at this school, is welcomed as an opportunity for creativity, initiative, and innovation.

The principal had a vision to create a "mold-breaking," nurturing school environment where all students, regardless of cultural and/or economic background, could fulfill their full potential. Along with a team of teachers, she set out to develop a proposal for such a school. The vision called for a school-empowered staff, with minimal bureaucracy, including minimal external oversight, fiscal flexibility with budget, programming, and staffing decisions. Budgetary flexibility, considered risky, required new ways of strategizing expenditures aligned to clearly identified priorities, both short and long term, while being responsive to emerging needs and quick midcourse corrections.

Bloom's "Taxonomy of the Cognitive Domain" and Howard Gardner's "Multiple Intelligences" served as the centerpieces to drive the teaching and learning philosophy. The proposal based instruction on critical and higher-order thinking through hands-on, culturally relevant, "active," experiential, and exploratory learning. Critical thinking and problem-solving skills were required across all disciplines. "We are teaching kids to read and to think" (Principal). Computer skills, deemed essential in our rapidly changing and technological world, were to be available in all the classrooms and used regularly to teach, perform assignments, and assess student progress. The notion that everyone has talents or gifts in some area(s) may not be new, but the creation of a school explicitly grounded in this notion and catering to the development of multiple intelligences was considered unique and innovative. The idea was well-received and waivers were grant-ed. The proposal came to fruition with the creation of a technology-based community school grounded in diversity of learning styles and acknowledg-ing varying forms of intelligences. With the approval, administrators were allowed much freedom to hire teachers who bought into the philosophy and "the majority of the initial staff is still here" according to the principal. Additionally, this is a SATELITE school (Students as Tomorrow's Economic Leaders in Today's Education). Local businesses assist with a school-to-work program, which provides concrete experiences to transition students from the classroom to the working environment. Students create items and en-gage in banking activities and postal work. They begin with the design pro-cess (of student-created products) up to the culmination of a product for sale in the marketplace.

Description of the School

The school was located in a "perpetually" growing community of single-fami-ly homes, rental units, and Department of Housing and Urban Development (HUD) subsidized housing for low-income families. The school building was specifically designed and built to meet the vision. The entire design was de-scribed as a learning environment. The building and campus was very attrac-tive and modern. The main office was brightly painted and colorfully deco-rated with stenciling. There was one main entrance, which made the building very secure. The hallways were roomy and created a sense of openness. To foster school pride and unity, students were required to wear uniforms; den-im jeans and/or inappropriate clothing were not permitted.

During the 2001–2002 academic year, the school served 1,300 students, including 8.9% non-Hispanic White/Caucasian, 3.5% Black/African Amer-ican, 84.8% Hispanic/Latino, 1.7% Asian American, 0.1% Native American, and 1% children of multiracial heritage. This enrollment placed the school over capacity. The school qualified for Title I funding with 59.3% of the students on free or reduced-price lunch. The school also reported 9.5% students with disabilities, 9% students classified as gifted, and 38.6% stu-dents classified as ELLs. The student population was extremely transient, with students moving in and out of the community, as well as back and forth to their countries of origin. The community, predominantly Hispanic/La-tino, was considered vibrant, with representatives from every Central and South American country, and with each bringing a bit of their culture to the school atmosphere.

The school employed 71 instructional staff, a principal, and two assis-tant principals. Faculty stability was 94.2%, and teachers had 5.4 average years of experience. The principal was the main administrator assigned to the school and worked with the two assistant principals. The principal and two assistant principals were interviewed together for our visit; henceforth, throughout this chapter, their comments are labeled "Principal" for those specifically attributable to the main administrator or "Administrative Team" for their collective ideas. The next section of this chapter addresses the themes that underpin this school's success.

Vision of Local Intelligence

Everyone in the school community possesses valuable assets, if not monetary, human capital, including culture and networks which, collectively, create a rich school environment supportive of instructional effectiveness and student learning. Central to this core school value is that every child is gifted in some way. It is then the school's obligation to address different learning styles and forms of intelligences to uncover each child's unique gifts and surface them, where they can foster achievement and success for each and every child and thus, the entire school.

The school mission statement, clearly visible throughout every area of the school, including every classroom and the school Web site, emphasizes this belief while focusing on students' achievement and preparation for an increasingly complex, interconnected, and technological world. "You can go into any one of the computers and the screen saver is our mission statement. When you go to the Web page, it is there" (Principal). Teachers, students, parents, and other staff are all well-aware of the school mission. Collectively, they review the mission regularly to "fully understand their part as a whole—everyone's part" (Teacher). The mission states, "Brightening the future through the power of knowledge using a multiple intelligence approach." Additionally, the school vision states,

> [School X3] will help individuals excel by discovering the full potential, experiencing the lure of the future, and dreaming of and actualizing the possible. The vision will be accomplished by: daring to dream; nurturing the intellect; expressing emotions; raising achievement; sharing responsibility; and fostering the love of reading.

Authentic, Exploratory, and Experiential Learning

Faculty agreed that academics "is not sufficient" for a vision of learning and realized the need to integrate the whole person to address the different learning styles of children by nurturing the whole child through fitness, the arts, the intra- and interpersonal, etc. They "spot" children who learn kin-esthetically, through music, and/or other modalities. While School X3 was specifically designed and built to implement different learning styles and multiple forms of intelligences, the school's philosophy is further grounded on eclecticism. With approximately 300 computers, 6–8 per classroom, and Internet access in every classroom, the school is virtually paperless. There are computers in the library that are also accessible to parents. Closed-circuit television and specially designated funding supports programs such as children televising the news each morning. A parent describes the involvement of students: "Our morning announcements are done by kids. There are kids in the library with the machines and everything, and they know how to do it. When we have open house, they're the ones who are running the cameras, and we're the ones speaking." All teachers have e-mail; all memos come through e-mail. The school has an impressive Web site, and many instructional programs can be accessed from home. The administrative team explains, "Students can access this server regardless of what program they're in, and the scores are posted in their classrooms. Every month we retrieve (the secretary does it automatically) those class lists and look up where the kids are reading or not reading, how many points they have earned, and how much progress they have made."

Technology is applied to all teaching and learning. Technology is used to keep "track of who's reading, who's understanding what they read, and how much they are reading" (Parent). The parent goes on to say, "Most of our teachers are accessible to their parents by e-mail. I'm always e-mailing them and they're letting me know if something is going on. If he didn't get the grade I thought he was going to get, I can always call and ask, 'What's going on? What does he need?' So, I think there's a very big—a lot of open communication . . . that really helps me to be on top of him."

Performance-based assessments are designed to supplement standardized tests and summative teacher-developed criterion-referenced exams, to actually allow students to demonstrate what they have learned and how they apply that learning to problem solving and everyday lives—the "real world." Children are able to express themselves musically, artistically, physically, etc.; they can choose different ways of presenting what has been learned and how they apply the knowledge. This gives teachers a better idea of what students actually know rather than "just the multiple-choice or written essay" exam. Teachers use assessments to "gear up" instructions; constantly using formal and informal assessments to determine where they need to take students from one year to the next. Both teachers and students employ Bloom's Taxonomy. Teachers keep cards detailing the questioning levels of the taxonomy to remind them; students have cards too. Teachers guide students in developing their own high-order questions so they better understand how to respond to them. They teach the children *how* to think rather than *what* to think, because "that's how they need to be in life," according to a teacher. Teachers state that their goal is to prepare children to become more independent and work well with each other because "there's not always somebody there." Furthermore, the principal serves as a role model; for example, modeling higher-order skills through her questioning of everyone from teachers to parents, students, and other staff. Students are prepared to be analytical, independent thinkers, through activities that engage their thinking, and teach them strategies for problem solving. One teacher describes as an example, the teaching of chess:

> I teach some of the kids how to play chess: "OK, this is what this piece does." Then at the end of the school year, when they're thinking three or four moves ahead of where I'm at, and I'm telling them, "This is going to help you in math, this is gonna help you in life 'cause now, instead of just thinking one step at a time, you're looking ahead to the future." Mr. [Teacher M] told me about the Academic Excellence Program, where they fund my program now. They're actually sending me materials, and I felt embarrassed at first because I was doing things with my hands behind my back, so to speak, in the beginning stages, and now they're giving me books. I was drawing boards on the [chalk] board, and now I have [real] chess boards.

The school culture and climate is very sensitive, inclusive, and responsive to the community and school demographics. In addition to Hispanic/Latino heritage, Black History is celebrated by bringing in speakers such as Miss Black America; and holidays around the world are also celebrated. Contests in writing, poetry, and oratory are another way cultural sensitivity is demonstrated. While the school affirms all cultures and exposes children to different cultural groups, even those not represented in the school population, it also affirms the commonalities everyone shares:

> We might be different by one thing, but in reality we're all human and it goes on every day. As a whole, the kids know, I may be different. I may be better at art than such and such, but he may be better than me in something else. Just because I'm from Peru doesn't mean that I have this stereotype. They know pretty much that we're all the same. We're all in this together, and we're here as a team to help each other out. (Teacher)

Community languages are also valued and considered assets to school success. ESOL instruction is provided for inclusion students who are ELLs, as well as dual and developmental bilingual education to foster bilingualism and biliteracy. Through dual/developmental bilingual education, half the children in the class are learning each other's languages; for example, half the children will be English-dominant and learning Spanish while half will be Spanish-dominant and learning English. The goal is to foster a learning environment where both groups serve as valuable, authentic, language models for each other. Each native language continues to be developed while children acquire second language proficiency.

Cascading Democratic Leadership

Representing a succession of stages, processes, operations, and units, each dependent on the preceding one and blending into each other to produce a culminating effect, cascading democratic leadership considers everyone a stakeholder—the students, the teachers, the counselors, and the parents. Although the principal is ultimately held responsible for decision making by the school district and never forgets that she is "getting paid to run the building," which means she'll "do the [final] decision making," every staff member at School X3 is involved in the decision-making process. Parents, noninstructional staff, and community members are also involved in decision making.

The school has several groups directly involved in the decision-making process. The Leadership Committee is composed of administrators, a secretary, a paraprofessional, a cafeteria worker, a custodian, two teachers, and a member at-large elected by their own constituents. Even staff who are not part of the committee can participate if they are interested, ensuring that everybody knows no one is excluded. The EESAC is composed of teachers, parents, noninstructional staff such as custodians and secretaries, and administration. The EESAC looks at all aspects of the school; what needs improvement, what seems to be working well, what can be done to benefit the children more, where to apply for funding. They're always trying to better things and "there's always an area that can use some improvement" (Teacher).

By the same token, the principal maintains that if people are going to buy into the decisions, the school must have some degree of consensus management. She has discovered that "most of the time it is easier to buy into consensus management." It is understood that consensus does not mean majority rule or that everyone has to be in total agreement, but that everyone agrees to support the decisions reached through the group process. Even at the grade levels, decisions are made democratically through consensus. Although there is a chairperson for each grade, that person does not decide.

We all decide as a whole. So it's evenly spread out. We have faculty meetings and we give her [Principal] ideas from the faculty, and then EESAC takes that back and makes the decisions. They have our input into it. It's not like they just get in the group and say, this is what's going to be done. You guys have to do it. Then we all get mad and don't want to do it. She [Principal] asks for who is interested and feels they can take this on. It helps us to feel like we're all part of it. Everyone has the opportunity to be a part of it. (Teacher)

For example, the school received FCAT award money and collaboratively decided how to use the funds. One teacher enthusiastically described the involvement of everyone:

We've got money! We've got money! Yeah, we got these nice shirts. We got polo shirts with an "A." We got a stipend. We got money! We all voted on who we want to include. Is everybody included in the process, right? Right, it had to go through EESAC. We included everybody. Everybody! Everybody! We voted on that because one thing that our school really believes is that we cannot work in isolation. It's a team effort and we go from the cafeteria to everywhere.

Another example of consensus management involved teachers and custodians. Teachers complained that the classrooms were not cleaned properly, while the custodians pointed out that the air vents were not working properly; even though they were cleaning through the inside with their hose, there was dust. The custodians also pointed out that teachers were not picking up in their classrooms. After democratic discussion of all concerns, it was agreed that the teachers were correct and the custodians were correct: They were cleaning, yet the classrooms were not as clean. The teachers were not keeping the classrooms as tidy as possible. As a result, they ended up with an improvement plan that involved everyone and benefitted everyone.

It is acknowledged that a well-informed school is essential to decision making through consensus. As such, information is widely disseminated among all staff and parents. The principal takes on the role of mentor in encouraging leadership. She'll spend time showing teachers the ins and outs of what she's doing "ALL the time." Teachers and parents attest that "quickly when you come into this building" everyone realizes that this is a school site where "everyone is expected to bring something to the table and all are allowed to share what they feel would be the best course." While all ideas presented may not necessarily be used, it is very encouraging that people at all levels (i.e., administrators, new teachers, experienced teachers, parents, staff, etc.), bring their ideas to the table. New-hires are assessed for knowledge and skills needed at the school and to ensure that they can support other staff members and contribute to the school's success. The importance of acclimating new personnel is explained from two different perspectives:

> You very quickly become a member of the family ... I know that parents and students we do not choose, but as far as personnel in the school, the administration of this school does a very good job of whoever comes in new, making sure that they are a member of the team very, very quickly. That's how I felt from day one, ... that I was a member of the team. (Assistant Principal)

> My first year working here, which was about four years ago, before school started when we all met as a faculty, the principal introduced me and walked me around to different classrooms, and I thought that was really special. We have happy hour (laughter). That's true. We do a lot of things outside of school together. Yes, we do, we do, we do—team-building activities. (Teacher)

The school conducts many surveys to ensure everyone's interests, needs, and perspectives are known. Parents, who are not on EESAC or any other school committee, are surveyed often to ensure their voices are also heard, asking their opinions on various items—from the open house to school security, etc. Information obtained is used to develop strategies and programs, purchase materials, send staff to professional development, etc. Even if staff expresses interest in areas in which they lack expertise, opportunities for further education and training are provided to enable them to grow in those areas and then share the expertise gained. As well, this models the initiative to take risks to acquire new knowledge and skills.

Parents confirm that there has always been an open door. "I've been at this school now since my son started in Pre-K; he's in fourth grade, and I've always found an open-door policy" (Parent). Parents can come at different hours of the day, even before and after school, and find teachers—someone to lend a helping hand. According to one parent,

> They're [teachers] always around. They're always participating. They get involved in our PTA. They get involved in the EESAC. They volunteer for the workshops, even though it's after school and we ask them to stay. They come and introduce themselves just to parents and say, hi, I'm the first grade, I'm the second grade, we're the third grade, we're the ... They're there. That's a lot of extra time over and above for them on top of the time that I know they need for, like, their continuing education credits and for all the different things that they need to do. It's like they're always there.

As such, School X3 boasts much parent involvement. As one of the assistant principals concurred, "We do not have any problem with representation and making sure that everyone has a voice. This has never been an issue and it prevents cliques. It spreads out over the population." The statement from the assistant principal is corroborated by a parent:

> Due to the fact that the teachers care so much and go out of their way, you can come here at five o'clock any given day and you'll find any amount of teachers on campus. I think the parents get more involved, due to the fact that they see other parents getting involved, and you speak to them and you see them the next time that they're here. At each meeting we find a new face. I would dare say it's contagious. It's something that really is contagious. People that don't socialize as much, because they think, "Oh, I don't have to," just by talking to other parents that have had involvement in the school they somehow show up later on. (Parent)

High Expectations for All

With very high expectations for everyone in the school, the selection criteria and process for hiring teachers were, and remain, very demanding. A teacher explains,

> Once she [Principal] starts to interview, she gives a tough interview. She really, really does. She'll make sure that she has the right person. I came to the interview and I was impressed that one of the first questions out of her mouth was, "What skills are you going to teach to my students?" Wow, I wasn't anticipating such a specific question. I thought maybe, what do you bring to our school? She wanted to know on a serious level what I brought to her school, to her program. It made me feel good because . . . she is very knowledgeable in a lot of [areas]. There have been instances when the district has tried to send teachers over that she really did not feel would work out well and she made sure that she gets what she wants.

In addition, teachers describe what else is needed to succeed at this school, noting that being a team player as well as working hard is critical. They also note that it is important to have a good sense of humor, be flexible, self-directed, and trust yourself to do the best for the students. The teacher further acknowledges,

> Everybody has a lot to offer and the kids are the first priority. We're not here for a job, it's we want to be here. You work 'til nine o'clock at night. You have to be self-directed and you have to be able to go and do your thing, knowing and trusting in yourself that you're doing the best for those kids . . . You can

have a master's degree and sit in your classroom and read the newspapers. Not here. That will not be accepted.

New-hires are expected to not only meet standards but to be above the standards set for the school. New staff automatically become part of the school and aware of what is expected. For example, special education teachers are expected to co-teach and be part of general education classroom instruction. High expectations are integral to teachers' self-perception, self-efficacy, and self-regulation. "There is a belief that we're going to strive for one hundred percent, whether we get there or not. At least…we're going to shoot for it. If you don't shoot for it, you're never going to get it" (Teacher). According to one teacher,

> Mrs. [Principal] is a strong leader and she sets her expectations for her teachers as high as her expectations for a student…Somehow she just fosters that. She gives you that encouragement to just succeed at anything for your students and at a personal and professional level, and we help each other too. We do a lot of monitoring with the new teachers or even teachers that are new to the grade level, who have taught many years but they've switched grade level. You know, we help them along.

Beyond external expectations and requirements, everyone strives for achievement for themselves. The principal and administrative team had this to say:

> They're always striving—we're always striving—to look what else we can do better. When the scores come out, we look to see where our weaknesses are.…We've been looking to see what we can do to strengthen the reading program in fifth grade because we noticed that's an area we need to work on. So, it's not where you say, "OK, we've got it and that's it." You're continually looking to see where there are lapses.

> The bar is set at a level which is not necessarily easily achieved by what we would consider to be normal for students. When you set the bar high, you get a lot more kids that are trying to achieve a much higher level of education than what would normally be occurring…because the standard is so high in this school, they must achieve at much higher levels nevertheless. So even some of our weaker kids are achieving at higher levels than other kids that would be labeled as…weaker in a [another] school. (Administrative Team)

As the principal stated, "We have done it for us." Teachers affirm, "The strategies used for FCAT were around long before FCAT was around." Even with the state-mandated standardized testing, teachers emphasized that they do not teach to the test. It is further held that the school's success is driven by the collective desire to succeed. Motivational outlook is believed to be the key to success. Motivation and generosity begin at the top from the school leadership. One teacher says,

> I know for a fact there are a lot of friends of mine that work at schools where they're saying, "You have to do such and do this," and they get frustrated. What happens is, they get frustrated, and it revolves down to the students. The students get frustrated. The students are frustrated, they don't do as well. I think [it] goes back to, from the top— how do they make you feel and then, how do you pass that onto the students?

Both administrators and faculty concur that all students will succeed regardless of what it takes. The school offers many opportunities for students to get involved, including before- and after-school programs, which include chess, a nature club, and content-area tutorials. They had kickboxing, camping, a carnival, tap dancing, even a scavenger hunt—all over the school. They also had someone to teach salsa dancing to the students. Students are motivated by being graded on both effort and achievement. For example, "When your children have won awards or whatever, we'll bring them up so the whole school can see the children and their trophy or awards," said one teacher. Teachers are also recognized. They hang a "banner outside to recognize teacher of the year, or National Board teacher." Teachers so enjoy working at this school, there is only one reason they leave, that is for promotions or a higher position in another place. Additionally, the school believes in growing their own. For example, "The principal hired a lot of student teachers or substitutes that we've had. On a daily basis she can really see how well they're doing and she observes the class. This was one of our student teachers (pointing to Teacher Z), and he was even an after-school care teacher before that" (Teacher).

New teachers receive much assistance through workshops in numerous areas, including classroom management and discipline. Additionally, new teachers and those having classroom-management difficulties are allowed time to visit other teachers for peer observations. All staff, instructional and otherwise, are expected to meet or go beyond requirements and are supported in attending various professional development programs, considered integral to school success: "Whenever there's a workshop, we're there. Somebody from our school is there, even on Saturday" (Teacher). Specially designated funds were set aside to attend local, state, and national workshops and conferences around the country. Although not required, when teachers attend conferences and workshops, they share the information learned so everybody gets a chance to see what's going on in the nation and/or region, and everyone learns from their experience. "I could not understand a school that did not put professional development first and everything afterwards. I think the attitude towards professional development keeps everyone in the building fresh and keeps them working as a unit" (Principal). One teacher shares her experience: "We went to Sarasota to a science conference recently, which was wonderful. There were teachers there that had to pay it out of their own pockets. Not her [Principal]. She took care of it for us, and we brought back things to use in our classroom, so that keeps us up."

In order to ensure that teachers are all on the same page and working together as a collective unit, they are assigned adequate team-planning time, which helps teachers align the curriculum both horizontally across and vertically between grade levels. The school has a Lead Teacher, who focuses on curriculum and performance between the grade levels, as well as between general-education classrooms and special education, bilingual education, and other programs. Teachers ensure alignment of tests and/ or authentic assessments with established curriculum. They use a spiral curriculum wherein basic ideas taught are reviewed repeatedly and built upon until the students fully understand and can apply them at higher and higher levels. Teachers also meet across grade levels to ensure they prepare students for what is ahead. This allows them to assess growth across grade levels. Even grades K–2 art, music, and physical education teachers, who do not complete state-mandated standardized testing, become familiar with the test and testing strategies because they agree that they must know in each grade level what the expectations are "down the road" in order to set their own grade-level goals and standards. Beyond regular articulation between fifth grade teachers and middle school teachers to prepare students for the transition, there is also much articulation between teachers across grade levels. They describe articulation and communication as formal and informal, between teachers at all times. One teacher says,

> We even articulate with teachers in the special areas [art, music, physical education], where we tell you your child has a problem, or whatever... I mean if they have low self-esteem. The music department does too. If they think that a child had low self-esteem. It's a miracle.... She was so proud that she had been in the chorus, you know, so they help us.

Grade levels are allocated professional development days where they meet together the entire day—even longer—to come up with plans and strategies that they will all use as a grade level, in order to give the children the same access to all the skills and knowledge that they are using in the individual classrooms. Grade levels and departments meet at least twice a year to discuss what has been learned and how they can encourage students to perform better. They look at scores from the year before—how they can improve them and come up with a plan. They ensure that everyone is doing similar things. The principal provides substitute coverage. "We have coverage and then we can meet. Sometimes we will only have free from three to five o'clock [provided by district] and you don't have the time, so this makes it a little easier" (Teacher). The teacher goes on to say, "Yeah, we can stay late until eleven. The first year here teachers were here until eleven p.m. Yeah. Wow! Most teachers are here until at least five p.m.—six, seven, eight p.m. We're talking dedication. Boy, I'll say. But you're not forced to do that; it's your choice. It's personal choice."

No one—teachers, principals, or anyone else on the staff—becomes complacent and satisfied with the school's high achievement. Teachers agreed that one of the most significant things they are doing is always identifying areas for improvement. No matter how much they improve, it always opens another opportunity for improvement. They feel that they must improve every year. This is evidenced by the following quotes from teachers:

> I don't think we're satisfied when 67% of our kids scored at Level Four. If thirty-one percent of our kids score a Level One, then those are the kids we're going to focus on. We'll have tutoring after school. Right now we have a program in place where some of the special area teachers in their planning time, they'll go into the classes and they'll pull those kids who will need the most and might benefit from one-on-one instruction . . . So it's not just about we're an A school because sixty-seven percent of our kids . . . You can get an A by having some good kids, right? But the fact is that the ones that might need most of the help are those ones who are not achieving. So those things that are put in place by actually helping all the ones that are below catch up to some of those higher kids. They might not get Level Four, they might not get Level Five, but their reading improved. We have the same standards for everybody.

> It's not difficult to leave those [students who are low achievers] and we're going to pull this on the good ones so we can get eighty percent do well and forget about the other twenty percent. There are things in place and we should phase in those twenty percent. We're going to push them along just as much as we do the other ones.

To establish high expectations and consistency, teachers develop assessments that are the same across the grade level. As well, grade level teams examine the curriculum to ensure consistency and similar expectations for all students. To further highlight this point, it was discovered that the curriculum for students classified as ELLs did not always match that for students proficient in English. The curriculum was not aligned with reading and language skills, and additionally, it was agreed that the materials and the assessment tools for ELLs were very weak in comparison to what all students were expected to do, both ELLs and students proficient in English. As grade levels, ESOL and non-ESOL teachers sat down to write more rigorous materials and assessment instruments that totally aligned the delivery of bilingual English instruction to that of the English instruction for students already proficient in English.

Like all staff, students are expected to go beyond regular expectations. Students are constantly expected and encouraged to improve, even when they are doing well and improving. One teacher says, "We do that with the kids. 'You wrote a great essay. That's not perfect, let's do it better.' The kids notice that nobody's perfect—I can still keep improving. Every year it's the same thing. This year we improve on those thirty, let's find another thing to improve."

Looping is considered an effective strategy whereby the same teacher(s) stay with a group of students for 2 (sometimes 3) consecutive years. Fourth- and fifth-grade teachers decided to do looping to really get to know the students over a 2-year period. This allows teachers to move on from where they left off the previous year. Additionally, teachers ensure that all content areas are integrated across all instruction. Teachers get together to plan what they can do to integrate all different aspects of each department [art, music, and physical education], which balances out the different strengths and weaknesses of the students. They incorporate the music and art teachers into classroom instruction as well as integrate classroom-content instruction into special music and art programs.

Rather than collections of "nice" work, student portfolios are designed to be self-reflective for both teachers and students. Teachers reflect on their instructional effectiveness and guide students in self-reflection to critically evaluate their own work: what they have learned, what they would like to learn, what worked, and what did not, etc. When it is noticed that a lot of students in a particular class are not making gains, "we start asking questions" and hold meetings with the teacher to problem solve. This is first addressed at the grade level before moving to the principal level. Teachers whose students are not making adequate gains must develop a professional plan for improvement of student achievement.

Teachers stay in close contact with parents. All communication is disseminated bilingually, in English and Spanish, since most of the population is Hispanic/Latino. School newsletters are designed to inform and encourage parent/community participation as well as provide practical strategies for implementation at home. A lot of the information focuses on research-based strategies for reading that the parents can practice at home. Furthermore, the school provides much access for parents to also reach teachers: through voice mail, e-mail, and telephones in each classroom. The school is opened the Saturday before the fall semester begins to welcome parents and help them feel comfortable at the school. This allows the parents and the students to come in, find their new teachers and classroom, and speak to the teacher about expectations for the year and try to get the child acclimated to the new surroundings. A parent shares his first experience:

> I was impressed with the principal the first Saturday that we came in prior to the school starting. We had this huge Saturday where we met all the teachers and everything else. Then at open house; the involvement of the teachers and how well they explained everything from PTA to the actual curriculum and everything else. My wife's a teacher herself and teaches students in [another community], and from being involved in her school and her activities, I can see this huge difference between over there and over here.

A profile is developed for each child, and individual progress is closely monitored. Profiles are reviewed and updated during the summer, and list the assessments the children in a particular class had and their scores. At the beginning of the school year, teachers receive the student's previous year profile; from there, teachers update the profiles throughout the year. Profiles are used to develop progress reports that are sent out to parents regularly. "At this school, that's done earlier in the year than in other schools where they wait toward the end of the winter nine weeks" (Principal). Daily and weekly reading logs, daily worksheets, and other ways to apprise parents of their children's progress are used. While it is up to the individual teacher to decide how often to send out progress reports, these are quite regular. Anytime a significant change with a child is noted, as far as academic performance and behavior, the parents are notified by the teacher and a conference is held.

As far as discipline, the focus is on the child rather than the problem—a child may have a problem, but the child is not the problem. "My position is that if someone is misbehaving, the child has a problem—emotional, at home, or instructional" (Principal). Grade levels help each other out in coming up with strategies to better handle the management of behaviors in the classrooms. When a student misbehaves or forgets his/her homework for the third time, "We pick up that phone and tell that child to tell their mother. If someone is behaving foolishly, we make sure the parents are aware of that. The teacher can call and make sure the child tells the problem to the parent" (Administrative Team). If a child is extremely difficult to deal with, it becomes a team approach, not an individual who deals with the behavior. Whenever a serious and/or recurrent problem is identified, whether it's behavior or learning, it is taken to the team to discuss strategies. The school has further developed a child-study team for alternate strategies. Counseling is an integral part of this approach. The school has counselors who are always available and "who actually work with students" (Principal). Teams of teachers analyze the student's behavior in order to develop behavior-management plans. They conduct functional assessments of their behavior to identify the cause of the challenging behavior. They understand:

> We can't just say..., "John is driving me crazy! That's not enough." We have to get down and figure out what the problem is, and we can't suspend a student ten times without having a functional assessment of behavior. We have to know what the cause of this behavior is, their special needs—are these being met. We need to go further and have a child-study team. We can't just say, "Ugh, not again!" and continually suspend the student. (Teacher)

Strategies are implemented for 4 to 6 weeks, and if they don't work they go back and try something else. The school has also adapted many strategies from Exceptional Student Education (ESE) to identify behavior and learning problems as well as implement useful remedial strategies. Yet the overwhelming feeling at this school is of genuine care for all children and letting children know that they are loved. One parent shares the following:

> You also hear the stories about kids being sent to the office. In the old days, like I remember...if someone ever told me I had to go to the principal's office, I probably would have been trembling. You see kids here all the time and going up to the principal and giving her a hug. They see her, and she goes into the classrooms and it's not the typical that I grew up with. They're not scared, right, no. They have access and they come and they talk and they're taught to do that.

Exemplary Professionalism and Commitment to Success

Teachers are treated and treat each other like professionals. A teacher says, "We're allowed to grow as professionals [and that] just makes our instructional knowledge better." She goes on to say,

> She [Principal] does treat us all like professionals. We buy into that and it makes you feel good...I'll be very honest. The...first week I was working...I just gave her an idea and immediately she got the ball rolling and things were changed. So, to me, what that did was, I'm important here.

From that day forward, I was hooked to do whatever she ever asked me to do … it gives you that professionalism and you know that her priority is what's best for the kids and I want input from everybody. So we feel like part of a family—it comes from the TOP. We feel like we're given the opportunity to do things. It's not just district says to do this. What it is, is you are a professional, you know how to teach those kids, get results, and you do it however you can.

The teaching staff is considered highly educated. The school has three National Board-certified teachers, with several going through the application process. They informed us, "We have a staff that is highly educated. Believe it or not, we all have more than a bachelor's degree. Well-rounded. Even our paraprofessionals have college degrees. They just really want to help and participate. We have a well-educated staff and Mrs. [Principal] always encourages, first and foremost, higher education" (Teacher).

As professionals, teachers are given the freedom to structure instruction in ways they know are best for their students. In the words of one teacher,

I credit our administration for really giving teachers the sense that they can go and do what they need to do for these students and not feel like they're being micromanaged. It may be an unconventional way of teaching, you may do something that the next person wouldn't do, but you're certainly encouraged to go ahead and do that. In the end, they trust that what you're doing is for the best … we have one position, but here at this school we can wear many hats.

Although the district does mandate the use of certain instructional materials, the principal allows as much flexibility as possible. Rather than selecting and mandating instructional materials and instructional methods for teachers as many other district principals do, teachers at this school are asked which of the state-adopted materials they prefer to use in their classrooms. Each year, teachers develop professional development plans and decide goals for their classrooms and what they are going to do professionally. These are valuable self-assessment tools for teachers.

Teachers are expected to be, or become, experts at something and share their expertise, including conducting workshops and mentoring other teachers. It is expected that teachers will learn from one another. Teachers, novice and veteran alike, are encouraged to mentor each other and ask questions of each other to improve their instruction. This helps them to realize and appreciate what they are doing well as they learn from one another. From two teachers' perspectives,

I might have been teaching a lot of years and this person might be new, but I haven't been back at school. Even though we get a lot of professional development, they have ideas that they're bringing in fresh, and we can stagnate. So not only am I giving them advice on what I see that they can do better,... They can give us ideas on something new, some type of research that they might have learned, and we're given that opportunity to go into their classrooms and they come into our classrooms and solve some of their doubts.

There's two people assigned to every new teacher and then on an ongoing basis. We'll go in and give them ideas and we'll see what they're doing. They give us time during the school day to sit in their class, see what they're doing, and give them advice. They can come to our class and see what we're doing. Not necessarily that we're better than them, but they can [also] give us advice maybe on something that we're doing. So they have the opportunity to mentor us.

Even students serve as mentors for other students. Kindergarten students and first graders are paired for mentoring, "Kindergarten students spend thirty minutes in the first grade reading class during the day, and vice versa" (Teacher). Third graders help second graders, fourth graders help third graders, and so on. A parent explains her son's experience:

Kids buddy up, like with someone in a class; like in fifth grade, my son will buddy up and he'll help someone in third grade to tell them about what's it going to be like when you go to fourth grade and then he learns what's it going to be like when you go to fifth grade. He's had that ever since he was here in Pre–K. They also do the reading program—the fifth graders who read to the ones in kindergarten. It's so cute. They have buddies; they're going, "Oh, my buddy."

Calculated Risk Taking

Fiscal flexibility allowed the school to request waivers to use staff development funds in ways other than those designated by the district at-large. They desperately needed professional development money that was not tied to district requirements or budgetary costs. They received a waiver and put the money that usually went to chairpersons into professional development. This is illustrated by the following quote:

Rather than our grade-level chairs receiving a stipend for doing the job, we work together so that everyone in the grade level has a commitment to helping out the grade-level chair, and those funds have been set aside for professional development. It gives us the opportunity to learn more of the new trends and styles that are going on...and then you're given opportunities for planning days. That person doesn't feel overwhelmed and inundated with work, we kind of all work together to [support the] grade-level chair (Teacher)

The school also wanted more flexibility in how to manage their time and internal affairs without constant external intervention. According to the principal, "You need to be creative at times. Manage your time...I learned very quickly. Every new regulation that comes in at the district level is forwarded to the school level. So it seems that every day you have new mandates. I don't think the district tells us how to manage our time. I can tell you what we want at the school is to manage our time." Fiscal flexibility and time management allow the school to prioritize and decide how to engage in self-reflection and renewal. Each year, grade-level teams establish short- and long-term goals. They use part of the professional development funds to give teachers planning time every grading period—also termed "adequate progress meetings." Rather than assess at the end of the school year, these meetings are used to assess progress toward meeting goals. The principal understands,

> You cannot expect teachers who teach a full day to come over and sit down for five hours and describe their class. They need a professional day to allow them sufficient time to benefit...The district has not really given us very much of a say of what you are supposed to use. So it is very important that the grade level has the opportunity and the time to come up with their criteria to determine this. So when they are questioned on a student that is or isn't receiving a D or F because they are below grade level, they have criteria that they have designed on their own that they can justify and implement. They have the time to do it. We are very fortunate in setting up the time for this.

The school also gets to decide how to spend other allocated funds. Technology remains a top priority. It is often stated at this school that the way to learn to read is by reading, so in addition to new computers and programs, and upgrading existing technology, it was decided to revamp the library. The school wants to retrain children to develop a love for reading and a desire to read whole books. They want students to read "for longer than five minutes, which is what most of these kids with Nintendo can do" (Teacher). They believe that many of today's television and computer programs for children train their minds to work on very brief time tidbits; within 5 minutes, with marketing commercials in between, children "beat the aliens" and move on to another different scenario. "We train their minds to be quick, everything's quick, everything's quick" (Teacher). As a consequence, today's children are not encouraged to spend extended time on reading, or concentrating on academics and critical problem solving.

Although special themed, School X3 is also vulnerable to districtwide budget crunches. Each year, district funds become less and less, and schools are expected to become more and more self-supporting. As a teacher states, "Our budget is all gone. One year of matching funds. We're scrambling to come up with matching funds" to keep up with technology needs. The two quotes below illustrate budget concerns from two different perspectives:

> At the school level we get to see fewer and fewer dollars, making it harder and harder to purchase those supplementary materials. You know, a book is gray but sometimes supplementary material adds a little bit of flavor. You need to have some of that; you cannot expect teachers to go home and create all of that. Which means it's really sad that the monies are not there. (Principal)

> Budget is a word around here that every time we hear it our hair kind of... (laughter). Each year we have less and less money.... Basically...you have to put on fighting gloves to be able to keep what we get...Sometimes out of the blue, they'll just come and say, "Oh, we're yanking this," or "We're taking this," or "You can't get this." It's already stretched, it's already below what it should be...we put our school first, and we did everything possible to make sure that we can plug in any hole that there is out there but, you know, we can't plug them all in. (Parent)

Fortunately, the school's PTA is very active and highly regarded nationally for their fundraising. A teacher bragged, "I heard that they were sixth in the nation." Faculty and parents have also become quite skilled at "begging" as described below:

> Through the PTA, through EESAC, we have business partners...A lot of it is just going and knocking on doors sometimes, and saying, "Look we need a little bit of help; can you help us with this?" Can our kids come here for a field trip; can they come here for a lunch? You know, going to [Business X] and saying, you know, "We have so many kids that can't afford to buy school supplies, can you help us out with that, or pencils, or the composition books? Can you donate or give them to us a little bit less than...your retail." (Parent)

The principal even funds substitutes for teachers to stay home and work on grant proposals. Teachers have become quite skilled at searching the Internet for available free resources and grants. Technology is effectively used to maintain databases on "almost everything that is going on" so it is always at the teachers' disposal. They are constantly searching online and informing each other via e-mail of what is available. A quote from a teacher emphasizes their pursuit of external funding:

> Grants—that's our favorite part (laughter). Get us that grant, girl! She's [Principal] the Grant Queen. We write a lot... To write a grant you probably have to write it at home. Sometimes they'll give you... [a] substitute so you can sit down and write your grant. You're encouraged to write grants—very encouraged to write grants. I know I've written thirteen and received thirteen grants. [Teacher X] has written seven and [Teacher Y] got the most. We know that we have to work hard for the money, but that is out there. A lot of it is because we're very aware of our community partners. It's how we find out so often about the grants and the funding, because we're so involved within the community. We're encouraged to get grants.

The administrative team agrees that "there are lots of resources at the tips of their fingers with the computer." Even parents are trained on using technology to locate resources. As a team, everyone supports one another, knowing that in the end everyone will reap the rewards and benefits. A teacher describes the support they receive from office staff:

> Our school, compared to other schools that I've heard of or been in, is very organized. Our office staff is very organized and when things come in, they get to us right away, unlike other schools where they'll find out three months later that there was a grant. They're very good about bringing us all the information, and not only that, they'll even write on it who it would benefit the most and they send it to that person. I think that we're a close-knit family, and we just share among each other... ways... we can find out about this.

Parents are encouraged to volunteer in a wide variety of ways. Volunteer breakfasts and after-school events, including field trips, are held for parents to have a social time where they get to know each other and feel more comfortable at the school. As such, parent involvement is high at this school. Parents are a common sight throughout the school grounds and, particularly, parents are seen in classrooms. This allows parents to observe the teachers at their regular times and routines and how they interact with each other. The school even has a formal group of parents in charge of fundraising. Additionally, parents assist with the annual career fair. The school hosts the fair to acquaint students with a variety of educational and career options at a young age—before they enter middle school, where their paths become narrower and more entrenched—through tracking the courses they choose to take or not take. For the fairs, they invite parents to conduct presentations for the students. A parent shares their experience: "A little session with the kids, it really helped ... I'm a mediator profession- ally and that's coming to the schools with conflict resolution ... how they could resolve conflicts."

Many workshops in English and Spanish are provided for parents, par- ticularly to acquaint parents with school and grade-level expectations and how to support students at home with specific skills and assignments: how to read to/with their child, how to motivate them, how to support with NCLB, etc. In parent workshops, students can also tell the parents about their instructional levels and points earned. "We don't hide it from kids. What is their independent level, what range of books they can read, and how they can find it in the reading center" (Principal). Significantly, parent conferences and workshops present excellent opportunities to also educate parents. According to one teacher,

> It's not just, come and see something beautiful your child has made. It's more of a lesson to the parents, where we use that opportunity to talk to the parents and relay the expectations, so that they understand what's going to be coming in the years as a part of our school ... for them to understand even the multiple intelligences. We always explain to the parents.

Parents also serve as advocates for the school at district meetings. This is made clear by a parent who said,

> We try and be vocal also. Sometimes you see the same group of us that tends to be involved in a lot. Like when we had the Attendance Founder Commit- tees, when we were a new school—what were our boundaries gonna be—we were there and we spoke up, and were saying, no way! We have enough, we have this, we don't want anymore. It's like when our teachers are tell- ing us our classes are at capacity, we can't do anymore; then the group gets together behind them and says, "OK, we're gonna go, we're gonna speak, we're gonna say this is what we have to do. Just tell us and we're out there." Or like, if there's certain legislation or anything that has to do with teachers, like we just had the class size, get out there and vote, get out there and do this ... We get the word out, whether it's through EESAC or the PTA or just through word of mouth in our community. So they [parents] usually get involved and they [teachers] don't get overwhelmed.

Regardless of deficits and declining budgets, the focus is on teacher effectiveness and student achievement. The school has been able to move funds around to balance and/or reduce classroom sizes to allow more effec- tive teacher-student ratios. If/when teachers express a need for something unique to support their teaching effectiveness, the principal finds a way to fund it. "Well, if you find something that's really beneficial, she'll find a way to get it" (Teacher). Both a teacher and a parent chime in about the budget:

> The budget is always there for us. We go full out...sometimes we go into buying music, buying instruments and things. She has the money for it; she makes sure the budget is geared for that. And field trips. When we need money for buses and travel, she has the money for it. So the budget is always there for us. She wants the kids to shine; she wants them to get on stage and shine. And they do. They always do. (Teacher)

> I'm going to take this opportunity to praise Mrs.[Principal], as far as her budget ability. I mean, if she ever left teaching, I think that I would try to propose to go into partnership with her in a business because she's a real magician with money. I know that, for instance, where my wife teaches, they get a lot more money because they're a needier school than this one. However, money's always missing. They're always in need of money over there, and they don't have enough to cover things that I think we take for granted here because somehow Mrs. [Principal] stretches her budget to make it happen. It's amazing how she does it. (Parent)

The School in 2009–2010

During the 2009–2010 school year, the school enrolled 583 students. Due to overcrowding, a new school was built nearby as a relief school. For this reason, the school experienced a significant drop in enrollment. While it was expected that enrollment would eventually increase as the area continued to develop and grow, the school had to surplus several teachers, and the school predicted more cuts with dropped enrollment. Due to severe budget cuts, the faculty voted to discontinue a School improvement Plan waiver that traditionally allowed professional development days for each grade level and department. As a result of the state- and districtwide budgetary crisis, the school did not expect to be able to hire the hourly teachers it had for pull-out tutorials.

Student demographics were as follows: 92.3% Hispanic/Latino; 2.4% non-Hispanic White/Caucasian; 2.9% Black/African American; and 2.4% combined Asian American, Native American, and multiracial. Additionally, 31% of the students were classified as ELLs and 9% were students with disabilities. The school was a Title I school with 74% students on free and reduced-price lunch. The mobility rate was 21%. Class size in the primary grades was 15.2 and 16.5 for upper grades.

The previous principal retired at the end of the 2008–2009 school year. The new principal was a Hispanic/Latino female with a master's degree and 16 years in administration. This was her first year at the school, having served as principal at another elementary school. The assistant principal held a bachelor's degree and had been at the school for 8 years. The school employed 47 teachers, including a reading coach and a math coach. Teachers with more than 15 years of experience and teachers with advanced degrees were both 31.9%, and 11 teachers were certified by the National Board for Professional Teaching Standards. There were no 1st-year teachers. Title I funds provided for a Community Involvement Specialist. Title III supported before- and after-school tutoring and needed programs for students who were ELLs. Title II promoted professional development focused on development of a Professional Learning Community (PLC) and facilitation of more effective work with parents.

Table 6.1 attests to this school's sustained achievement. Indicators of high performance include achieving and sustaining a school grade of "A" for the past 8 years, 70% or more students scoring Level 3 or above on the

TABLE 6.1   School X3 Indicators of High Performance

Academic year	Adequate yearly progress met	School grade	Students scoring Level 3 & above on FCAT		Students making learning gains	
			Reading	Math	Reading	Math
2008–09	Yes	A	92%	94%	82%	80%
2007–08	Yes	A	86%	86%	67%	78%
2006–07	Yes	A	89%	85%	77%	68%
2005–06	Yes	A	89%	84%	71%	75%
2004–05	Yes	A	86%	82%	76%	84%
2003–04	No[a]	A	79%	78%	69%	71%
2002–03	No[b]	A	77%	70%	75%	75%
2001–02	NR	A	70%	72%	67%	74%
2000–01	NR	B	67+%	72+%	NR	NR
1999–00	NR	A	67+%	61+%	NR	NR
1998–99	NR	C	NR	NR	NR	NR

Note: NR = Data not reported

Source: No Child Left Behind School Public Accountability Report.

[a] 97% of AYP criteria met. Students with disabilities did not meet math proficiency requirement.

[b] Percentage of AYP criteria met was not reported. ELLs did not meet math or reading proficiency requirement. Students with disabilities did not meet math proficiency requirement.

reading and math FCAT for the previous 8 years, 67% or more students making learning gains in reading and math, and the school also has the distinction of meeting the federal requirement of making AYP for the past 5 years.

The school had also been the recipient of the prestigious Governor's Sterling Award (GSA). This highly coveted award is recognized as the preeminent state award in the nation. The Florida Sterling Council assists organizations through implementation of proven standards of excellence to enact improvements that generate better operations, customer value, and overall results. Since 1992, only 42 Florida organizations have been recognized for improvement and achievement of performance excellence. Of these, only two have been school districts and only nine individual public schools (Florida Sterling Council, http://www.floridasterling.com/recognition.html).

So what else made this school successful with the same student population other schools across the district, state, and nation are unsuccessful with? A teacher articulated this well:

> I think the environment of our school... translates itself to the children, the way we feel about each other, the way we feel towards our children. Something you can't put on paper. I really believe that's a big factor in our school that has helped us to achieve what we've wanted to achieve because our children feel cared for, our children feel loved, and they know how much we celebrate their success and how we celebrate each others' successes. When one of our teachers wins an award, one of our students wins an award, when our school gets a good grade, everything's celebrated here. We care for them, they see how hard we work.... they want to do well for you because you want it so badly for them. We encourage each other, our classes work together. Her class will come to her ESOL class, they will come to my class and will help her students, and her students will teach my students something.... Yeah, it's like a family. We can't put into words. Basically the fact that there's cohesion and not a single department is now working in isolation.

Parents also stated their perception of what made this school so unique and successful. When asked, "Are there any other factors that you feel have contributed to the school's success?" they quickly responded: "US! (laughter). I would agree with that, and administration and teachers working together have created this school. We're here because we're welcome, we care, but we also feel welcome." Another parent said,

> I call it the family approach. I know we all work and strive for the same thing... I think a lot of them [teachers] are unsung heroes. I have a full-

time job and I put as much time as I can here, obviously not as much as I would want to. Usually I'm here early mornings, and they're usually here even before the bell rings. You see them sitting around and talking, sometimes it's about a student, sometimes it's about a project. If I come after work, sometimes it's five, five-thirty when I get here—they're still here.

Questions for Discussion

1. What are some of the key elements making this an effective school in spite of its lack of fiscal resources? How can these elements be developed in your school?

2. How can school communities identify, develop, and pool their local intelligence and human capital? How can this human capital serve to enhance limited fiscal resources? How can human capital sustain an atmosphere of collegial unity and professionalism?

3. How can a school identify and develop a unifying theme (or themes) to propel and drive its entire teaching and learning environment?

4. How can schools prepare parents and community members as public advocates, frontrunners, and protectors of the school? How do you create this advocacy without giving rise to an angry or hostile reputation for the way parents and community members advocate for the school?

7

Nothing Succeeds Like Success

Anyone we hire, we try and set them up for success. If someone comes in and says their strength is kindergarten, we're not going to put them in a fifth-grade classroom. If they succeed, we all succeed. (Principal)

We have been able to move our children up and still have them be very comfortable and be successful, because nothing works better for a school than success... Morale is very high. We are quite competitive. We know we are the best in the business. (Principal)

Introduction

The adage that nothing succeeds like success permeates this school. School climate and overall collaborative professionalism helps set the foundation for this school, labeled X4. Administrators, teachers, and parents share a strong belief that they are the best and expect all of their students to achieve. Everyone at the school, from principal to parents and other support staff, holds personal responsibility for high student performance and utmost confidence in their ability to achieve it. Annual grades from 2001 through the 2008–2009 school years are reported in Table 7.1, "School X4 Indicators of High Performance," located at the end of the chapter. For the

Leadership from the Ground Up, pages 111–136
Copyright © 2012 by Information Age Publishing
111

interview with administration, the research team met with the Leadership Team, which included the principal, assistant principal, reading leader, and curriculum coordinator.

This chapter discusses the major themes that collectively propel this school to sustain high achievement: school/community/university partnership; academic teamwork; transparent shared leadership; growing their own successful staff; and fiscal entrepreneurship. This school is definitively an innovative groundbreaker, being the first school in the district and state to establish a school/community/university professional development school (PDS) partnership with a major research university. Academic teamwork is exemplified through a closely monitored and coordinated seamless curriculum. While the lead principal, as all principals in the district, is ultimately responsible for decision making, this school exemplifies shared leadership that is extremely open, multidirectional, and managed through consensus. The school also distinguishes itself in its ability to mentor and grow most of its own staff. Most teachers come through the university partnership and complete their clinical field experience at the school. Other staff members are former students and/or parents of students at the school. This creates a close-knit community with a vested interest, who "own" the school, joined through a common vision and goals. Everyone's creativity in locating and securing extra funding and resources is skillfully honed and snowballs into a shared entrepreneurship. Indeed, this school has crossed over into an exemplary model for demonstrating fiscal entrepreneurship and resourcefulness.

Description of the School

This community school was located in a rapidly growing low-socioeconomic area. The community was composed of residential homes and apartment complexes. There was a large community park near the school, allowing students access to a pool and other amenities. The school was the hub of a predominantly Hispanic/Latino community and served children from a variety of Central and South American countries. At the time of our original visit in December 2002, the school was housed in two buildings: the original, older, structure and a newer wing that housed the administrative offices, the media center, and special areas (computer lab, science, music, and art). The school had been retrowired to provide Internet and intranet access to 100% of the classrooms. The media center housed a state-of-the-art closed-circuit television (CCTV) system and Internet access via all computer stations. There were four portable classrooms. The atmosphere around the school and the main office was very pleasant, courteous, professional, and welcoming. From the onset, the school mandated all students wear uniforms.

What does this mean?

No students were transported to the school, which in 2001–2002 en-rolled over 960 students. A total of 97% were Hispanic/Latino; 2% non-Hispanic White/Caucasian; 1% Black/African American; and 1% com-bined Asian American, Native American, and multiracial. The average class size (K–5) was 30.7 students. Students classified as ELLs were 31%, gifted students were 9.8%, and 4% were students with disabilities. Students on free and reduced-price lunch were 78% of the student population. Many students came from single-parent homes. Title I services had been received for many years, but incoming students were increasingly poor. As well, many parents worked more than one job and had limited ability to communicate in English. The mobility rate was high at 26%. A sizeable proportion of the student population was new to this country and expe-rienced communication difficulties and adjustment problems. Due to the sustained high academic achievement record of this school and the feeder middle school, many out-of-area children were in attendance: "We're an "A" school and everyone wants to send their children here...We have some students here that are out-of-area. We don't know they're out-of-area, we find out in their last year when we plead and beg for them to give us their real address so we can send their cumulative folder to the middle school they're going to" (Principal).

The school employed a total of 71 full-time and 31 part-time staff mem-bers. There were 2 administrators, a principal, an assistant principal, 45 classroom teachers, 5 special education teachers, 1 guidance counselor, 13 hourly classroom paraprofessionals, 4 clerical employees, 8 cafeteria work-ers, and 6 custodians. The guidance counselor held extensive orientation sessions with all new parents and students. With the exception of reading, a curriculum coordinator orchestrated the various instructional programs and provided reading comprehension instruction to selected critically low-performing students during the school day. This teacher also provided after-school instruction for the Academic Excellence Program, enriched instruction for high achievers in grades 2 through 5. Most of the teachers had been at this school for many years and held an average 12 years of teaching experience in the state. As parents stated, "Teachers have been here forever." A total of 26 teachers had advanced degrees and 1 was certi-fied by the National Board for Professional Teaching Standards.

The principal was a non-Hispanic White/Caucasian female with a mas-ter's degree. As of 2002, she had been at the school for 22 years and held 29 years of experience as an administrator. This was her first principalship, and she was very pleased with the opportunity to stay at one school and real-ly help shape a culture of professionalism and success. "They haven't been able to pry me out of here." The assistant principal was new to the school.

As a Title I school, a reading leader was allocated by the district; this teacher supervised, monitored, and coordinated the reading program and the many facets of remediation offered. Title I also funded a Community Involvement Specialist (CIS) who worked with parents and the community through the Parent Outreach Center. This CIS conducted informative staff meetings and parent workshops, and made home visits. The CIS also sought community resources. The school had a very extensive school volunteer program through the Title I coordinator and did orientation sessions on a monthly basis, "because we're always getting new volunteers" (Principal). The school had received numerous awards, including the Golden School Award, based on exemplary parent volunteerism.

This school had been the first—the leader, the groundbreaker, the pioneer—in many areas. It was one of the first schools in the county to put in an after-school program, a full science lab, a technology paperless classroom, and distance learning. From its inception, the school was quick in establishing partnerships with other schools in the area on an algebra action research project, which brought algebra into grades K through 12. They sent teachers and students to the middle school, and vice versa. "We have quite an active articulation program" (Teacher). One of the most outstanding pioneering accomplishments was the establishment of a school/community/university partnership with a major local research university, "one of the premier partnerships with a university in the United States" (Principal). Additionally, this was a *SATELITE* school (Students as Tomorrow's Economic Leaders in Today's Education). Local businesses assisted with a school-to-work-program that provided concrete experiences to transitional students from the classroom to the working environment. Students created items and engaged in banking activities and postal work. They began with the design process up to the culmination of a product for sale of their student-created products for the market place.

School/Community/University Partnership

The partnership was established with X4 as a Professional Development School. The university also had a partnership with another elementary school, a science lab school of choice, as an experimental research facility providing a clinical environment for psychological and educational research and development. Parents of students at the lab school granted the university and school staff permission for their children to be involved in educational research. Professional Development Schools (PDSs) are innovative institutions formed through partnerships between professional education programs and P–12 schools to provide support for professional learning in a real-world setting in which practice takes place. PDS partnerships have a four-fold mission: the preparation of new teachers; faculty development; inquiry directed at the improvement of practice; and enhanced student achievement. (NCATE, http://www.ncate.org)

The PDS partnership presented a uniquely outstanding opportunity for both groups. The school provided training for university preservice teacher candidates, and the university provided professional development and education opportunities for school teachers. University students completed their field experience internships for teacher preparation courses as well as their clinical preservice student teaching at the school. Many school teachers attended courses at the university, including the master's degree program. In addition, the university provided on-site inservice staff-development workshops for school teachers and parents. Both the university and the school ensured that parents and community organizations partook of the collaboration. A university professor was assigned to the school as Professor-in-Residence. The professor coordinated grant activities, offered inservices, supervised student teachers, and engaged in and coordinated research projects with school teachers and university faculty. The research not only examined but improved school programs and added to the scholarly literature on actual site-based effective practices.

It is significant to note that this partnership began through the school's needs and initiative. Because the school is one of the first to implement inclusion programs for students with disabilities, they soon realized that they needed assistance. Initially, the school did not have much support from the district or a clear understanding of the program itself: how inclusion is implemented most effectively, what practices demonstrate effectiveness in inclusive classrooms, how inclusion impacts the attitudes of teachers and students, etc. In fact, the principal stated, "We were the only school in [the county] doing inclusion and with really not any district support per se, and we had to fly by the seat of our pants." Since the university was doing research on inclusion, the school approached them for suggestions through a few professors they knew who were involved in this research area. Initially, the professors indicated that they really didn't have time to work with the school but "would come out and chat." They did, and the school "kind of hooked them in." The school is proud to state that is where the partnership emerged. Both the university and the school learned much about effective inclusion instructional programs and practices. The inclusion program served as a model for the district. The school principal said,

It was just amazing to me when I read the research on this, that not only did our ESE students benefit from inclusion, but the attitudes of the general education students in the classroom just showcased a very effective school climate in those rooms. It was amazing that when we compared the test results of our inclusion classrooms with noninclusion classrooms, the students in the classrooms with ESE and general education kids outperformed ... classes on the same grade level.

Soon, other projects emerged. For example, when collaborative strategic reading and the impact of cooperative groups on students who are gifted and students with disabilities was being researched by the university, it was researched at the school. The school and university also became heavily involved in research concerning the paperless classroom. How effective is a class infused with technology compared with students in classrooms without the same level of technology? As a result, the school boasted a state-of-the-art paperless classroom lab. Later they became involved with the impact of aesthetics on education. Their involvement with a university included

Our professor-in-residence, who roped in the departments of art and science down there at [university X] and brought out their professors in theater, dance, music, and our teachers were in inservice training with students. Then they went down to [university X] to work down there. That's quite an important project that we're continuing, because it's important to tie in aesthetics with the arts to improve our reading program. (Principal)

The university secured a federal grant of several million dollars to support the partnership, and a sizeable portion was designated for the school, which put those funds toward technology, with updated equipment and software. Developing the grant proposal was also a collaborative effort, as described below:

We sat with them, and when they wrote the grant, we had to put in our piece of it, what we would do. [The university's] whole umbrella was teacher training and how to make the school of education better. They received the money, and our part of it was focusing in on technology, and also another aspect ... which we wanted to do, was to establish the first paperless classroom. (Leadership Team Member)

The school shared the knowledge and skills gained with other schools across the district, state, and nation. On the national level, school administrators and teachers were involved in conferences and teacher training on the effectiveness of teacher training programs. In the area of technology,

Parent Magazine identified the school as one of the top 10 schools in the development and use of technology in the United States.

In relation to school and community partnerships, the school created an open school environment. Parents described the school as being very open, "everyone knows what's going on and that helps a lot." Staff members are all out in front each morning before school begins. There is a family atmosphere where parents are welcome. Teachers expressed that parents are very much involved—very active, very engaged—in "all that we do." At any time in the morning and throughout the day, you see parents walking around. Most parents do not need to make an appointment; they just approach school personnel outside, "because all of us are outside every single morning before school opens" (Teacher). Much of the communication with parents is "one-on-one." Parents really do trust school personnel as professionals, "and you can see it." Teachers state that there is a mutual respect and that parents treat them as professionals. Parents describe the atmosphere as one of respect and mutual support. Parents indicate the teachers are most responsive, returning calls quickly, and meeting with them at the slightest hint of a problem or decline in performance.

Cultural sensitivity is demonstrated by sending everything home in both English and Spanish. The school supports its goal of preparing global citizens by affirming the local and national population and groups across the world. The school regularly promotes activities that showcase other cultures, although the school is predominantly Hispanic/Latino. Everyone is involved, from classroom teachers and students to media center specialists, the office staff, and even the cafeteria staff. The school library has a wide variety of books that have been written by Hispanic authors, African American authors, etc. It was emphasized that,

> We should not get all hung up on Hispanic culture, which is the one that's most represented here. We do have multiple activities that cover all other cultures and religions, and we deal with Kwanzaa now, with the African Americans, and the teachers and paraprofessionals cook and prepare some of the foods. It's incorporated daily into the lessons. (Leadership Team Member)

The community really takes ownership of the school. This is clearly seen through the significant participation of parents in all areas of the school. Also, it is clearly visible in the physical maintenance of the school. Everyone ensures that the school grounds are kept clean and attractive looking. This is also evident in the low level of graffiti and any other vandalism this school experiences in comparison to other schools in similar neighborhoods. Another way the school promotes a strong sense of community within the school and the community is through the required school uniforms. Even though most students come from needy households, all the students wear the school uniform. "You walk through our halls and see our students; we present an image of being certainly midstream America, because our students are in uniforms" (Leadership Team Member). They have noticed the positive effect that uniforms have had on the children, especially instilling school identity and pride. The school has developed a "bank" of pre-owned uniforms to ensure that all students have them, regardless of family income. The principal explains, "We don't just give them one uniform, which is unrealistic. We give them two or three because we want our children to come to school with clean clothes, and we want them to feel part of our school and part of the group. That's very evident when you walk through our school." When students outgrow their uniforms, the parents give them back to the school. The school has also negotiated a generous arrangement with the uniform company. Each year, the school conducts a general school climate survey that the parents take, which is also published districtwide. This allows everyone to know "how the school looks from the inside" but also from the outside in perspective.

When it was found that many parents did not understand the banking business, the school created a partnership with a local bank to address this community need. This partnership has helped both parents and students and is described below:

> We have a student-operated savings bank here at the school. We found that many parents themselves were afraid to go to banks, and they opened accounts right here at the school. Every Thursday is bank day. Our students are trained by the bank, how to operate it. Sometimes the bank officials come in and take a look at it, or they go to classrooms and do presentations on credit and saving. At the same time, they showcase our students' artwork at the bank. (Principal)

Academic Teamwork

Student achievement is linked to effective teaching, and teachers at this school are a prime example of effective teaching. As shown earlier, all instruction is collaboratively coordinated and supported by research-based practices through the PDS partnership. All teachers hold high expectations for themselves and their students and are driven by enhancing student achievement. Academic teamwork begins with everyone, from instructional to noninstructional staff and even parents, being experts at something. Everyone's success is celebrated as a success of/for the school and, importantly, success is modeled for the students. "We celebrate everything and feel that everyone is an expert in something, and that all have something to contribute. It's important that as teachers we show our students that what's important to them is also important to us" (Teacher). Parents also conduct workshops; for example, "workshops with the parents of the very young children about helping them read, to get involved in their education" (Parent). Along with this, students are expected to lend their expertise through peer-mentoring, in class and across grade levels.

The schedule is designed to provide teachers at each grade level with an hour of common planning time each day. This facilitates utilization of consistent curriculum through seamless articulation of instructional programs, professional development, networking, and sharing of materials, resources, and ideas. Contiguous grades meet at the end of the school year and again early in the next to talk about student performance the previous year and the things current grade-level teachers need to emphasize. Midyear, teachers further look at the programs being implemented to see if they're successful or not, if revisions are needed, or if these programs need to be dropped altogether. They are not "charmed" by new ideas that have been found to be effective in other places but are not considered appropriate for their students. This perspective is confirmed by the following quote: "We don't have a lot of fancy programs here. I'm really not impressed by schools that tell me they're using this and that program. One presentation I listened to in one elementary school, they rattled off about ten different programs, and I just shook my head, because basically, what you need is effective teaching going on in the classroom" (Leadership Team Member).

The entire school has learned the value of meaningful data, from student attendance to academic performance. Data guides instruction; it lets students know not only how they are doing but what they need to be doing. The principal supports teachers by collecting and updating various data on student achievement, graphing data, and ensuring teachers have the most current and detailed information to constantly see how students are doing over a period of time, from one assessment to the next. Some of this data is provided by the district online; for example, specific skills on the FCAT. Teachers meet regularly to review data on student progress: data from the previous year's performance in order to identify what the problem areas are, what they need to work harder on, and where they excel. They design or revise their instruction based on specific students' needs. Data are discussed extensively with parents at conferences. Data are used to assist in grouping for instruction, including after-school tutorials, and to determine if additional assistance is needed to accomplish grade-level goals.

Data are also used to apprise parents of student attendance, which is the principal's "pet project." She considers data the base of everything they do. "Her foundation is attendance, because if they're not here, they can't learn—a lot of emphasis on attendance. I can vouch for that. I just came back from doing home visits to talk to parents about attendance" (Parent). All staff reward students who attend school each day. Teachers with perfect attendance are also recognized. As a result, the school boasts very high student attendance, being number one in the district numerous times. Frequently, the principal writes letters to parents whose children's attendance is not up to par. She prints the child's attendance profile and includes that. Yet the principal is quite cognizant that student attendance begins with parents. She said,

> All of this goes for naught unless students come to school, and that means come every day and come to school on time...We found a long time ago that in elementary school, children are really not responsible for their own attendance. Parents are responsible, so we work extensively with parents to make sure they bring their children to school every day, tell them to try to schedule doctors' appointments after school, and if they can't, we tell our parents to take your child to the doctor but bring them back.

The principal meets with teachers twice a year—with grade groups in January to look at students' progress: where they're at currently, whether a child-study team has met with the teacher and students, what kind of strategies have been provided, whether a need exists to make a referral for testing, if they need to get an idea of a child's benchmark level in reading, and what is the latest information—to come to some kind of decision about what needs to be done to provide some help for students who are not being successful.

In addition to required district pre- and progress tests in the areas of reading and mathematics, teachers do their own criterion-based pre-, progress, and posttests to assess skills being taught. This also occurs in reading where every 9 weeks, teachers keep their own "running records" to check students' comprehension of what they're reading. Teachers themselves administer regular weekly tests to make sure that children master other skills taught that week, and, if not mastered, quickly move into remediation. Teachers generate many criterion-referenced tests to measure student achievement across the content areas through critical thinking and higher-order tasks that employ "holistic scoring." They are critical of tests that are mandated by the district, which are content-based or specific-strategy based and don't necessarily measure critical thinking. In fact, the school insists that "teaching to the test" is not a recipe for success. "Schools that teach to the FCAT are not going to be really successful" (Principal).

A pacing schedule assures a sequenced learning plan for all students. Instructional pacing charts track all skills prior to the start of school, and each grade level checks off and works on a particular skill assigned to that particular grade, thus ensuring that everything that needs to be covered is addressed. They use pacing schedules for reading, math, science, and social studies. Even physical education, art, and music teachers have some sort of pacing covering the skills and reinforcing those skills taught in the classroom. This school prides itself on student achievement with the same student population with whom other schools in the district, state, and nation have not reached success. Expectations are high and come down to students doing well. "We can tell right away when a child [from low SES, ELL, and ethnic and racial minority backgrounds] has transferred in from another school. . . . We can tell right on the spot, academically and behaviorally, and then we can bring them up to speed by enrolling them in all the programs that we have. But they stand out right away" (Leadership Team Member).

The school ensures that grade-level materials are used with all students. Even though they work at students' skill levels to bring them up, teachers expose all children to grade-level material. As such, no student is denied the opportunity to experience grade-level material. Teachers use different strategies every year across the school, in every grade level. They use collaborative strategic leading, or student instructional leadership, for the intermediate grades. This involves not only collaborative and problem-based learning, but peer tutoring within and between grades. Teachers who teach special areas include reading strategies and math strategies in their curriculum. They provide an example with this quote: "If you go, for example, into a Spanish language arts class, they're basically using . . . the same reading strategies. Everything we're teaching them in English they are also reinforcing in Spanish, and those skills transfer, so that's added assistance for our children" (Leadership Team Member). All teachers use in-class groupings, which is part of the Comprehensive Reading Plan. This is a district-generated plan emphasizing guided reading. It promotes heterogeneous grouping, trying not to have students of the same ability together because "then they won't go anywhere" (Teacher). Same-level grouping is used with guided instruction wherein the teacher aims to bring up the skill levels of specific groups. Then the students are regrouped in mixed-ability groupings. There is also flexible instructional grouping across all other content areas. It is agreed that there is no valuable research-based reason to always keep a child in the same group if they're ready to move on. Their dedication to flexible grouping is illustrated with this quote: "We've even had children at one grade level that we were unable to accommodate at that grade level, they were too advanced. We would get together with the next grade level and find a time . . . we would send that child to another grade level to receive instruction. It's very difficult to do that for one child, but we've done that" (Leadership Team Member).

Clear standards and expectations are established for each classroom, and the children participate in putting them together, "even the little ones." This ensures that behavior problems are kept to a minimum. The school has learned that when students are interested and actively engaged in "what's happening in the classroom," discipline problems "virtually disappear." Most of the behavior difficulties encountered at the school deal with socialization skills that students coming from other countries or environments may lack. Of course, the school has strategic plans to address these needs and help all new students transition into the school culture. At any time of the year, new students are provided with an extensive orientation program and buddies. The guidance counselor takes them on a school tour and provides special sessions in her office. Further, the counselor is involved in having ongoing meetings and training with the parents, providing basic information about the school and different skills and strategies they can use at home. This is ongoing on a monthly basis, at the school and at the parents' homes. A parent leader, who is a parent volunteer, works through the Outreach programs and also meets with new students' parents to help with their transition to the school and encourage them to volunteer.

The entire curriculum is "opened up" with many different activities to focus students' energies and interests within very engaging programs. Further, students are motivated and rewarded through many contests, "which gives them a chance to put their muscle in and go beyond the basic" (Leadership Team Member). One of the Leadership Team member confirms, "We buy ribbons to go home with report cards; we buy medals and trophies for our end-of-year extravaganza so the kids can be awarded in different areas. Certificates, plaques, field-day events, treats, anything they have we take advantage of . . . We showcase students, even at the classroom level, sometimes with a certificate, or plaque, but it's ongoing." Every student is involved in some way in either before- or in after-school programs. They participate in the music club, the art club, and many other activities. The school even has special before- and after-school programs for ESE and ESOL students, and even a program for students who are gifted. Before school, there is a computer lab and media center open for students, which especially works for all students doing research. Parents are encouraged to use the computers in the media center and/or to check out laptops for use at home.

To promote productive citizenship, the school recognizes the need for critical thinking. They want all students to be independent analytical thinkers who can problem solve. As such, one of the first things they did was "absolutely banned the ditto." Experiential and hands-on learning activities are the pedagogy, not the exception, for instruction designed to engage students in authentic learning relevant to their lives and futures in a highly technological global society. The goal is to prepare students to think independently, apply learning strategies to real-life situations, and make informed decisions rather than teach to a test. Since a large portion of the student population is comprised of students who are ELLs, they felt that "busy seatwork," for example, giving students a pack of work to do at their desk, did not allow students who are ELLs to hear and interact with the English language. Dittos and meaningless busywork is perceived as depriving all students, ELLs and English speakers alike, of the enrichment that comes from active and authentic engagement with language through constant interactions, listening, and speaking. Instead, they say, "We expect our teaching staff to provide the kind of hands-on learning that is absolutely vital for a second-language student population, which we have. We want active participation. Our [ELL] students need to hear English being spoken in the classroom. They need to be able to speak themselves, in a give-and-take exchange through discussion" (Leadership Team Member).

Technology plays a part in all subjects, all grade levels, and all curriculum groups. Every classroom has between six and eight computers. Teachers are well-trained in the instructional use of computers to reinforce classroom activities, broaden students' knowledge base, and move them forward through different skill acquisition. There is a lab with software specifically designed for students who are ELLs, and another lab with open access in the morning. Staff personnel are paid supplements to run the lab as well as the media center. Teachers sign up for the lab to do large group projects. Although there is a large number of computers in the classroom, there are occasions when the teacher wants all the students to be on computers at the same time. An extensive closed-circuit television system provides opportunities for unique experiential, hands-on learning. Students are involved in many video production projects, including moviemaking. The principal recounts the following experience: "When they came here to do repair work, they told me that our studio is the most sophisticated studio in all of [the] county schools, including high school magnets.... We take our cameras on-site. I remember when the big ships came into [X county], we sent our TV crew down there filming."

The school developed the first paperless classroom in the county. They used the funds received through the PDS university grant to establish this state-of-the-art computer lab. It cost close to $80,000 to put the classroom together. In this lab, the children are instructed using technology, both at school as well as at home. Teachers post all the assignments online, the students do their work online, and very little is done in the way of textbooks or paper and pencil. They also have a science lab that teachers can access for hands-on learning projects. Well-trained paraprofessionals work with students and teachers in preparing and conducting activities in the computer and science labs. Paraprofessionals prepare lessons, organize materials, and order appropriate software and other needed items. In addition, there is distance learning: "We have embarked on distance learning with [county X], so we have several distance learning projects going on.... We have about five distance learning programs weekly, to deal with reading, math, social studies.... We have ideal learning for ESE, across the whole curriculum" (Leadership Team Member).

One program that is boasted as having made the most impact is the Comprehensive Reading Plan. From the onset, the school chose this reading plan. The components of this plan are a 2-hour block for reading, direct instruction, guided reading, and other research-based strategies known to be effective in promoting student literacy. To enhance student motivation to read, the school started the RIF program (Reading is Fundamental), where second graders take home free books that they own. The school held a "big extravaganza for this, with ice cream; the children went up and selected their own books" (Leadership Team Member). They also host book fairs where students, parents, and community members may purchase books. This has also been a great fundraising activity for the school. Another big impact on reading and math has been to maximize the use of teachers who teach in special areas, including teachers of students who are bilingual and teachers who teach art, music, and physical education in coordinated curricular integration across grade levels and content areas. "To me, that and staff support, communication among the teachers: sharing best practices—what works with this group; what doesn't work—that in itself has had the most impact in reading and math" (Principal). All of this is further coordinated with before- and after-school programs, and the student's home. The principal goes on to say,

> Sometimes I'm amazed at all the things that we do and how, even though we do a lot, it's not stressful. It just becomes routine. It's nice for me to know that everyone takes seriously providing support. I go into the classrooms and see what the after-school teachers are doing, so I monitor that. I pay attention to their delivery and the activities they use after school. I make sure that they're not just busy activities, but meaningful activities. I see how some of those teachers even give homework, and people say, "Who's ever heard of homework from after-school?" They really take it seriously and want to go beyond and reach into their home time.

Both before- and after-school tutoring, plus Saturday classes, are provided for identified students by certified personnel. Even the principal is involved in teaching Academic Excellence after school. In addition, the school established an Intensive Care Program, which was originally created by the district. Intensive Care Program teachers are very well-trained and have a 3-day lesson plan targeting certain skills, like comprehension and vocabulary. The program is twofold. The principal pulls children who have scored below the 25th percentile during their physical education time, so as not to interfere with the classroom, "to truly supplement, but not supplant." She works with these children in the very skills they need, particularly in small groups that are known to be more effective. The Title I reading leader instructs students with low-level reading scores during the school day. In addition, paraprofessionals work with students during the school day, mostly in the classrooms alongside teachers or pull-outs.

The school works closely with the parents in letting them know where their children are, if there's a need for interventions. They provide parents with strategies and books and activities, like task cards, so they can work with the children at home. They recommend participating in tutoring if they're not able to attend the after-school tutoring program. Sometimes they contact college and high school students to help. At the beginning of the year, primary-grade students are administered an assessment dealing with basic skills such as phonemic awareness. Based on the results of the assessment, the school targets children who are working below where they need to be and has tutors work with them. At the end of the year, they're tested again to assess improvement. On a weekly basis, the principal goes to the fourth-grade classrooms and works with students on FCAT skills. On a week-to-week basis, she makes a chart for the children to see what they have done, how they have improved, and how the other classes are doing, so it becomes quite a big competition.

The school has two kinds of programs serving students in ESE programs: inclusion and pull-out. Agreeing that not every student with a disability belongs in inclusion, decisions about placing students in full inclusion classrooms are carefully scrutinized and individually based. Staff work extensively with teachers who teach in ESE programs to select students who they feel will benefit from inclusion. Instruction across programs is carefully coordinated to ensure students are not missing essential instruction. "We try not to work against each other....My instruction is very specialized, because I pull them out, but I am not robbing them of classroom instruction.... I work with the classroom teacher's plan, what she is teaching" (Leadership Team Member).

Furthermore, the issue of state-mandated retention is dealt with through internal collaboration and decision making about what is best for their students, especially since many students who are served in self-contained ESE classes and students who are ELLs are retained. It is perceived unreasonable to expect the same kind of performance from those students that is expected from students in other groups. Instead of using retention as a punitive measure, this school uses it as an effective strategy. The quotes below illustrate two perspectives about retention:

> Retention is a definite strategy that we use here...to help children progress. We find that if children are not ready to go to the next grade level, that's where you lose children. To just mass-promote children who cannot work comfortably with the materials, if you continually do that throughout the child's career, you're going to find that the child's school career is very short. So what we do is use retention as a tool. If children are not ready...we retain the child... At any given time, once the child...is ready to go on to the next grade, we promote him right then and there. We don't wait for that child to have to spend the whole year in that grade, but we are ready to promote right then and there. (Leadership Team Member)

> We have been able to move our children up and still have them be very comfortable and be successful, because nothing works better for a school than success. Nothing can doom you as much as a child meeting constant failure, and that's why I think there are a significant number of dropouts. Children are pushed into situations they cannot handle, they are bored and they check out. (Principal)

Even with state-mandated tests, the school is very sensitive to students' feelings and needs. They try to have their ESE or ESOL teachers test those students so they feel comfortable and "not just thrown into a room with a stranger on that day" (Principal).

The principal is a strong believer in having parents read to and with their children at home. When parents state that they have no books at home, the principal takes them straight to her office and they walk out with a stack of books. In addition, the principal and the entire school believe in the power of developing literacy and family bonds in the children's home language. The principal emphasizes her point:

> Especially with our population, that's very important...because I've been at other schools and other administrations where they just deal with English. Reading skills transfer and you have parents coming in frustrated that they don't speak English and they can't help their child with reading. We say, please read to them in Spanish, question them in Spanish about what they're reading, anything you do with them in Spanish will transfer to Eng-

lish. That is one strategy I would definitely use with our parents, because most of them don't speak English.

Growing Your Own Successful Staff

Staffing the school is really not a problem, because we're staffing it with the teachers that we're training, so they fit right in with the [school] philosophy" (Principal). This is true at all levels of the school. Many parents are former students, and the school ensures that when they hire paraprofessionals, cafeteria positions, or other positions, they hire former students and parents who have children at the school. Great efforts are made to hire skilled professionals and place them in their area of strength, as described below:

> It just happened recently that we were interviewing one of the people that we hired, and she was interviewing for a position, it was actually a bilingual position. We saw that her strength would be more in a classroom than in the bilingual program, so we approached another teacher who was all for going back to the bilingual program, so we accommodated. We were able to give the new teacher a regular education assignment. (Leadership Team Member)

There are high expectations for all staff, instructional and noninstructional, and anyone hired is immediately set up for success. "If they succeed, we all succeed" (Leadership Team Member). The principal describes teachers as "better today than they've ever been. They are better trained and prepared. Their delivery is far more perfected." She adds that some of the paraprofessionals are working on their degrees, and they have such expertise that they are "like having another instructor there." Paraprofessionals literally work with children in the classroom and have specific responsibilities to assist with student growth. The principal further attests that teachers and all staff at the school are highly competent with high expectations and sound judgment, and they should select the colleagues they want to work with. As such, school teachers conduct all the interviews and make the selection of new teachers. The principal explains, "Consequently, for the last several years, I have not done teacher selection here, I have not hired teachers. Our teachers are the interview committee, and they do their own selection of colleagues that they want to have on board to work with. The last two teachers that we hired a couple weeks ago, I met after they were hired."

When a custodian had to be hired, the custodial staff did the hiring. Everyone is quick to point out that they have very low tolerance for colleagues that are not putting forth the same efforts that they are.

To further support cohesion, they allow the children of teachers and staff to attend the school, even if they live out of the area or district. As a result, the school has put together a strong, cohesive staff with a vested interest in the school's success. It is not at all surprising that the school has developed the reputation that few staff leave. Even when the district offers substantial bonuses for teachers to move to low-achievement D and F rated schools, teachers at this school do not want to leave. On the few occasions when a teacher has left, it has been for a promotion or better-paying 12-month employment. When two new teachers were offered positions by their home schools to stay, they elected instead to take the new positions at this school. The principal is not surprised, because of the reputation the school has of going out of their way to effectively support new personnel— to support the success of all teachers and staff—and thus, support total school success.

The school is very positive about the strength of their new teacher-mentoring process. The support system includes a mentor teacher, a professional development team, a curriculum coordinator, etc., all of whom are assigned to work with the new teacher. Even the principal is actively involved in training new teachers. The principal is an "avid reader" and enjoys placing valuable literature with personalized comments in teachers' mailboxes. If new-hires are experienced, coming from a different school and a different culture, they are still assigned a mentor teacher, someone whom they could relate to or discuss things that are particular to this school and its population. New teachers are not allowed to start teaching in isolation. The school tries to provide a transition period wherein the teacher being replaced and the new-hire work together. If a teacher is having a problem and someone on the grade level can give support, the team teacher is released to do this. Often, a substitute is hired to release somebody to provide support, sometimes for up to a week at a time.

Professional development linked to academic goals is a major priority. There is ongoing staff development at the school, with the university and school teachers providing many workshops. One example of university-provided professional development is described with this quote:

> Another thing you see across grade levels and classrooms at our school is research-based strategies that we got from the university. We were trained in making words, and [the Professor-in-Residence] has trained and retrained teachers and starts the programs up for them. For our first graders, you'll see them making words, then you go into a fourth-grade classroom and those teachers are using the same strategy at a higher level. It's continuous. (Principal)

There is even a program to support paraprofessionals in pursuing degrees to become teachers. A major support is to provide training for paraprofessionals so they have skills to work effectively with students. "They are not here to grade papers and do clerical kinds of work" (Principal). If a large group of teachers needs some special training, the workshop is brought to the school. The teachers take great advantage of the Saturday in-services. Teachers who attend conferences and other workshops also conduct in-service workshops at the school to share what they have learned. Teachers are very generous and share all they can, from materials to ideas. All staff personnel are included in professional development workshops. Teachers are very open with each other and not at all ashamed to say they want to learn from each other. They model lessons for one another. The teacher of the program for students who are gifted is an expert in writing and has put together extensive high-quality bulletins that could be published. The technology teacher put together several workshops on different technology skills. With a school focus on technology, they ensure that they always have someone attend state and national technology conferences and workshops. Grade levels are divided into teams that facilitate professional development through a common planning time. If teachers go to a workshop that is specific to their grade level, they have an hour each day to share and practice their strategies. There is also some professional development going on in almost every teacher planning day. The principal brags, "you would not believe the fabulous presentations they gave with PowerPoint, very professional. We have evolved with our staff development, from total group staff development, to [specific ones] depending on the needs. . . It has evolved to exactly what our needs are [and doesn't] put staff members through things they don't need or things that they already know."

Transparent Shared Leadership

The principal has learned not to micromanage. Instead, she trusts her staff and assigns projects to them. She does not need to restate her expectations, because everyone is well-aware of the high expectations, so when the staff puts something forth, "it is always the best." Then, as she states, she does not "think about it until the plans come in. I take a look at it; this looks great. I don't think about it until it's completed." She says however, that it has been a learning experience:

> I started doing extensive monitoring and extensive curriculum reform here ... when I arrived. Things were not in place as I felt comfortable with, with my vision. Consequently, many staff members felt comfortable seeking employment at other school sites, and so I have evolved now where the

leadership is a shared leadership and not so much a me-directed thing. . . At different times, different faculty members take the leading role. I am very well-aware who is ultimately responsible for the whole organization of the school. I know that an effective leader cannot be in isolation, doing the job alone, so my leadership style has evolved to a kind of shared leadership; also, providing opportunities.

Teachers describe the principal's style as resourceful and highly effective, with high expectations for all: "She has a vision and tells it like it is. She shares her expectations, knows that we'll get it done, gives us her trust as professionals, and lets us do our thing." The principal is very accessible. Parents and teachers alike feel they can walk freely into the office at any time and know they will be supported in dealing with problems or any other help needed. Parents agree that a big factor in the school's success is the principal: "I think that our big factor is the principal. She is very good, just out there, involved with the parents" (Parent).

Teachers concur that they are made to feel comfortable assuming leadership roles and that everybody is a leader at some point or in some activity. Each committee is established ensuring representation of diverse groups and voices. To assist with administrative decisions, the principal has established a Leadership Team composed of herself, the assistant principal, curriculum coordinator, reading leader, and ESOL chair. In addition, there are many committees, and every teacher is involved in a long-term and a short-term committee. All teachers either chair or participate in these committees. There is a very strong EESAC committee composed of the principal, five teachers, six parents, one student, one education support employee, and two business/community representatives. Even parents who are not members of EESAC often initiate recommendations that are taken to the staff for discussion and consideration. There is no union steward on the EESAC, because there are no union members at this school. The principal comments about this:

> I'm very cognizant of the contract and that we follow it. If I have a question, I run it by the teacher that used to be the union steward. I think that's why a lot of our teachers, despite why people dropped out of the union, weren't afraid to do it because everything here is done by the book and we know that it's not going to be done any other way. We don't have to worry about being a union member. It's not an issue.

All areas of concern are shared with the staff, including difficult financial decisions. Situations are openly explained and the staff asked to decide which option is most beneficial. The quote below describes one such situation:

> This year, we worked with a budget crunch and we had to make some decisions. The decisions were, do we want an after-school program or do we want to bring back the paraprofessionals who provide daytime support during language arts time; and we allowed the staff to make that decision. The decision was, we're going to go with the paraprofessional support . . . rather than buying items or things. (Principal)

Almost anything that needs to be discussed is brought before EESAC; they make recommendations, and the EESAC chair brings recommendations to the staff. The staff then has a chance for discussion, to come up with alternate viewpoints, and take a vote with the entire staff. While the principal attends faculty meetings, she no longer actively manages them. Usually the EESAC chair handles faculty meetings; whatever is on the agenda, whoever has input on the agenda chairs the faculty meeting. "I think that's what shared leadership is all about. I have the utmost confidence in our staff and in our teachers who are in leadership positions. They certainly have all of the tools necessary to do a fine job" (Principal).

The school budget, allocated and discretionary, is presented to EESAC to discuss and make spending recommendations. The entire pot of FCAT award dollars went to staff bonuses, and the EESAC and staff determined the allocations. Bonuses included all part-time and full-time staff, paraprofessionals, custodians, teachers, and clerical and cafeteria staff—everyone with a role in the school. EESAC puts together goals and objectives for the school, which are then reviewed at the EESAC meeting. It reviews the mission and vision for the school: where do they want to be at the end of the year and how to get there. Whenever extra funds are secured, through grants and other sources, teachers are asked what they wish to do. EESAC also monitors the school improvement team process, which includes a representative group of teachers, not only by gender, but also ethnicity and grade-level configurations and across the different disciplines. Within the school, there are also content-area teams, and it is expected that every teacher will serve on at least one content team. The point is that everyone is involved in some level of school improvement and decision making.

Grade-level chairpersons are volunteers, and the principal makes the final selection. They are rotated annually so everyone has the opportunity to serve in this capacity. The chair schedules and plans the meetings; yet, for the most part, every team works collaboratively so the chair is not doing the work alone. Many times, the principal meets with them to share information. Sometimes they request the principal's presence to ask questions and obtain information specific to their team. Grade-level meetings are also a great time for professional development. The team decides how to spend allocated funds and what materials or professional development are needed. While the state and district have specifications and provides a list of adopted materials, the school does not mandate the use of any materials. They are very cognizant of the reasons why materials do not define the teaching: "You know, there's a way of using materials, and there's a way of using materials" (Leadership Team Member). Another leadership member adds, "It's never mandated, which is not a good practice, because why should they mandate what we're using when we're out in the trenches? We know what's going to work best with our children, and we have the ability to make those choices, and we're allowed to." At the end of each school year, teachers are surveyed to determine their thoughts about materials and/or programs. Decisions regarding continued implementation are made based on what's helping them meet their goals with their students.

Fiscal Entrepreneurship

> We are really limited in the kinds of decisions we can make in terms of funds, because the funds aren't there. When you have the district pulling twenty percent of your discretionary money out prior to you getting it, and then, like last year, come February, taking your budget and leaving you with just enough money to last you to the end of the year, there's very little that you can decide upon. (Leadership Team Member)

The district is described as a "budgetary fiasco." The principal is the "master of funds" and the "budget wizard." Linking the budget to academic goals and student achievement is the underlying goal of utilizing all resources available. The school wants to provide whatever teachers need. The entire district-allocated budget is spent on teachers and students, "period." Additionally, the school uses discretionary funds to support classroom instruction to every extent possible. They also use all available funds to make sure teachers receive added support through paraprofessionals, the curriculum coordinator, and the reading leader. Title I dollars are always spent on things, such as personnel, that directly impact students. Each department makes its own decision. The department for students who are bilingual gets a separate budget and these teachers decide what they want. Teachers who teach students with disabilities get a budget, and they completely decide what it is that they want, even if they want to pool their money and buy an additional computer, curricular materials, or things for students to take home. The Advanced Academics program for students who are gifted also provides earmarked funds for materials.

Educators at this school also want to provide opportunities for extensive inservice training. The PDS partnership provides fiscal support for the school's technology mission. The PTA is "terrific" and lets teachers put together wish lists of "everything they need under the sky" (Principal). They do many activities: dances, fundraisers, "all kinds of things." The school tries to maximize dollars through matching funds and goes "after any kind of grant we can think about going after" (Principal). Usually, toward the end of the year, teachers submit different items they need during the year. Here is where staff, parents, and the community come in to find resources they can bring into the school. Everyone has become quite astute at making connections, developing networks, and "begging." Parents work with hospitals and churches to get donations for needy school families. Teachers have become impressively skilled in technology and online searches for anything and everything that will benefit the school. They have even been able to find places where they can get computers "for close to nothing." Paraprofessionals are also involved in these endeavors: "Our science lab paraprofessional, who is involved with the banking activities, has contacts. One time she contacted someone in south [X county], and they were willing to donate things for our science lab. We went there and brought back two truckloads of stuff" (Leadership Team Member).

They effectively advertise themselves and spread the word that the school needs and accepts all the help possible; and abundant help does come in regularly from local clubs, private businesses, and organizations across the district and state. Numerous business and community partnerships and contacts have been initiated by school personnel, parents, and even the students themselves. Educators receive funds, toys, bikes, instructional materials, even volunteers. Often it is not a one-time thing; organizations return many times with more contributions. The school raised close to $3,000 to buy musical instruments for the music program, which was one of the wishes of the music teacher. The music teacher was willing to put a band together but needed more instruments. The principal laughs,

Our students have a lot of moxie. They won't hesitate to say something. One of our students wrote to the commissioner that she needed a new computer, and the [commissioner] called me up and said that she received a letter from a student who was really needing a computer. She said that she had an organization that is donating a computer for the student and can it be picked up? Of course it could be picked up! Our students don't hesitate, and neither do our teachers, to ask anybody for the assistance they might need.

It is quite apparent that the entire school has a lot of "moxie." The principal continues,

> A few years ago, we went after the Retrofit grant. We pulled it in from the state, and the first year we applied we didn't get it, so I called...wanting to know why not and inviting their person down here....He walked in with a roomful of parents and teachers looking at him, and also a room piled high with computers saying, hey, we need a network. The next year when we wrote our Retrofit grant, we got it.

Another clever way to add to the fiscal pot is through district resources such as substitute days available through the regional office—"and this is where we really do well" (Principal). The principal went on to say, "Not only do we use our substitute days, but we find that there are neighboring schools that aren't using theirs and we go after them. That's the big-ticket item. Training is really free, it's there, but you have to provide substitutes to provide access to the training. To do that, we squeeze sub days out of the district and the region." Overall, the morale and collective school efficacy that has resulted at this school are very high. There is a palpable sense that everyone is in this work together for the effectiveness of the entire organization, every part of it. There is a belief that everyone is needed and everyone contributes to everyone's success. Parents are integral components to the success of this school and are welcomed as assets to the school's collective efficacy for taking action. This united identity has been a main ingredient of the school's sustained high achievement and has empowered the entire organization to become self-motivated, self-propelled, and self-directed.

The School in 2009–2010

The evidence of 9 years of data is confirmed in Table 7.1. Indicators of high performance include achieving and sustaining a school grade of "A" for 8 of the previous 9 years, 70% or more students scoring Level 3 or above on the reading and math FCAT for 8 of the previous 9 years, and the school also had the distinction of meeting the federal requirement of making AYP for the previous 4 years. The school's grade configuration changed to P/K–5 during the 2002–2003. It had Internet/intranet access in all classrooms, with four computers per classroom and a teacher station. The mobility rate remained high at 21%. Student enrollment was impacted by an influx of immigrants in the upper grades, who entered at various times throughout the school year. This variable influx had an impact on student achievement at those grade levels. As stated in the annual 2009–2010 School improvement Plan, "some enter after the first semester of the school year and are still ex-

TABLE 7.1 School X4 Indicators of High Performance

Academic year	Adequate yearly progress met	School grade	Students scoring Level 3 & above on FCAT		Students making learning gains	
			Reading	Math	Reading	Math
2008–09	Yes	A	72%	72%	68%	67%
2007–08	Yes	A	73%	73%	73%	69%
2006–07	Yes	A	71%	71%	80%	77%
2005–06	Yes	A	77%	70%	71%	74%
2004–05	Provisional[a]	A	81%	75%	76%	80%
2003–04	No[b]	B	65%	64%	59%	64%
2002–03	No[c]	A	74%	77%	67%	82%
2001–02	NR	A	72%	71%	77%	76%
2000–01	NR	A	77+%	77+%	NR	NR
1999–00	NR	A	59+%	75+%	NR	NR
1998–99	NR	C	NR	NR	NR	NR

Note: NR = Data not reported.
Source: No Child Left Behind School Public Accountability Report.
[a] A provisional AYP may be assigned if a school did not meet AYP, but received a school grade of A or B.
[b] 93% of AYP criteria met. Students with disabilities did not meet math or reading proficiency requirement.
[c] Percentage of AYP criteria met was not reported. ELLs and students with disabilities did not meet reading or math proficiency requirement.

pected to perform and meet the same proficiency requirement as non-ELL students who have benefited from a full year of instruction."

The average enrollment during the 2009–2010 year was 870 students: 98% Hispanic/Latino, 1% non-Hispanic White/Caucasian, 1% Black/African American. The proportion of students on free and reduced-price lunch was 84%, about 5% were students with disabilities, 38% of students were classified as ELLs, and 7% of students were classified as gifted. To maintain small teacher-student class ratios, Title I funds were used to hire two full-time teachers for the 2009–2010 year. Title I also provided a reading coach. As a result, less Title I funds were available for paraprofessionals and supplemental materials. More reductions in paraprofessional hours were anticipated in the future. It was feared that additional budget cuts would hinder the school's ability to secure grants to continue the Saturday and/or before- and after-school tutorials. The absences of these services would undeniably have a negative impact on student achievement. The school had a different principal. The principal was a non-Hispanic White/Caucasian female with a bachelor's degree, who had been at the school for 3 years, and had 20 years of experience in administration. The assistant principal had been at the school for 10 years, with 8 years in administration. The school had 64 teachers: 26.56% had over 12 years of teaching experience, 32.8% had advanced degrees, 4.7% were certified by the National Board for Professional Teaching Standards, and 76.6% were ESOL endorsed.

The PDS partnership continued and really had a significant impact. It shaped the whole philosophy of how this school grew and nurtured better staff, instructional and noninstructional. Teachers were provided many extra resources they can turn to, whereas "a lot of schools don't have that" (Teacher). Everyone in the school, from instructional and noninstructional staff, office staff to custodians and cafeteria workers, parents and community, all shared in the responsibility of academic excellence, before, during, and after school—in and out of the school. The infusion of technology had an enormous impact on the outcomes that we saw. Children were motivated to read, because everything they did with technology required that they knew how to read. While technology had been a focus, another focus had been improvement of reading and hands-on science instruction. In 2009–2010, the school boasted a new partnership, in its 3rd year, through a NASA Explorer Schools Grant, with an emphasis on enhancing the teaching and learning of mathematics, science, technology, and engineering.

Questions for Discussion

1. What are some of the distinguishing characteristics of this school, particularly in regard to how this school builds capacity through its human and fiscal resources (i.e., hires the right people and builds academic teamwork and also advertises and markets itself to increase community support)?
2. What types of connections did this school build with the community to get them to work as partners in learning?
3. How did this school identify and successfully go after resources internal and external to supplement its limited funding?
4. Describe how mentoring and supporting new teachers has been a successful strategy, which is part of the larger philosophy, for how the teachers and the administrative team sustain learning and growing at this school?

8

We Focus on ALL the Children

I think that depends upon the philosophy of the school and if from the top down, every person who works with every child believes that every child can learn and that every child is important then its [equal access to knowledge and skills] taken care of automatically. Here at this school, we focus on the children. (Teacher)

Well, when you talk about equal access, you really need to look at individual student needs because what you have to ensure is that the curriculum is being delivered in a way that addresses the individual needs of the student. (Principal)

Introduction

This school focuses on the overarching theme of a strong inclusive philosophy for all the students in the school. The teachers and administrators embrace not only the cultural and ethnic diversity of the student body, but also the diversity reflected in the range of ability levels of their students. Perhaps it is because of the depth of the diversity of their students that they acknowledge openly a commitment to the philosophy that is expressed in the two quotes that open this chapter. That is, every child can learn, every child is important, and the curriculum must meet the individual needs of each student. Therefore, the focus at all times must be on all the children. Further, this school embraces the emotional and social aspects of learning within a family culture and climate to address the needs of a diverse neighborhood community of students. They are committed to meeting the needs of the whole child, not just their academic needs. A teacher made the following comment:

> One key element is that I think all of us here really try to intimately know the students, their families, think of very humanistic feelings within this building, and I think that helps a lot. People go above and beyond, you know, your family situations and being able to assist not just the academic ways but in emotional ways, social ways, and I think that that's really the very key of this particular school.

The teachers believe they are responsible for the progress of each and every student, and they emphasize that "we work for the students, parents, and the community." There are four major themes that reflect the practices that have sustained the high achievement in this school: a philosophy of inclusiveness; professional teamwork; a culture of involvement and shared decision making; and an integrated use of technology in teaching, learning, and communicating.

As stated above, this school serves a student body that is culturally and linguistically diverse and offers special programs that reflect even more diversity. For example, the school offers programs for students with learning disabilities, severe emotional disturbances, students who are gifted, and for students who are ELLs. It also offers a program for pre-kindergarten students with special needs. But programs in and of themselves do not speak to the underlying practices that guide the actions of the educators in this school. The beliefs and attitudes reflected in the statements made by the teachers and administrators, and the practices they use demonstrate clearly a philosophy of inclusiveness that permeates the school and is central to how this school is organized. The principal and the assistant principal promote professional teamwork as a way of encouraging teachers to share and help each other as they work in unison to accomplish the high goals that they set for themselves and for their students. A culture of involvement and shared decision making indicates a recognized value in involving parents and the community in the school, thereby producing a school that is made better because the administrators, teachers, parents, and community work together for the common good of meeting the needs of all the students. Finally, the last theme of how the school has successfully integrated the use of technology in teaching, learning, and communicating informs the other areas and the progress of students. Succinctly, this chapter will demonstrate how these four themes work together to support an overall school culture and climate that embraces diversity and involves both the family and the community in a partnership to meet the needs of each and every student. At the time of the initial site visit, this school had been designated an "A" school and had consistently sustained achievement at a high level for the previous 9 years. It has been labeled X5 and the annual grades for the school can be found in Table 8.1, "School X5 Indicators of High Performance," located at the end of the chapter.

Description of the School

School X5 was opened in the fall of 1959 and located in an older residential neighborhood. An addition to the school was built in the mid-1970s. Although the school was aged, the outside of the school was well-kept and the office, media center, and art room were renovated in 2002. Of the 600 students enrolled at this school at the time of the initial site visit in 2003, 53.5% were Hispanic/Latino, 21.5% non-Hispanic White/Caucasian, 14.8% Black/African American, 5% Asian American, 0.3% Native American, and 4.8% multiracial. Students on free and reduced-price lunch were 53% of the student population. The average class size in grades K–5 was 22.3 students. The school housed the regional program for students classified as gifted and served over 200 full-time students, who made up 34.5% of the student population. The percentage of students who were ELLs was 29.5%, and 8% of the students were classified as having disabilities. The stability rate of 91% indicated that the majority of students enrolled in this school in October remained enrolled in February.

The school employed 2 administrators and 37 teachers; 17 were teachers of students in exceptional student education programs, and 20 were teachers of students in general education classrooms. The teachers had an average of 13.9 years of teaching experience, and 70% held advanced degrees. The principal was a Hispanic/Latino female with a master's degree, 8 years of experience as an assistant principal and more than 2 years as a principal. The assistant principal at the time of our visit was a Hispanic/Latino male who held a master's degree. In addition to the principal and assistant principal, the leadership team included four teachers, the primary and intermediate grade chair persons, and the chairs of the gifted and special education departments. The school also employed a guidance counselor, a media specialist, six classroom paraprofessionals, six clerical employees, and five custodians.

A Philosophy of Inclusiveness

The student population at this school is diverse in a unique way. Its diversity is reflected not only in the ethnic and SES backgrounds of the students, but also in terms of the diverse ability levels of the students. In the preceding description of the school, it was noted that 34.5% of the students are identified as gifted, 8% have disabilities, including learning disabilities, emotional disturbances, intellectual disorders, and physical impairments. The school also provides a pre-kindergarten special-education program for students with varying exceptionalities.

This school shares an underlying philosophy of inclusiveness as it embraces the diversity of its student body. It participates in a Multicultural Exchange Program with four other schools that celebrate and highlight the many cultures represented in the four schools' populations. Each participating school represents a different culture and shares programs, with the other schools addressing the differences and similarities of the diverse cultures. The principal and a teacher share their perspectives:

> We are truly a multicultural school. We really are like a slice of the community. We have every type of ethnicity and mix within our school. And this school has gone through a lot of changes actually. It's very interesting; the population of the neighborhoods has changed, and we also have a program for kids who are gifted. So a third of our kids are brought in from various neighborhoods and then we have the community kids and we have a mixture of Hispanic, we have Black, we have Anglo, we have Indian, we have Hindu. We have everything. So for us, it's kind of easy. We also have a program, multicultural program, and the children are teamed with the kids from these schools. One is a Black community, one is Haitian, one is Hispanic, and they meet throughout the year for various activities. We do a lot of things within the curriculum to address cultural sensitivity, but in a sense we live it because the kids get to know each other and they are all from different areas. (Principal)

> Yeah, we have a very diverse population, so we, by nature, need to be very culturally sensitive, and we do that on a daily basis. We have programs, assemblies, and for example, our holiday program is very multiculturally based. We just constantly are . . . keeping aware of things that are happening within different cultures and, you know, we are sensitive by nature as I said, because of the population. (Teacher)

The school motto, "Many Faces—One Goal," epitomizes the school's appreciation of its diversity and cultural richness, while at the same time emphasizes its high expectations for all its students. The underlying assumption of the school's motto is that while the students they serve have faces that reflect numerous cultures, the teachers and administrators have the same goal for all students; that is, to achieve at the highest level of their abilities. One teacher says, "Well, if you don't reach higher than whatever the highest standard is, you won't make it. For instance, [regarding the FCAT] if you reach for a six, you might make a five. If you reach for an imaginary seven or an imaginary eight, then you're going to go higher. So you always have to challenge the students to reach higher."

As a testament of their commitment to higher-order thinking for all students, they sought and received additional funds (by writing and submitting a grant proposal) from the district through the Excellence Program to "encourage higher-order thinking from the kids within everything we do" and not just for the students who are gifted, but for other students as well. The program is designed to provide enhancement services in language arts for children who are functioning high academically but do not meet the criteria to qualify for the program for students who are gifted. The program is implemented during school hours with second and third grade students. This provides a double bonus, because while those students are being pulled to receive their additional enrichment activities, the teachers are left with smaller classes to work with the students who need additional help. The principal says, "If the child is able to go beyond, then we move them beyond. Our program for students who are gifted was on a higher academic level, not necessarily the grade level, and now perhaps a more enriched version. The same is true in the general-education classroom. If there is a child who demonstrates a need to go beyond, we go beyond." A teacher echoes the principal:

> We have been supplied with an incredible amount of research-based materials to access. Many teachers have been trained in . . . how you use higher-order thinking skills across the curriculum in the classroom, and then we use questioning paradigms when we work with the children so that they are challenged to use higher-order thinking. So they are challenged to analyze, synthesize, evaluate across the curriculum. Everything that we do is discussed with the children, and they're asked to draw conclusions and share those with each other.

The inclusive philosophy of this school extends to the way in which it addresses the needs of its special-education student population and its students who are ELLs. While acknowledging that these students need additional supports and therefore may be better served using strategies that group them together to better meet their academic needs, they also exercise flexible grouping to accommodate the needs of the individual child. Once again, the focus is on the child, not the child's label or background.

The philosophy of inclusiveness extends to all students and is illustrated superbly with these quotes from the principal:

> Based on the student needs and school level, and they [instructional grouping] are absolutely flexible, within the classroom, the teachers identify, for example, guided reading groups, and those are based on not necessarily instructional load per se, but perhaps [to] strengthen skills; or I need to enhance comprehension of this particular group or whatever it may be. And, yes, [reading groups] are definitely flexible. Within our ESOL program, the ESOL instruction is presented either in the classroom by the teacher or as a pull-out by the ESOL teacher; so for example, we may have some children that may be have been identified as a Level Two, let's say, which right now we would pull out, but the teacher's going to say, "No, this child is going to do better if he stays here because he's capable of continuing with his curriculum the way I present it." So we make the decision based on the child.
>
> Same thing with children with disabilities or learning disabilities, ESE students. . . . There may be some emotional issues, things going on in the home that are affecting the children's performance in the classroom. So basically, when you talk about equal access, you're looking, at least from our perspective, you meet with the teachers regularly and look at the kids that are having difficulty showing us progress and try to figure out why and what are the teachers doing to address those issues. Also, whatever programs are available in the school, we make sure that they are available to all kids.

The school as a whole embraces the idea of making accommodations for ESE students, but within the understanding of "equal access" that the principal stresses above. One teacher states, "[We provide] a setting in which they feel comfortable. And it's a smaller setting, and I believe that there's flexibility there. Accommodations are made for the students." This attitude is confirmed by the principal, who made the following statement: "There are some allowable accommodations. We see the advantage to children, we feel that they need these accommodations and basically through the classroom teachers' observation and recommendations, they've somehow worked with the child . . . we allow the accommodations." Ultimately, the educators in this school reject the notion that labels and/or educational programs (e.g., learning disabilities, ELL, special education) dictate what students are able to accomplish. Instead, they set high expectations for their learners and embrace a philosophy of inclusion that welcomes all students. These educators accept the challenge to meet the needs of each learner and emphasize that instruction should be based on the students' abilities, not their disabilities, nor limited by assumptions about their cultural or SES backgrounds.

Professional Teamwork

School X5's teachers are considered and treated as professionals. The open-door policy of the administration establishes an atmosphere of collegiality and professionalism. The school functions like a professional team led by the principal and assistant principal, whom the principal describes as "a very effective assistant principal." The principal shares a similar sentiment about the teachers: "I'm dealing with professional people that are doing a great job . . . an excellent job, and my role, I think, is to make that easier for them to do. Whatever help they need, then provide it."

The principal and assistant principal work closely together; they conduct daily walk-throughs and know what teachers are doing in their classrooms. Teachers are comfortable with these visits and enjoy having the administrators provide feedback on their instruction because they know their administrators use classroom visits as a way of seeing how they can assist teachers, help students, and generally provide support. One teacher says, "Our administrators walk into the classroom frequently just to visit. It's a comfortable situation. They may even involve themselves in what we're doing in the classroom." The principal put it this way:

> I think, particularly, the climate that we're in now for education can be very stressful, and I think that my role, and my assistant principal has the same philosophy, so we kind of try to facilitate that to the teachers and we kind of buffer that instead of add to it; so when we present information to the teachers or when we share or work with them to try to improve the school, it isn't done in a pressure-filled type of atmosphere. It's done in a collaborative-type of atmosphere and more in, "Okay, this is where we are, this is where we need to go. What do we think we need to do to get there and what can we do to help you achieve that?" So we offer help, we don't demand from them. So I think maybe that creates an atmosphere that people are comfortable with.

As professional educators, the administrators and teachers work collaboratively to analyze student data and develop strategies or programs to improve teaching and learning, as is so aptly demonstrated by this quote from the principal:

> Well, with each of the subject areas, as I mentioned before, we do meet with the teachers periodically and what we do is we review those assessments that the teachers have administered throughout. For example, in reading, we have the Accelerated Reader program, and that provides us with a reading level through the "Star Test," and the teachers administer that three times per year. So that gives us an opportunity to gauge student progress in reading. With writing, we have monthly prompts that the children have written

and we strategize together: "Okay, let's review this response. What kinds of strategies does he need in the classroom?" We, the principal, the assistant principal, and the teachers [do this together], usually by grade level...for this year...We have smaller groups of teachers, plus they are able to pinpoint specific needs of the development of the children of that age group....We gauge with periodic assessments.

The administration capitalizes on the strengths of the staff members by providing ample time for teachers to share their expertise and knowledge with each other. A teacher shares an enthusiastic comment confirming this. "Our assistant principal is phenomenal at making those schedules so that we can have the opportunity to work together. It's an art! It certainly is!"

The administration believes in making every effort to maximize instructional time for students. They use the budget to creatively reduce class size to accomplish this. According to the principal,

Basically, what we do is we look at what little money we have available and we see where the grade is needed. In this school, for example, we find that one of the best things that we can do for our kids that are having problems is to pull them out and address them in a small group environment. So, as an example, in terms of budget, the money that is provided by the state for enhancement, I turn that into substitutes and I hired, actually, a certified teacher who comes in and substitutes every day that I pull out of that account and she pulls my group. She targeted the kids that are in the most need. She pulls about five or six at a time and she works with those kids to enhance their scope. Most of the funds that we have available are used that way: an hourly to assist small groups of children.

There's a genuine feeling of camaraderie that exists among the staff. The teachers "get together on their own" to plan and to monitor student progress. The principal says, "I'll walk through a first-grade classroom...and see that there has been some communication among those teachers. You see it in the curriculum; you see it in the classroom." The teachers speak of mentoring each other. "The principal or assistant principal may ask a teacher to buddy up with another teacher and work together on this or work together on that...we mentor each other constantly." Another teacher describes the camaraderie this way: "I think that again goes back to the philosophy that the administration has. We have a comfortable working atmosphere here. We're happy working here. We enjoy coming to work. We like working with the other people on our staff." When new personnel are hired, they are encouraged to "buddy up" with veteran staff members to learn about the culture and teaching methods of this school. This buddy program also encourages new staff members to feel at home as part of the team. The staff is a proud team that works very hard to meet the needs of all students. There is a "collective pride" felt in this school. Respect, courtesy, and professionalism are valued.

The concept of teamwork is extended to the parents and students as well. Parents are invited in before the school year begins and are given an orientation tour of the school. New parents to the community are paired up with other parents to help them become familiar and comfortable with the culture and operation of the school. Students also participate in a buddy program that pairs new students with a buddy who helps them feel welcome and teaches them the ins and outs of the school. A teacher describes their buddy program:

> Well, for students, when there is a new student, if by any chance they know someone that maybe they know from . . . [the] neighborhood and you buddy them up with the person that they already know. We give them a buddy for the first day and usually you talk to that one student that you know that's very outgoing and very sociable so that that person will introduce the new student to the other students so that they have a comfort level like when they first come.

The administrators at this school have created an environment where teachers are supported, valued, and treated as professionals. It has been clearly communicated that administrators, faculty, staff, and parents are all members of the same team, with the same goal, that is, to assist the students to achieve to the best of their abilities.

A Culture of Involvement and Shared Decision Making

This school has created a culture where parent and community involvement is welcomed, and educators give credit to the parent commitment to help out and be actively involved in their children's education as a key ingredient in their success. Over a third of the students are bussed in to this school, yet the parents take a very active role in the school. They support the school through volunteer work. In fact, the school has documented "about 13,000 or more" volunteer hours from parents in one year. One popular volunteer program is the school's "Lunch Bunch" program, where parents come to the school during lunchtime and read to their kids. The parents confer with the teachers regarding which books might be appropriate choices to select and the result is "a beautiful thing, you go out there during lunchtime to speak with a kid and there's a parent reading to them. It's reading for enjoyment" (Teacher). Additionally, the PTA provides financial help to the school through its fundraising activities. For example, the Multicultural Exchange

Program is "completely funded by the PTA. They fund $3,000 per year" including the funding of the field trip that they sponsor for the participating children. In addition to that, "ribbons and any incentives, reading incentives that we have for the kids are funded by the PTA." They also "give an allowance to each teacher for classroom supplies and pay for the agendas (planners) that are distributed to each student. However, it is important to note that the PTA activities go beyond fundraising; they also plan many activities to get the community together. The principal states, "We have a very active PTA. We have a lot of activities which the PTA puts together as social affairs, social events. We give this community an opportunity to come together and have some fun. We're not always doing fundraisers. They do things that just bring people together." Another example of the culture of involvement that exists at this school is the numerous partnerships with businesses in the local community the school has established. These business partners have provided financial "bonuses" for teachers to help pay for supplies and contributed volunteer hours to assist teachers in the classroom.

Coexisting with the culture of involvement that is cultivated at this school is the principal's leadership style, which invites shared decision making. The administration encourages staff to assume leadership roles, respects the work done by teachers, and involves them in the leadership process and decision making. In addition to the principal and assistant principal, other leadership personnel at this school include the chairpersons for primary and intermediate grades and the chairs of the departments for students who are gifted and students who have disabilities. These teachers meet with administration on a monthly basis and/or as-needed basis to partner in making decisions that affect the school. The principal describes her leadership style in the following manner: "I think I'm the kind that likes to involve, see I like to facilitate and guide. I like to get input from those that I'm leading. I involve them in whatever the problem may be, the solution may be, and I strongly feel that I'm dealing with professional people that are doing a great job." It is clear that the teachers feel they play a leadership role in the school and share in the decision making. Teachers feel that they have latitude to make decisions that affect their ability to teach in their classrooms. They feel they have a critical voice in the use of curriculum materials that fit their teaching and the learning styles of their students. They especially are proud of their involvement with selection of new teachers and programs that are a key to the success of the school. The following statements are from teachers:

> I believe one doesn't believe one is greater than the other. Everybody needs to share their ideas and are able to express their concerns. . . . Somebody

may be in charge of a program or something that's going on, but everyone pitches in and helps out.

I think that we have a lot of leaders within the school. It seems like almost every staff member takes on some sort of leadership role in one area or another. In other words, whether it be the union steward, whether it be somebody who's handling the America Reads program, there are a lot of [leaders] in this school in terms of staff.

A mechanism that involves parents in the decision-making process is the EESAC, which is described by the principal as a "demographically diverse group" that consists of parents, teacher representatives, and school administrators. According to the principal, this committee is involved in

All major issues with regard to student improvement, planning assessments, strategies that will be used, even financial budgetary decisions are addressed with the EESAC. Parents there have an opportunity for input. Also, with the teachers, I believe very strongly the teachers need to be involved with the decision making and need to buy into whatever programs we decide to implement so when we meet periodically, it's not a meeting where we dictate this is what we're going to do. It's more a meeting of this is what's going on. "What do you think are ways that we can address this? What are things that we can do?" So it's really just the atmosphere and the culture.

Finally, the PTA is also "active in decision making" at this school. "They are always made a part of decisions that are made here" (Teacher). The educators at this school have demonstrated to parents that their involvement in the school is valued and appreciated. They welcome parent involvement, and the principal's open-door policy invites parents and teachers to share in the decision making. The administrative style of the principal, which is also shared by the assistant principal, encourages teachers to assume leadership roles. Teachers' work is respected and their voices are heard.

An Integrated Use of Technology in Teaching, Learning, and Communicating

School X5 is one of the most advanced technologically equipped schools in the region, because of technology grants and additional resources from the community. The school emphasizes that its use of technology is integrated into teaching and learning and in communicating with parents and each other. Uses of technology in the classroom are confirmed by this comment from a teacher: "I'll tell you what; every classroom has five or six computers, pretty much state-of-the-art. We've got scanners; we have visual cameras, a lot of that came from our PTA. Most schools don't see that." All

say that is a big deal.
odd

computers are linked to the Internet and technology is used as a tool for finding information; the students can use the computers to "do research there through the Internet." They also use computer programs as a means to motivate their students in the areas of reading and math. For example, teachers use computer-assisted instruction assessments to determine what books are appropriate for students to read. Students' reading progress is monitored through the Accelerated Reading Program, which is maintained in a database on the computer. This program allows students to see their progress and motivates them to achieve at higher levels of reading.

Electronic gradebooks are used by teachers and monitored by the administrators and guidance counselor to ensure successful student progress. Constant monitoring of data, which is managed and maintained electronically, gives the school a good picture of what is happening in the classroom and how goals are met. This approach helps to track what the students are learning and what specific things they need to work on. The principal described it this way:

> One of the things about us monitoring student performance also is that we've now moved over to the electronic gradebook. So basically I can go to my computer and pull up any teacher's gradebook and see if they are keeping up and how is Johnny doing. If I was worried about a particular child, I could go in and see how that child is doing and if he has shown some improvement and so forth.

> I keep a log and I meet with teachers by grade level. I keep a log of those kids that I'm concerned about, and I have a database of a list of those children. I don't just go by a particular summary of those meetings, I look at the report card grades and the kids; I have a printout of the report card of the kids that are making D's or F's in critical areas. I'll add them to my log even if the teacher has not mentioned that child, and I'll say, "OK, this child seems to be having difficulty. What have we done about it? Have we met with the parents? What strategies are you using? What can we do?" So I review the report card, I review any test results that I had from prior years. Those are the kids that we take the time to monitor.

Additionally, child-study teams access data to help make decisions on educational goals and plans for students with special needs. A variety of data sources are used to select and develop interventions to meet the needs of students who require additional support. "We're provided information from the district with regard to the students' results from all of their testing; test results and test scores and how the kids have done throughout the years." The teachers in this school have an appreciation for data. They "look at where the kids are and what areas perhaps are showing a need for improvement" and use the data to make "instructional decisions." Data about students is shared with parents on an individual basis, and parents can access schoolwide data online, including the school improvement plan, from the school's Web site. It is interesting to note that this school so values the use of technology that

> Technology is part of our student school improvement plan. We have a budget for technology, and so every year there's a group of teachers that get together and talk about what we need. Do we need word processing programs . . . and we come up with a list of software and then that's purchased. We have a server . . . on the computers at school so we can put a lot of that software on the server and [make it] available for anyone to use. (Teacher)

The teachers in this school appreciate the advantages of technology. They use it in numerous ways, including for instructional purposes, as a means of keeping parents informed about their student's progress, and as a way to manage and access data so that it can be used appropriately for instructional decision making.

The success of this school contributes to the conversation that all students can be successful when teaching is adjusted to meet their individual needs. The educators in School X5 have embraced wholeheartedly a remark articulated fervently throughout the field of special education: "all means all." This statement expresses the underlying philosophy of the inclusion movement: ALL means students with disabilities too. These students do count, as do students who are ELLs and students who come from culturally and linguistically diverse backgrounds. Teachers must be held accountable for meeting the needs of every student, not just held accountable for meeting the needs of the general-education students. There is a heightened awareness across the United States that many general educators say they agree with the statement, "all means all," but often educators' daily actions say otherwise, and students with special needs are not included.

On the contrary, when the educators in School X5 say "we focus on the children," their actions demonstrate that they mean ALL the children. They have created a culture of inclusiveness that extends to students who are gifted; students with disabilities; students from culturally, linguistically diverse, and low-SES backgrounds; in other words, students who are often not included. Further, their philosophy of inclusiveness entails setting high expectations for their learners and accepting the challenge to meet the needs of each individual. They work together as a professional team to analyze student data and develop strategies or programs to improve teaching and learning, including the use of technology. Finally, they get involved in the leadership of their school and share in the decision making as they work in partnership with their parents to support the learning of all their students.

The School Today

The data in Table 8.1 verifies the sustained success of this school. After dropping to a "B" during the 2008–2009 school year, School X5 regained its "A" status in 2009–2010, resulting in the overall achievement of a school grade of "A" for 8 of the previous 9 years. Additionally, 70% or more students scored at Level 3 or above on the reading and math FCAT for the previous 8 years, and 70% or more students made learning gains in reading or math for the previous 8 years. The enrollment during the 2009–2010 academic year was 507 students, including 46% Hispanic/Latino, 24% non-Hispanic White/Caucasian, 21% Black/African American, and 9% of stu-

TABLE 8.1   School X5 Indicators of High Performance

Academic year	Adequate yearly progress met	School grade	Students scoring Level 3 & above on FCAT		Students making learning gains	
			Reading	Math	Reading	Math
2008–09	No[a]	A	81%	77%	74%	67%
2007–08	No[b]	B	80%	73%	64%	70%
2006–07	Yes	A	83%	77%	75%	72%
2005–06	Yes	A	86%	80%	76%	79%
2004–05	Yes	A	85%	77%	70%	74%
2003–04	No[c]	A	80%	74%	71%	73%
2002–03	No[d]	A	79%	75%	62%	77%
2001–02	NR	A	80%	73%	73%	79%
2000–01	NR	A	70+%	64+%	NR	NR
1999–00	NR	B	65+%	62+%	NR	NR
1998–99	NR	C	NR	NR	NR	NR

Note: NR = Data not reported.
Source: No Child Left Behind School Public Accountability Report.
[a] 97% of AYP criteria met. ELLs did not meet reading proficiency requirement.
[b] 90% of AYP criteria met. African American and economically disadvantaged students did not meet reading or math proficiency requirement.
[c] 93% of AYP criteria met. African American students and students with disabilities did not meet math proficiency requirement.
[d] Percentage of AYP criteria met was not reported. ELLs and students with disabilities did not meet reading or math proficiency requirement. African American students did not meet math proficiency requirement.

dents who identified as Asian/multiracial. Students on free and reduced-price lunch accounted for 45% of the population, 6% were students with disabilities, 19% were classified as ELLs, and 33% of students were enrolled in the program for students who are gifted. The school experienced a declining enrollment trend during the last 2 years, which would potentially have an impact on the funding structure to the school. It was expected that the school would receive less funding for resources and surplus employees, which would result in higher class size ratios. The school had a different principal who was hired during the 2009–2010 school year. The new principal was a non-Hispanic White/Caucasian female with a doctoral degree who had 10 years of experience in administration. The assistant principal, also a non-Hispanic White/Caucasian female, had been in this role for just 1 year and had 4 years experience in administration. The school had 40 teachers: 30% had 1–5 years of teaching experience, 32.5% had 6–14 years, and 37.5% had more than 15 years of teaching experience. Some 35% of teachers had advanced degrees, 10% were certified by the National Board for Professional Teaching Standards, and 62.5% were ESOL endorsed.

Questions for Discussion

1. Why are inclusive practices essential in today's schools? For example, what does this mean in how you can work effectively with parents to successfully educate students with special needs, students who are ELLs, students who are culturally and linguistically diverse, students who are gifted, and students who are at risk?

2. As an educator, what are your responsibilities for addressing the needs of all the students in your classroom? How can you ensure that you establish high expectations for all students regardless of cultural background or ability levels?

3. What is the role of the principal in fostering collaboration? How can teachers work together to ensure their collaborative efforts will be successful and incorporate best practices for collaboration between schools and families? Schools and communities?

4. What are some ways that technology can be used to enhance teaching and learning? How can schools that don't have access to the level of technology available in this school create opportunities for students to gain access to technology? How can teachers keep abreast of new technologies in order to benefit students?

9

Professional Development

This Is My Job!

My job is to support and to make sure that everyone is receiving the training and staff development that they need, and there is support with parents and students and with student management behavior. We try to set up the school so that children know what the expectations are. It is real clear, there is no confusion. (Principal)

I think teachers feel comfortable because it is such a nice staff—everyone gets along and if you need help with something, you can ask and you will get the help you need. (Parent)

Introduction

This school focuses on the overarching theme of professional growth of teachers by directing its annual resources toward multiple venues of professional development and support of its teachers. Annual grades from 2001 through the 2008–2009 school years are reported in Table 9.1, "School X6 Indicators of High Performance," located at the end of the chapter. The principal utilizes the district's diverse professional development op-

Leadership from the Ground Up, pages 153–170
Copyright © 2012 by Information Age Publishing
All rights of reproduction in any form reserved.

tions for her teachers and staff as well as other professional development choices that add value to the school. She believes that by supporting continuous professional development, she is encouraging ongoing learning. The results are visible in increases in student achievement and through the greater breadth of instructional strategies and innovations that are being implemented by the teachers in their classrooms to enhance learning. Because professional development is at the heart of this school, human resources are the key leverage point to promote ongoing change, learning, and shared dialogue across several grade levels and within the greater school. Notably, the principal views professional development as the learning capital for investing in gains in intellectual capital for her faculty. She stresses that it is her job to ensure that staff receives the appropriate training and professional development for the school to be successful. This translates into how the principal recognizes how the human resources within the school lay within her purview to positively influence so that she sees that people are her greatest resource. Consequently, she chooses to enrich her faculty, staff, parents, and students, as her chief starting place to foster optimal conditions to encourage, sustain, and promote continual school improvement through learning. As the quote at the beginning of this chapter suggests, this principal believes that professional development supports teachers who support students. Creating an environment where growth is central implies a leadership philosophy where the principal's support of the educators in her school in turn provides similar support and sustenance by the teachers to the parents and students for their ongoing growth and learning. The results are apparent.

Everyone is clear about what is expected of them for their students to be successful at this school. The parents relate what this means to them by saying that in attending this school, they understand what is expected because it is very well-organized, and the educators are unambiguous about what is important. Hence, teachers understand that their ongoing learning is pivotal to sustaining a school culture where building a strong academic community enhances this school's capacity for working together to solve problems. Teachers discuss the numerous opportunities afforded them to avail themselves of professional development. These same teachers identify the multiple benefits to them personally, their teams, and the overall school, but ultimately and most importantly, they note the benefits to their students because of their shared focus on professional development and learning. Altogether, high expectations, coupled with strong support for ongoing professional development, engage these educators in trickle-down learning that extends to their students and parents—and to one another.

There are four major themes that reflect the practices that sustain the high achievement of this school: professional development, strong academic culture, leadership of high expectations, and focused utilization of human resources. These four areas work together to enhance overall student achievement. Professional development is the lifeblood of this school. It is seen as a resource used to affect the academic culture in positive ways. Strong academic culture drives learning through professional development. An example of this is the use of technology to access online information systems where data is warehoused and utilized for planning, assessment of students and programs, and making decisions to foster school improvement. All teachers have access to these data; it is a click away. Teachers also understand they must use these data in thoughtful, meaningful, and strategic ways to make critical decisions about how to group students and to monitor students' learning. Although teachers use data to identify areas of need, they also use data to build on students' strengths. Moreover, teachers use these data to plan lessons thoughtfully that reinforce students' higher-order thinking and questioning skills, building on students' prior learning. Simply put, these teachers use the technology available to them as a means to enhance the strong academic culture of learning, to augment instruction, to engage in ongoing assessment, and to continuously monitor their students' learning.

Importantly, teachers feel that in this professional culture, administrators treat them with respect because they are partners in learning and decision making about instruction. Deliberately, the leader's high expectations translate into a teacher culture where teachers openly acknowledge how everyone knows what the goals of this school are and actively seeks to meet them. Or, as the principal states at the beginning of this chapter, "there is no confusion" here. This is a school culture where the school leadership of high expectations translates into beliefs that enable its members to have a clear direction to focus their energies on results that engender student achievement. The connections between learning and ongoing professional development, high expectations that support a focused utilization of human resources, also serve to highlight how this synergy among these four mutually reinforcing practices have worked over time for this school. Arguably, however, it is the last theme that unmistakably reveals the power of a leader's high expectations, coupled with the intentional utilization of human resource capital, through targeted professional development, which buttresses this school and builds its capacity over time to meet and sustain its vision, mission, and goals.

Description of the School

School X6, an older school was built about 45 years ago. Three permanent buildings housed 24 classrooms and a new fine arts/media center suite. Six portable classrooms housed special area programs. At the time of the study, the school's construction project costs were in excess of $100,000 for technology. The school's local bonds provided an additional $195,000 for technology equipment, support of programs, and staff development.

The school was located in a predominately Hispanic/Latino neighborhood with many apartment buildings and single-family dwellings. The school enrolled approximately 550 students at the time of the initial visit in 2002 and maintained an enrollment of close to 600 students for a number of years. At the time of this initial site visit, the majority of the students (86.9%) were Hispanic/Latino, 10.2% non-Hispanic White/Caucasian, .9% Asian American, .9% multiracial, .8% Black/African American, and .2% Native American. Students on free and reduced-price lunch were 54.1% of the student population. The average class size in grades PreK–5 was 19.7 students. The school housed the regional program for students who are gifted and served approximately 170 full-time students, who made up 35.7% of the student population. The percentage of students who were classified as ELL was 29.9%, and 9.9% of the students were classified as having disabilities. The stability rate of 79% indicated that the majority of students enrolled at this school in October remained enrolled in February.

A total of 58 full-time staff members and 17 part-time staff members were employed at X6. The school also employed 2 administrators, 22 classroom teachers, 9 additional teachers who were certified in special education, bringing the total number of teachers to 31, with one guidance counselor. Additionally, there were four full-time paraprofessionals, seven hourly paraprofessionals, five clerical employees, three cafeteria workers, and six custodians. Of the teaching staff, 12% were new to the school, with the average length of time in teaching of 12 years. A total of 59% of the teachers held advanced degrees.

The principal had been at School X6 for the previous 6 years and was a veteran educator with 25 years of experience, with a master's degree. There was no demographic data to report her race or ethnicity. The assistant principal was a female and had been at X6 for 10 years and held a master's degree. The vision of the school addressed promoting learning, academic excellence, and assisting students to develop critical decision-making skills through problem solving and creative approaches to foster the productive use of leisure time as well as developing effective conflict-negotiation skills. The school's mission emphasized cooperative work with the parents and the community and to prepare its students academically, socially, and emotionally in a positive and safe learning environment to meet the challenges of the 21st century. Within the school, values of diversity, respect for the rights of others, and thinking globally were all stressed.

Professional Development

The first theme of professional development is pivotal in the way that the principal sees her role. She directs many of the school's annual resources toward multiple options of professional development that are provided in the district, or through other professional networks, and/or through the hiring of key people for certain needed skill areas such as technology that teachers are required to know or she wants them to learn. In-house professional development and learning are also an integral part of this school's normative culture so that teachers learn from each other in concert or alone with other professional development activities.

In regard to technology professional development, the principal hired several technology specialists to provide assistance to the teachers at the level they needed and to bring all the teachers up to par with everyone else so that the school could operate at a certain level of proficiency. This is important to note in this school because of the wide array of technology services found within the school district of which teachers can avail themselves. Additionally, the recent investment in the school's technology infrastructure through grant monies and bond levies, coupled with district technology resources, shows why it is important for faculty to have the latest knowledge and skills necessary to access information systems available to them via technology to support student learning and other management systems at this school.

Moreover, the principal shares that she asks teachers what they need and want to know overall to plan forward for professional development with them. She understands that not everyone requires the same level of professional development. She discusses how professional development should differentiate among various levels of knowledge and skill development to be effective. The principal illustrates, for example, with the technology professional development, that there are general information sessions for all teachers and staff to attend and after the initial session, there is a customized menu of options for teachers and staff to select from in order to tailor their individual professional development specifically to their needs. This type of professional development goes even further and takes into account personal one-on-one sessions for more direct assistance, schedules permitting. This multilevel menu of professional support clearly demonstrates that the philosophy of professional development at this school is not a one-size-fits-all approach but a model based on individual needs. In fact the principal states as much regarding the professional development of teachers with specific reference to technology:

> We do have different levels and as they know, some of them are wonderful [speaking of teachers' differing comfort levels with technology use]. They use their technology all the time. We have others who are a little less comfortable with it, and I certainly understand it. It took me a long time myself, but we try to encourage one-on-one. We have a wonderful technology person, and we have a lot of teachers that are supportive and very helpful to other teachers. So they get right in the classroom and help them and show them. And we now have a new microsystem's technician whom we are very pleased with and whom we interviewed. He is very sensitive and very understanding that some people do well when you get one-on-one with them, but everybody receives the general training.

Educators at this school peruse weekly professional development opportunities that may benefit them. They let the principal know what their needs are for their professional development. In turn, the principal supports any professional development that would enrich each individual teacher's growth, their team, and/or the school. Professional development conducted by the teachers and administrators at the school encourages less formal means such as mentoring, coaching, and teaching others in areas aligned to an individual's strengths.

Manifestly, the principal espouses a strong belief that the district Language Arts Department supports high-quality professional development backed by research. She bragged, "It was the best professional development in the world, with suggested research strategies that work." She also said,

> I think this district has the best reading/language arts department in the world. [They are] the absolutely top-notch people [that] I have ever worked with. I have worked with several people for years. They are so well-informed and so well-trained that it amazes me. So that has trickled down, and they have chosen the right people to bring it to us—the right people who have the personality and the ways to motivate teachers. So they have done a wonderful job in looking at these people they have out here and bringing them out of the classroom and sending them out to train. Our teachers come back from those professional developments, the reading institute, for example, and they are all dying to go to their classrooms and apply what they have learned. The district has gone throughout the country and found programs that work. The district has spent a lot of money training people, the right people to get out and show us how to do it [teach reading]. And that has made a major difference in the way we teach children.

The school values what the district provides them in terms of quality professional development and sees this professional development as relevant to their school improvement. The principal also notes that although the district has identified areas of need for professional development across the district, the conversation about what is important for teachers at this school is one that the principal personally engages in with teachers every year. She wants her teachers to offer her ideas related to the school goals. She emphasizes that there are certain areas in which everyone is focused. "The last couple of years, technology has been a very important one (area). Everyone's professional development plan has been [focused on] technology and services." There are several other areas that the school focuses their professional development on such as inclusion and reading. The principal notes, "Right now, we have had a lot, like I said, [of] inclusion training with the teams." She also relates that "We have had a lot of training in reading too." Through the reading professional development, the principal believes that the teachers have increased their ability to ask much higher-level questions. "I will tell you what it has done, as I observed. It has shown teachers on the spur of the moment how to ask . . . higher-order questions." The principal summarizes that when "We talk about it [professional development] at the beginning [of the year], we identify where we are headed with it, set it up, and plan for it, and then [we anticipate] there will be some differences for different people."

To recap, several points are central to understanding why this school's professional development approach has been so instrumental to its success. First, professional development addresses current needs but also anticipates future areas teachers identify as upcoming needs. In other words, professional development is proactive, not reactive. For example, the principal states, "Science is coming our way; that's something you need to definitely practice on, but teachers will often ask, if they see something they need. . .We encourage teachers to take action on their own." Second, everyone in the school is involved in some type of professional development. As noted, the district, state, and national professional networks, and in-house training are part of this school's use of a network of professional growth opportunities they avail themselves of to enhance their knowledge level and skills as educators. The principal models for her faculty how she is an active participant in learning. She personally takes professional development through the leadership offerings from the district and shares how professional development builds her capacity to be a better leader for the school. She encourages her faculty to look forward and identify areas for potential growth. Third, parents and teachers participate in professional development as part of their role in school improvement. They learn about school improvement and what it means to be on the school improvement team. This results in teachers and parents attending training together through the district that expands their roles and results in increased participation in school improvement efforts in ways such as (a) reviewing school and classroom data, (b) monitoring student learning, (c) evaluating how instruction is paced, and (d) presenting data to their colleagues. The principal observes that the bulk of professional development encourages teachers, parents, and staff to work together "to know they are on the same page." Fourth, professional development lays the foundation for the second theme of a strong academic culture. Because the teachers are learning and growing together, they are making improvements in their daily work that positively influences their academic culture.

In the case of this school, the principal has established professional development as a proxy for the learning culture. She understands that high-stakes testing can work against involving teachers in professional development, but argues, "You have to let people out of the building; unfortunately, you have to do that. But it is worth it in the long run." She goes on to say that the school benefits. However, because of the school's success, the principal has made a defensible argument to the school district, which not the case for all schools. The principal sums up what professional development means at this school:

> We do a couple of things. First of all we are very, very clear on professional development and professional growth. If on observation or noticing something else that comes up, we see if there is a concern, we talk. We always confer with a staff member who may need to talk with us, but primarily we depend on professional development: coaching, mentoring, and professional development. Almost everyone can and will perform well when they have that kind of a situation going on. However, in the years that I have been here, it has been necessary to take appropriate action for personnel that are not complying with a number of issues. We do follow professional standards and document as needed. But the balance is in other things—professional development, coaching, mentoring, that is what it is all about.

Again, the principal praises the role of the district in providing a process for mentoring new teachers but cautiously notes, "There is a fine district policy in place for mentoring and coaching. Now, how far the school takes it and uses it, that depends on the principal of the school." Because this principal believes in supporting her teachers, she views mentoring as another tool to use with her new teachers for ongoing professional development. She says, "Even though we are small, we are always bringing on somebody new. So, we want to make sure they have the full support of the department chair, the teachers around them—that they have a group that is supporting them. Yes, coaching/and mentoring is all part of that."

Strong Academic Culture

The strong academic culture of this school is driven by the level of commitment that the educators in this school make to their profession and daily work. The principal states,

> You know it all boils down to commitment. Now more than ever we need people that aren't...just [here] because they can't find something else to do. We need people who make an active choice to teach, because that's what they know they can do. They know they can do it well, they want to do it, and they are committed to doing it. Without that, they are not going anywhere. So, to me that is the key. They are not going to make a lot of money at it, but right now we have teachers here who would not do anything else. They are here early, and they are here late, and they love it.... But it is what drives them. That's what you look for.

With commitment comes the dedication evident to parents in the systematic way work is organized in this school. Parents are very aware of this organization. One parent said,

> My kids were at another school before, and I don't know exactly the curriculum, but I see that [there's] a lot more work at this school. They are a lot more organized. I can tell you that much compared to the old school. I think that the organizational part of this, honestly, would help and the way that the teachers share the curriculum. I think by presenting their organized structures and everything, you know what they want to teach the children. I think that that comes across for the homework and then you also see that there's times that they'll have a higher level of homework or there's a mistake or some other thing but I think that it kind of helps child to do enough at school but also at home, and get the parent involved again.

Parents have access to teachers on a regular basis and enjoy this ongoing communication that keeps them abreast of their children's progress. Frequent communication about students' progress with parents in both Spanish and English creates strong bonds between these parents and their children's teachers. Parents report that they know what is happening in the classroom because of this routine communication about their children's progress. One parent acknowledged, "I think the educators here are very caring. They really care a lot about the kids. They're very organized and we have a really good group here. Everyone pretty much gets along and tries to help each other. I think that makes it really special because, you know, when there's a lot of friction you don't get a lot of things done, so I think it's really important for everyone to get along." The relationships that educators have with one another are visible to the parents and are perceived as caring. Creating a caring academic culture is important to this school and to learning. Communication is important in this school. The principal illustrates how the communication process involves listening to parents and responding to them. She said,

> We have gotten feedback from parents saying that it [the progress report] is too general. We are listening to that and revising it to make it more specific.... We always, always tell teachers that they must talk to parents regularly, before the interim report comes out and after the report comes out. So we rely heavily on parent/teacher conferences, on communication. We keep parent logs. One of the first things I look at when I go into a classroom is the parent log—communication log.... Many teachers offer a checklist to parents to help them keep track of their child's work. Another that I think is wonderful is the planner. Each child has it second to fifth grade. And that planner is a form of communication. The child writes her homework and the parent can respond, can see what the child needs to do, can write a note to the teacher. The teacher can write back. It is a form of communication daily. The other thing we do, we have everybody online with schoolwork. com. Everybody is on, and we also encourage parents to go there and check for projects, homework assignments, and upcoming events. You can go online with schoolwork.com with our zip code and you will see our school has more than everybody else. PTA is on there. Parents can get on there and maybe they can't talk to us every day, but they can get on there and write us back anyway we can do it. We want to do it.

The principal adds that teachers and staff are always working together to figure out the best ways of keeping parents informed. This administration also stays informed about what is happening in the classrooms through frequent monitoring of lesson plans, observing and attending team and staff meetings, talking to students, observing teachers in their classrooms, and also monitoring teacher and parent communications.

Communication is also part of a strong internal academic culture. Every teacher is part of a team that works to incorporate the practices of cross-level grade dialogue to ensure consistency throughout the grades for what is expected. A number of programs address individual and student group needs, such as the program for bilingual students, a full-time program for students who are gifted, character-education program, community school program, and other programs that add to the school's impressive array of educational opportunities for advancing learning. There is also tutoring for students who need additional support as well as before- and after-school care services for parents who work.

The students at this school are required to wear uniforms to minimize status differences. There is an awareness of diverse groups at the school that range from students who are gifted to recent immigrants arriving from other countries. Although curriculum is guided by the assessments of state standards, teachers are also sensitive to the diversity in their classrooms. They choose not to teach to the test but rather to use assessment data to drive instruction and decision making for flexible grouping. They also work on higher-order thinking skills and work on their questioning skills to engage students in critical inquiry. The principal comments on assessments used routinely in the school:

> We have very basic assessments that we follow for early learning readers. The basic process we use is not necessarily mandated, but we use it because we need to have that available for the classroom. We have regular writing assessments. They are not mandated every week, but programmatically they are here. A child's portfolio shows writing at a certain period of time; it will have reading assessments. It will have math assessments that are stronger. We use technology. We have an accomplished learning program, which also assesses children. It is not mandated, but it is a program that we use for reading, math, and science. We have some science going on now.

Assessments are part of a strong academic culture. Assessments help teachers in their classroom instruction. But assessment is not always formal. Teachers develop and use informal assessments within their classrooms at grade levels. The principal said, "I'm seeing that they [teachers] are trying to work together at grade levels to develop a consistency on how to assess the children. They have to determine, it is not formal in the books, but they have to do what they need to do to informally, assess as they go." Assessment and reviewing assessment data are what members do in this school. The principal adds, "Once again, I think it is because we talk so much to the staff. We spend a lot of time planning and interacting. I'm not sure it is just because we are small. I think it is just because it is a pretty good community of people." This ongoing dialogue compares what the school is doing with their data and how the data serve as information to raise specific questions for this educational community to wrestle with. The principal summarizes,

That's data. We have to go back and look and see; compare what we have done, what we are still doing, and what we need to do. We have to get specific with it. First we get the data. We get the journals. OK, you got this score, you got this score, [to] which you have to go back…and take a look at the specifics. What are the skills that you need? As a team, that is what we have to look [at]. OK, this is going to kill us if we don't get busy on pumping this up. We have to look at it like that. That has to be done every year. This is what we have to do, because in the past it has been delayed in coming. You get the general scores and then you would get the hard copy. Now we can start setting it up in the systems on the Internet. We can get to it real quick and that will be good for us.

The academic culture of this school is enhanced because of the district technological infrastructure, which can disseminate data from the state much more efficiently now than in the past. The school, in turn, has provided professional development to support its teachers accessing these data, leading to quicker response times for accessing their assessment data to make decisions that impact classroom instruction.

The principal understands that there are multiple uses of the data, from instructional and programmatic decisions to affecting school development and improvement plans. The principal says, "We make a lot of decisions with the data and on planning for development." Yet the nucleus of this school is that the teacher is the one who must decide how to use the data to make instructional decisions for their students. The principal expresses that there could be a number of educators involved in making instructional decisions for a student, such as the general-education teacher, the ESE teacher, the ELL teacher, and an administrator. She declares, however, that "It varies, but the responsibility falls on the teachers to make the final decisions."

Parents concur that they too are involved in instructional decisions with their students. They realize that "most kids that have their parents involved do much better." Parents report that teachers work hard at this school to ensure that the students have the background knowledge to be successful. The teachers talk with each other and the parents and the students to find out what they know. The principal relates that this is "something that she is seeing more and more of at this school." An example is how the principal describes the process that a teacher might engage in to make a packet of learning sources for a parent to use with their child. In other words, "the classroom teacher trains the parents how to make flash cards and how to play games with their child." Again, this reinforces the learning partnership between the school and parents.

Strengths in this academic culture highlight a tight coupling of instruction from the annual plan and the goals for the school's improvement. A parent says, "I find a real priority in this school that you don't see in every school and it's a definite plan for the year." The principal confirms that the community is involved in the plan because they are members of the school improvement team, and the plan is disseminated to the greater community too. The programs at the school, the use of data, the community and parent involvement, the school arrangements that encourage horizontal and vertical communication within the school, and the faculty teaming and sharing of instructional strategies and practices to make decisions with each other and the parents, all add up to a strong academic culture. The recognition of students through a variety of incentives rewards positive student behaviors. Citizen of the Month, good cafeteria behavior, and attendance recognize and reward behavior and academic improvements. Various clubs and groups, such as the Chess Club, French Club, chorus, Crime Watch, student patrol, and string group offer other areas in which to engage students. The strong academic culture builds on what the school has to offer. In turn, the school brings students of various ability levels together so that students classified as gifted work with general-education students to strengthen the overall academic culture, celebrate its programs for students who are bilingual and ELLs, and create an academic culture to support shared decision making and participation from each and every person.

Leadership of High Expectations

The third theme is the leadership of high expectations. Teachers recognize that they are involved in shared decision making at the school and that the chairs have a lot of responsibility. A teacher agrees:

> There is a department chairperson. They have a lot of the responsibilities, but then we have opportunities to sign up for different things too that are delegated to different committees based on who has expertise. We have two types of chairs: chairs for different groups and grade-level chairs; and besides that, we all have five committees. Everyone knows what we have worked with and what we need to do.

The principal stresses high expectations for her staff and students. She acknowledges that the school has maintained an "A" grade and that because of that grade they have had more freedom to explore the best alternatives for them to grow professionally. The principal talks openly and frequently with the faculty and staff about how best to investigate the means for them to continue learning for professional growth. Her expectations for professional growth are translated into ongoing planning with the faculty to provide them with a clear road map. As noted earlier, she encourages and supports a culture that promotes mentoring, coaching, and working collaboratively with colleagues to achieve the high expectations that she expects. She says, "We ensure that all departments are looking at the same high expectations. The bilingual department, the exceptional students' department, early childhood, everybody knows what our goals are, and everybody knows what our standards need to be, and everybody received professional development across the board." The principal wants to "make sure that no one feels that they are alone here." The collective work that the faculty engages in is part of what makes the high expectations achievable. Faculty are supported in working together. No one department or group is given special preference over another. In fact, the principal wants to ensure that each person has equal access to training and strives for the same high expectations. She believes that by upholding equity for faculty, that faculty will endorse and sponsor equity for students. The principal ensures her expectations

> By making sure that all departments within the school have equal access such as training, professional development, and ensuring that faculty knows that all students ought to have equal access. Well, once again, it goes back to the same concept. We assure that all departments are looking at the same high expectations. The bilingual department, the exceptional student's department, early childhood, everybody knows what our goals are, and everybody knows what our standards need to be, and everybody received professional development across the board.

The principal sees that language is not a barrier to sharing the high expectations with parents. The principal explains, "We meet with any parents that are coming in new, and show them the school. We try to be available, even if they come on the spur of the moment." She elaborates that she has staff that are bilingual who are available to translate. The principal emphasizes, "We are open to them (parents) to come in and speak to us. We ask for an appointment, of course, but we try to do whatever we can [to accommodate]." Finally, as part of the literacy emphasis in the school, there are high expectations for reading outside of school. The principal states that "students have to read eight books. I forget the name of [the competition], but last year was the first year we entered and our school won." The last theme presented is focused utilization of human resources.

Focused Utilization of Human Resources

The principal in this school focuses on the utilization of human resources. The principal has built a powerhouse of human capital to tackle the tough work in this school. She recognizes that because the school has done exceedingly well on accountability measures, the personnel are free to be innovative. Her strategic focus on personnel, to train and develop them, capitalizes on the strong orientation toward professional development within the district that maximizes existing resources for school improvement and school effectiveness. Results of the 2001–2002 school-climate survey resoundingly report that this school is a great place to work. Furthermore, teachers describe their access to a number of learning resources that support their work and instructional practices with students. The principal encourages connections with local resources such as universities where interns and student teachers are willingly placed within the school with seasoned veterans. Also, the school has a number of retired teachers and administrators who volunteer to tutor students, once more illustrating the use of human resources. What is more, paraprofessionals work in classrooms with teachers and provide support for student learning. Parents too, volunteer—an additional human resource network this school taps.

Almost everyone has leadership of some sort in this school, and everyone has the opportunity to be involved in different areas of the school that they feel particularly committed to wanting to impact. The principal says, "Everyone has the opportunity to be involved in different stuff in the school that might have control in their destiny." It is the human resources in this school that make the difference, not the grants that the school has been awarded. People use their information-rich environment to make decisions about instructions and programs. Once again, it is the principal's directing of resources and energies toward professional development for teachers in order to develop their capacities collectively as a school, nurtured the priorities that focus on pedagogy, curriculum, and the monitoring of performance targets, that has led to their ongoing success. Leadership guides the school-level resource patterns of established routines that have sustained a clear integration and coordination of professional development, a strong academic culture, and leadership that fosters high expectations. This interplay among these various factors results in a focused utilization of human resources that over time is the signature of this school's success.

The School in 2009–2010

The school in 2009–2010 had the same principal it had when we began this study; this was her last year. The school student population was shrinking in size due to the changes in community demographics and an overall loss of student enrollment throughout the district. This year the school had a 60% free and reduced-price student school lunch population and was designated a Title 1 school; this was a notable change. The school lost three teaching positions and its overall student numbers were down approximately 100 students from when we began this study. With only 447 students, the average class size was less than it had been during the previous decade with approximately 16 students per class in 2009–1010. Further, the educators advocated for smaller class sizes at this school to ensure their students had as much one-on-one assistance as possible. Of the students attending, 92% were Hispanic/Latino, 6% were non-Hispanic White/Caucasian, 2% were Black/African American, and 2% were Asian/Native American/multiracial. Although the school mission remained essentially unchanged across the previous decade, things around the school were changing rapidly as school competition increased and the poverty rate of the student population increased too. Explicitly, the school competed with magnet and charter schools nearby for the same student population. Yet the school facility itself continued to be upgraded and maintained so that the school remained attractive. To illustrate, the entire school was repainted inside and out, classroom white boards were installed, and a school marquee outside of the school was donated by the PTA.

This school was proud of its sustained achievement and outstanding recognition from the state. At the time of the initial site visit, the school had been designated an "A" school and had consistently sustained achievement at a high level. For the previous 6 consecutive years including the 2009–2010 year, the school earned an "A" grade and was recognized as one of the top schools in the state. Data in Table 9.1 reported 70% or more students scoring Level 3 or above on the reading FCAT for 9 out of 10 years that data was gathered, with 91% of the students scoring at a Level 3 or above during the 2008–2009 school year. In math, the trends were similar. For 7 out of 10 years, the data indicated 70% or more students scoring Level 3 on the math FCAT, with 91% scoring at Level 3 or above during 2008–2009. Moreover, the school also had the distinction of meeting the federal requirements for AYP for the previous 6 years.

The mobility rate was 15%, which was lower than the district average. Attendance was higher than the district average and the school had a process in place that it followed with fidelity with any absent student. The school process included communication with the student's parent or guardian on the day that the student was absent or tardy, flagging students who needed to be referred to student services or an administrator to identify how to work with the parents and student, and implement a reward and recognition system to reinforce the expected behaviors. Announcements promoted students' punctuality and attendance, and awards signaled the

TABLE 9.1   School X6 Indicators of High Performance

Academic year	Adequate yearly progress met	School grade	Students scoring Level 3 & above on FCAT		Students making learning gains	
			Reading	Math	Reading	Math
2008–09	Yes	A	91%	91%	80%	82%
2007–08	Yes	A	85%	81%	74%	65%
2006–07	Yes	A	87%	88%	89%	72%
2005–06	Yes	A	86%	81%	70%	74%
2004–05	Yes	A	89%	84%	77%	79%
2003–04	Yes	A	80%	78%	76%	77%
2002–03	No[a]	B	67%	63%	58%	63%
2001–02	NR	A	75%	70%	78%	83%
2000–01	NR	A	75+%	66+%	NR	NR
1999–00	NR	A	72+%	54+%	NR	NR
1998–99	NR	B	NR	NR	NR	NR

Note: NR = Data not reported
Source: No Child Left Behind School Public Accountability Report.
[a] Percentage of AYP criteria met was not reported. Students with disabilities did not meet reading or math proficiency requirement.

importance of student attendance and punctuality in relation to their academic achievement.

The school continued its focus on reading and was able to hire a reading coach with Title 1 funds to assist teachers in their classrooms with reading instruction and teaching strategies. In total, there were 35 staff at this school. About 60% of the teachers had 6 or more years of teaching experience, and 37% held advanced degrees. A total of 65% of the teachers were ESOL endorsed. The number of students who were ELLs remained similar to the year we began this study at 36%, but there had been a noticeable decrease in students who were identified as gifted to only 11% of the student population, and an increase in students classified with specific learning disabilities to 16%.

The school attracted more fiscal resources. As such, the students classified as ELLs benefited from a grant that enhanced their reading comprehension through the reading of nonfiction and the purchase of these materials. Additionally, the ELLs were awarded a computer program that improved their conversational skills. Teachers in Pre-K, Gifted, and Spanish classes were awarded funds to enrich their instruction. Local businesses contributed to the media center to support literacy programs for purchasing additional books. Overall, the number of partnerships and collaborative relationships added in this school increased the school's connections with external partners substantially.

Perhaps the biggest change was the focus on response to intervention (RTI) visible in the school. The principal noted the existing leadership team was a natural fit for the RTI process. Chairs were able to assume the responsibility of collecting data to evaluate their team's academic programs and progress immediately. Processes for data analysis of student achievement and programs were firmly established. Succinctly, this school's human resource capital was equipped to meet the new challenges of RTI. Importantly, however, the school was collecting data on the RTI teams to assess how effectively they worked together to solve problems and their effects on positively influencing student achievement gains. This school organized itself around some self-referencing principles that had sustained its achievement over time while simultaneously allowing the school organization to remain flexible and responsive to changes occurring within the school and outside of it. The focus on professional development continued to sustain this school's strong academic culture. With the changes in the principal, the hope was that the new leadership would continue to build on the strengths within the school culture that set this school apart from others.

Questions for Discussion

1. Why is professional development so important to this school's success, and how is this school's professional development different than some other schools that you might be familiar with?
2. What role does the principal play in this school to foster and support conditions that have enabled the success of the school overall? The teachers? The students? The parents?
3. How does the role of parents at this school appear similar or different from the other cases you have read? In other words, as you look at what makes up the school and contributes to why it is successful, how does this influence what and how parents interact with the school?
4. How does professional development recognize and build on the value of human resources? How can professional development help a school be proactive and anticipate future changes in the school milieu?

10[1]

The Learning Partnership Tree

Three theories-in-use emerged from analysis of the schools in the study and provide a backdrop for interpretation and discussion of results. First, systems theory frames how these schools worked in collaborative partnerships to shape and improve their "work systems and services and to assess the quality of effects on those being served" (Snyder, et al., 2000, p. 211). Next, power theories clarify how educators constructed "partnership power beliefs" within their unique settings. Lastly "additive schooling" explains how these schools were able to sustain high achievement over time with diverse populations. The schools used information systems to respond to changes in their environment in natural ways. Organizational theorists (Senge, 1990; Wheatley, 1992) suggest that healthy systems can promote disequilibria in natural ways through the sharing of information and ongoing dialogue. Information can be used to respond to subtle environmental changes, stimulating variable and adaptive growth. This ability is more likely to happen when power is disbursed and shared broadly throughout the organization.

Leadership from the Ground Up, pages 171–189
Copyright © 2012 by Information Age Publishing
All rights of reproduction in any form reserved.

The Power River

Drawing on a metaphor of power, "the power river" illustrates power relationships along four places: *power over, power to, power with,* and *power through* (Snyder et al., 2000). *Power over* and *power to* are set within a bureaucratic and dominator framework, while *power with* and *power through* are set within a contrasting framework of partnership and community power socially constructed between educators and communities. The first place on the river is *power over,* the most limited use of power, with restricted access to resources and opportunities within a hierarchical, top-down, controlling, and bureaucratic perspective. *Power over* is increasingly exercised through federal and state threats of punishment for districts' and schools' failure to produce changes within acceptable levels and timelines. *Power to* represents the dominator bureaucratic power framework that begins to unleash its hold over resources and opportunities to develop the skills of others and share some access to resources; power appears more widely shared than it is. Only when the power river shifts its energy and direction beyond the bureaucratic and dominator paradigm does power give way to *power with.* This changes dramatically the way people work together to solve problems and extends access to the broader community. There is an underlying belief in the expertise of the internal community that builds a collective sense of purpose. Finally, *power through* is enacted when power is loosely coupled with everyone, including parents and the community, working as partners to build learning communities through shared expertise and vision. There is an ethic of care and concern for each person connected to this broader community vision (Beck, 1994; Noddings, 2006).

Partnership practices seem to underpin additive schooling, the third theory-in-use within the schools. The focus of the seven schools was on the communities' culture(s) and language(s). This was termed "additive schooling" by the researchers. Drawing on the work of Valenzuela (1999), the assumptions underpinning subtractive schooling, and its converse, additive schooling, were examined. Subtractive schooling posits that today's schools work to fracture communities' cultural and social capital. Several well-established notions drive additive schooling. First, it has been demonstrated that school cultures do make a difference in "the lives of children and also in a school's ability to meet accountability requirements" (Snyder et al., 2000, p. 202). Furthermore, students from culturally and linguistically diverse backgrounds perform better in nurturing environments that embrace and affirm their heritages (Beck, 1994). The goal must be to narrow the gap between teachers' and students' social and cultural differences (Banks, 2001; Nieto, 2001a; Sleeter, 1992). As long as those in charge are uneducated in the needs of either ELL or culturally marginalized students, schooling has the potential to continue to subtract resources from them (Valenzuela, 1999). On the other hand, embracing students' and communities' cultural and social capital as integral components of the schools' network leads to a joint and reciprocal effort to educate everyone in the organization: children, community members, and school personnel (Valenzuela, 1999). Mutual trust is guided by the belief that both schools and parents have genuine interest and agency in children's educational and social competency. Parents must trust schools as places where their children are safe and educated as wholesome individuals who value themselves and their communities, and others in the world beyond (Espinoza-Herold, 2003; Valenzuela, 1999).

A New Model Emerges

This study found support for schools as nonlinear, less bureaucratic, living systems capable of self-organization (Meier, 1995). Learning organizations are enabling, capacity-building, human energy systems empowered to mediate external controls. Although the schools existed within a *power over* paradigm, they were organized around partnership and constructivist relationships. The original model (SAM) had to be reconceptualized to account for the theories-in-use. The new model depicts both sets of constructs as interconnected, interactive, and interdependent parts of a dynamic living system. The outer core was reclassified from standards-based reform variables to organizing variables. The inner core was renamed from embedded variables to sustaining variables when it was found that, while these variables often function in less observable and quantifiable ways, they are essential for the healthy life of the entire learning organization and were, in fact, the synergy driving the entire system. In the words of Meier (1995), it would take a "strong storm" to "uproot or break" strong learning organizations. The sustaining variables, then, are the fuel driving the organizing variables. They create the synergy to transform the organizing variables into practices that better meet the needs of students. The organizing and sustaining variables became the lenses through which beliefs and practices were examined.

Organizing Variables: School Practices

Accountability. In these schools, accountability is driven by the internal core values and vision of the organization. In one school, this is expressed as, "You never settle for what you have, but always strive to be better"

(Principal). The school works together to analyze the needs of students and look broadly at what is required to help them achieve. Most of the information gathered internally assists to evaluate student achievement. Monitoring techniques include pretests, progress checks, performance assessments, portfolios, weekly progress reports, and pacing charts for long-range planning. In several of the schools, survey feedback keeps the pulse on the academic climate to see what resources are needed in classrooms, including professional development and/or planning time. Sharing high expectations built a culture where learning was central to how teachers, principals, and parents talked about the school, particularly student learning. Accountability for excellence was one of the internal norms bonding everyone. Teachers considered their commitment and dedication to collegiality as contributing to their success. The schools educated parents on what standards meant for their child's learning.

Most of the schools relied heavily on the knowledge and expertise of teachers within the building. In all the schools, standards were aligned across grade levels, along with the grades above and below. Notably, when principals were asked how they held teachers accountable, they stated that they ensured teachers had the necessary resources and professional development to be successful. The focus was not on surveillance or monitoring, but direct instructional assistance when students were not achieving. It was clear that all educators shared a common sense of accountability and responsibility for successfully educating all children, including working with the child and the child's family. Principals kept books in their offices and freely gave them to parents. School media centers were open in the evenings for parents and students. "The priority is that students are going to succeed regardless of what it takes for the administration, faculty, and parents" (School X2).

Resources. Although districts provide a so-called operating budget, all the schools agreed that the district, state, or federal government did not generally fund schools that had been graded "A or D" adequately. After paying for staff, supplies, materials, and operational expenses, very little is left. As funds dwindle each passing year, schools have a harder time purchasing basic instructional materials. All schools reported budget cuts, forcing program and instructional personnel reductions and increased class sizes. Although all the schools received "FCAT Merit" funds as reward for high marks according to the A+ Plan, most reported using these funds to purchase basic instructional materials and support tutorial programs, especially with third graders, who are at risk for mandatory retention if they fail the FCAT.

All schools reported that their allocated budgets were insufficient to maintain and upgrade technology. Although expected to integrate technology in instruction, most stated that districts generally did not fund technology sufficiently to stay current. Schools varied widely in their technology programs and ability to obtain outside funding for technology. Moreover, some of the principals reported funding teacher, student, and parent recognition awards from personal income. The principal at School X2 personally conducted her school's Saturday tutorial because they had no funds to pay teachers. The role of principals and leadership teams has expanded to include, in the words of a principal, "begging." Specifically, this principal said, "I never thought that being a principal meant begging." Criteria for school effectiveness have grown to include individual schools' ability to aggressively secure external funding. For many schools, this really means balancing the negative equation created by deficit funding; not to enhance, but survive. This assault on schools' financial viability escalates as higher-SES communities add significantly to their schools' budgets, even doubling them through monetary and in-kind contributions.

All the schools depended on volunteers to supplement insufficient staffing, assist classrooms, and tutor students. The ability to secure volunteers is tied to the community's resources as well as parents' work and family demands. Schools in communities that could not contribute significantly, financially, or in-kind were forced to secure resources through grants and/ or partnerships. Although many districts have partnerships with local businesses, contributions tend to be limited (food, school supplies, etc.) and are chased by far too many needy schools. Add to this the reality that external funding is closely related to the skills and connections of leadership team members, and a truly disproportionate picture unfolds. Some educational leaders, be they teachers, parents, or principals, become adept at grant writing and/or hold personal connections to external funding sources (Brown & Cornwall, 2000).

Some schools attracted funding by establishing reputations as effective spenders. School X7, which had already secured an excess of $1.3 million dollars in grants over a 3-year period, received an additional $10,000 when a district agency discovered unspent money. This school leader received an unanticipated phone call and was asked to spend the money before weeks' end. In his words, "I was called because people knew I could spend money well. Many other schools cannot put together a spending plan that quickly." Although all the schools agreed that what really mattered in school effectiveness and student achievement was teacher quality, many openly expressed that schools perceived as having the most resources and community support tended to attract and retain the best teachers.

Instruction. Each of the seven schools stated vehemently that they "don't teach to the FCAT" but rather teach students to think. To quote a principal, "Schools that teach to the FCAT are not going to be really successful." While all the schools agreed that the FCAT provided them with information, they overwhelmingly disagreed with how it was used to penalize students and schools. Schools aligned their curriculum and assessments with the district's standards, which in turn aligned their standards to the state's. These schools, however, consistently developed curriculum beyond the core academics and agreed, "Students need the arts, the fitness, the intrapersonal and the interpersonal" (Teacher). Schools offered before-, during-, and after-school programs that included tutorials, fine arts, dance, chorus, chess, videography, cheerleading, etc. An important observation was that the schools consistently related the curriculum to students' lives and needs, and their future as productive, socially conscientious citizens. This made the curriculum relevant to empower students as problem solvers within their own communities and beyond. Instruction included environmental concerns, as well as local, national, geopolitical, and economic issues (Meier, 1995).

Schools employed many assessment strategies and tools, including teacher-developed tests and in fact, indicated that they were already utilizing a variety of assessments, particularly authentic assessments, to monitor student progress and self-reflect about their own organizational effectiveness, before the FCAT. Some of the externally mandated assessments were described as content-based or specific-strategy-based and not accurate measures of students' critical thinking. Schools geared much of their in-house assessments to higher-order thinking and targeted various forms of intelligences. Schools focused on literacy across all the content areas. Although districts heavily controlled instructional programs and materials, these schools selected strategies that supported the unique needs of their students. Students who are ELLs were supported through numerous research-based strategies and assessments that, while effective with most students, have been demonstrated as uniquely valuable with second-language learners. Most of the schools indicated that their teachers had much instructional flexibility; a principal says to her faculty, "If you want to teach in a tree and that works, you can teach in a tree."

These schools promoted infused multiculturalism on a daily basis throughout the school year to affirm students' cultural assets and validate other cultures (Banks, 2001; Sleeter, 1992). Many had multicultural committees to implement special programs such as assemblies and festivals. Teachers purchased culturally authentic materials, and libraries stocked a wide variety of books by authors of diverse backgrounds. The schools hired sufficient teachers proficient in students' native languages to provide self-contained bilingual and/or content area education, especially in math, science, and social studies, along with English literacy. Two-way bilingual education was found in the majority of the schools. Two-way bilingual education integrates students who are language minority students (English-language learners) and students who are language majority students (English speakers) to develop bilingualism and biliteracy in English and another language. They also included students who are ELLs in general education classrooms, where they were provided with additional English instruction. The model used widely in the state is the traditional ESOL pull-out program with no support in the student's native language. This least effective model was not employed in any of the seven high-performing schools. Team teaching and articulation within and between grades ensured that students who were bilingual ELLs and general education students were instructed in the same content and with the same grade-level materials and expectations—the curriculum was not "watered down." Because of mandatory third-grade retention disproportionately impacting students who are ELLs whose FCAT scores count after only 1 year of Bilingual/ESOL education, retention is often used districtwide to coerce a focus on English language skills, even at the expense of other content areas. Yet, in this study's schools, retention was neither used to coerce nor punish; once the teacher ensures that the student is ready to move on, the school promotes the child without forcing the child to spend an entire school year in the third grade. Thus, while adhering to the state's third-grade retention law, learning is recognized for students who are ELLs.

Information management. The ability to have a good information-management system was directly related to schools' ability to be accountable and responsive. This fostered autonomy and flexibility for success beyond the status quo and compliance requirements. Schools demonstrated valuing information/data as part of their ongoing self-assessment and improvement. Accountability was driven by the internal core values and vision linked to information management. One principal states, "So in addition to whatever the district has identified, we also decided what tools we were going to use and how we were going to use them. But we have done it for us." Schools employed numerous methods and formats, including quantitative and qualitative, to obtain a broad range of credible, relevant, and timely information/data from within and outside. Members became their own internal evaluators. Self-assessment included School Climate Surveys for teachers and parents. Although assessment data drove instruction, decisions on students were made on an individual basis. All the schools had already established information management processes before the FCAT was mandated. Data provided through the state and district were viewed as additional information to support organizational growth.

Personnel. Across most districts, principals are assigned and can be reassigned or removed at any time. Although schools are given some flexibility in the selection of instructional staff, it is not uncommon for teachers to be involuntarily transferred from one school and reassigned to another, regardless. Principals expressed looking for teachers wanting to be part of a community and having a real need to see children succeed. Most schools experienced very low teacher turnover. Teachers described schools as families supportive of them and their work. In School X3, teachers left only when promoted; then the staff commiserated on how much the person was missed. These schools made a conscious effort to blur the boundaries of seniority between faculty with newly hired faculty immersed into the school culture at once. Teachers saw themselves as lifelong learners, involved in providing in-house professional development, and attending state and national conferences. Repeatedly, teachers stated that their professional development was linked to student learning and needs. They were encouraged to try new things such as team teaching, looping, and observing peers. The school cultures encouraged inclusiveness, consensus building, openness, and sharing. Teachers talked about feeling motivated to seek creative and alternative ways of reaching students and to assume greater personal responsibility for the school's well-being. A teacher in School X2 said, "The principal just fosters that; she gives you the encouragement to just succeed at anything for your students and at a personal and professional level."

Embedded Variables Become Sustaining Variables: School Practices

Culture and climate. The core culture of learning organizations is reciprocally shaped by the sustaining variables and particularly, the organizational leadership style. All schools demonstrated a culture unified by common family/team spirit, where each member is a valuable and essential asset and leader, whether openly designated or not. Teachers addressed themselves and were addressed as professional by the school's designated leaders and parents. A strong sense of collegiality permeated the school culture. Teachers expressed high levels of ethical and professional expectations, standards, and motivation. This was matched with high expectations for everyone in the learning organization, especially students. They openly affirmed each other's expertise in numerous areas and willingness to work collaboratively. Teachers mentored new faculty and each other and were not inhibited and/or threatened by visiting each other's classrooms to provide support. While everyone recognized that their job was "very tough" and "even harder than most other schools," they defined it within a positive challenge paradigm, seeing the numerous obstacles as challenges they could overcome through teamwork. All of this led to productive synergy sustained through incentives and celebrations of achievement, even approximations. Continually, teachers, students, and parents were recognized. Consistently, a significant finding in all schools was a strong sense that the students and communities were an asset, including their culture(s) and language(s) (Cummins, 1996; Nieto, 2001a; Valenzuela, 1999). Relationships with students and communities were premised on authentic caring. Our findings demonstrated that to the extent the schools embraced and validated students' cultural and linguistic backgrounds, respect and trust were reciprocally established between schools and communities.

Leadership. The formal leadership in schools was affirming, nurturing, inclusive, and willing to share power with teachers and/or parents. In all but one of the schools, teachers described leaders as democratic, consensus builders, and participatory. Principals were attuned to moving their schools forward rather than resting on their laurels. Instead, they sustained the energy for ongoing improvement through professional dialogue and collaboration. Teachers were given common planning times within and across grade levels, and with feeder schools. Repeatedly, parents commented on the schools' access to them and willingness to respond quickly to their needs. One parent talked about how in a previous school, it took weeks for the teacher or principal to get back to her. In these schools, however, teachers and principals were in daily contact with parents and responded to concerns immediately. Principals recognized that teachers were key to successful learning cultures in all of the schools. There was an expressed view of teachers as capable. "I like to find the strengths in the teachers and build on that" (Principal). School leadership was not vested only in the principal. The administrators at School X2 described the leadership like this: "We have a leadership team. Everyone basically in the school is a leader . . . I think that, very quickly when you come into this building you realize that this is a building where everyone is expected to bring something to the table, and they are allowed to share what they feel would be the best course. And so it's very expected and very welcomed when people bring ideas to the table." Leaders encouraged teachers to talk about the school, not just their individual classrooms. This collective vision evoked language such as "we are all in this together" and "we work hard on school improvement here." Teachers were willing to share resources, prioritize them based on school needs, and dispense with the idea that everyone getting whatever resources they needed was equitable. Leadership was seen as collective accountability for student learning.

Decision Making. Staff perceptions were valued over external judgments. Table 10.1 reflects how power was enacted within schools and communities. For example, School X2 had a second-year principal who moved the school's relationship with parents from *power with* to *power over*. The school culture acquiesced to the principal's dominating power and relationships with teachers also shifted from *power with* to *power to*. These parents were ignorant of school leadership processes, decisions, and the school mission and improvement plan. They expressed that their involvement in decision making was minimal and limited to a small group of parents. Teachers expressed a shift from the previous administrator's practices of more involvement. School X3 had the most developed partnership culture. The principal envisioned a "break-the-mold" school of empowered staff, minimal bureaucracy, and achievement focused on integrating multiple intelligences into all aspects of the curriculum. The vision focused on democratic processes and consensus. The leadership team was composed of administration, a secretary, a paraprofessional, a cafeteria worker, a custodian, two teachers, two parents, and a member-at-large.

Communication. Communication with parents was strong in all schools. Information was sent home in student's native language and English. Parents often attributed few discipline problems to the robust communication. Teachers communicated to parents that they cared about their students. Frequently, parents commented on the accessibility of the teachers and administrators: "They are always at school." Teachers displayed student work prominently, communicated weekly student progress, held frequent

TABLE 10.1 Power Relations Between the Administration with Teachers and Parents

School	Power Relations	
	Teachers	Parents
X1	Through	With
X2	To	Over
X3	Through	Through
X4	Through	With
X5	Through	With
X6	Through	With
X7	Through	With

parent-teacher conferences, and generally created openness for parents. Parents could verbalize the missions and knew how decisions were made in all schools but one. Parents and teachers shared how their input was always welcomed, if not sought, except in School X2.

Parent and community involvement. Research supports that students whose parents are consistently involved in their education attain higher academic achievement levels. Programs with high parent involvement are more successful than those with less involvement. The effects of parental involvement linger through the middle school level (Decker & Decker, 2000). Learning organizations ensure significant parent and community involvement. All the schools supported bilingual communication with parents, including translations during meetings. Parent and community involvement specialists, which included school counselors, made home visits, arranged workshops for parents, and secured speakers from the community. Parents were provided opportunities to enhance their native-language literacy, English literacy through ESOL, computer skills, parenting, and behavior management. Parents in all schools were provided instructional materials and strategies to support their children at home. All the schools indicated willingness to teach parents how to get involved in an equitable manner to the maximum extent possible according to their work and family responsibilities. With one exception, all schools continually worked to augment parents' abilities to participate in decision making. Training included information about how the school and district works and where information is located about their child. All schools encouraged parents to continue speaking and reading to their children in their native languages. They believed that parents were essential partners in developing foundational concepts in the native language that could transfer later into English. Support for the home language sent a strong message to students that they were valued and respected.

Establishing Schools as Learning Partnerships

The Learning Partnership Tree (LPT)

The emergent framework, termed the LPT (see Figure 10.1), describes how the organizing and sustaining variables were found to work in concert in the seven schools. There was little, if any, vertical alignment between districts and schools on the organizing variables except for information management and accountability. Schools perceived that the sustaining variables were not considered as significant within the state-mandated framework, which sought to focus on the quantifiable constructs and centered on accountability and information management. Contrary to the state focus,

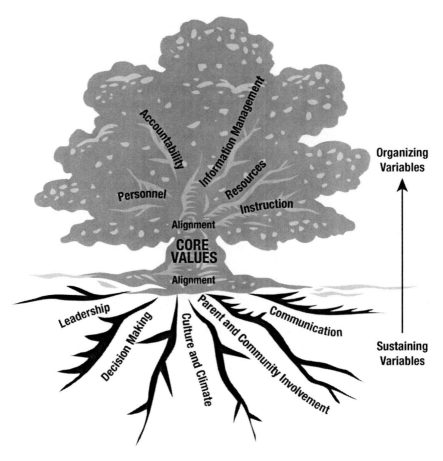

Figure 10.1 The Learning Partnership Tree (LPT). The LPT emerged from the data collected in the initial study. It represents schools as dynamic positive energy systems that are nonlinear and self-organizing around their core values. The LPT represents "a holistic approach to school effectiveness and educational reform focusing deeply below the surface, on those not-so-apparent structures and processes, which hold the sustaining nutrients to keep the entire system moving in responsive directions" (Acker-Hocevar et al., 2005/2006, p. 265).

the framework that emerged from the findings is grounded in strong vertical and horizontal alignments between internal accountability measures reflecting how beliefs were constructed and power shared within these systems. Externally mandated accountability measures were integrated within the core beliefs and selectively negotiated by each school to serve its unique needs and objectives.

Represented as a tree, the trunk is above the ground (organizational core values) supporting the branches (organizing variables) and canopy. The trunk (core values) must be structurally strong to support the branches and entire system upright. The organizing variables, while essential to the system, fluctuate at different times, depending on the system's interaction with its surroundings. All the organizing variables are interrelated, interdependent, and aligned at the juncture with the core values, signifying the system's internal determination of when and how to access the organizing variables according to priorities mediated through its core values. The organizing variables are the parts of the system most visible, concrete, and quantifiable, and thus, most focused on today.

Below the ground is the taproot (culture/climate), with its branching secondary root system (sustaining variables). The sustaining variables, while also essential to the system, exist in fluctuating proportions at different times and act in response to numerous factors found in the underground environment. Often, these components are less focused on, as they tend to be less visible, more abstract, and less quantifiable. All the sustaining variables are interrelated and interdependent and aligned at the juncture with the grounding organizational culture/climate. This juncture signifies the point where incoming nutrients merge to sustain the taproot (culture/climate) and develop into the core values that contributed to additive schooling.

While all the variables are essential to the whole system's health, the system is critically dependent on the sustaining variables, which provide the nutrients essential for a strong culture/climate. As the taproot grows, so does the trunk, and vice versa. As the core values evolve through interaction with the outside environment, the organizational culture/climate responds in tandem. The upper part of the system reaches out to the surrounding environment, and it too receives sustaining nutrients. Healthy systems use information and resources to move flexibly; failure to do so could destroy them. What must not be ignored is that the overall health of the upper tree cannot be sustained without a strong root system. Often, what surprises unaware observers, is that the root system (i.e., an organization's culture/climate and other sustaining variables) must be equally as large (or even larger) and equally as strong (or even stronger) as the parts above the ground. Another surprising aspect of this interrelationship is that as long as the root system remains healthy and strong, it can often re-sprout to re-create the tree. An extension of this to the upper tree is not always the case, for a trunk and branches cannot often re-sprout roots. There exists an interrelated and interdependent connection between organizing and sustaining variables. The trunk and canopy cannot continue growing indefinitely without the growth of the roots. And so, schools' organizing variables cannot be sustained without strong structural and supportive core values grounded by a strong culture/climate. Additionally, the organizing variables cannot be imposed on the system without the existence of this strong structuring and grounding.

Conclusion

This study supports the view of schools as living, natural systems that cannot be dissected into isolated parts (Snyder et al., 2000). When we engage in educational reform, we must look at the entire system and not simply those parts that are most apparent and quantifiable. A principal's knowledge is no longer "sufficient to actuate change" (Snyder et al., 2000). Effective change is created and sustained through team effort and shared leadership. Leadership requires principals working through democratic processes and consensus. Power must be distributed, accountability shared, and the work equitable and collaborative. Evidence of collegial norms encompassing attitudes and beliefs of support, trust, and openness to learning, with dedication to collective responsibility and accountability, seemed to assist these schools in adapting their work context to high-stakes testing and standards-based instruction. Yet the traditional role of principals remains entrenched in a bureaucratic, managerial model that most districts reinforce by not accepting a more distributed leadership model. By holding principals accountable for "running" the building and answering for all the decisions made in the school, the power of synergy among parents, teachers, and leaders is ignored.

Furthermore, the view of schools as natural human systems requires relationship building, self-reflection, mutual respect, and core values grounded in "inquiry as well as responsibility" (Meier, 1995). It is evident that this is crucial for low-performing schools, where principal turnover occurs with abnormal frequency. With each new principal, there is also staff turnover and the anticipation, with the remaining staff, of surviving yet another principal. Such schools are not able to establish supportive organizational core values and stable shared leadership.

Two major, albeit misguided, assumptions undergird the current state-mandated framework. First, that school improvement must be driven by top-down and external vertical alignment of the organizing variables between districts and schools. Specifically, this means that the district superimposes, for example, an information management system, and so forth, for each of the organizing variables. Significantly, this hierarchical approach also assumes that while both sets of variables are necessary for school effectiveness and improvement, the organizing variables take the front seat in educational reform and school effectiveness, particularly information management and accountability. A second major assumption is that school improvement is then driven by increased external domination and supervision over schools and classrooms through the organizing variables, particularly accountability and information-management systems, perceived as being responsible for "tightening the screws" on educators. This ignores all the other variables that make schools successful and is conceived narrowly within a highly technical and rational *power over* system of control. This contributes to the dysfunctional fragmentation of today's educational systems. A hidden, highly detrimental, assumption of the state-mandated model is that schools lack the know-how and/or motivation to effectuate improvement on their own. This perception reinforces negative perceptions of those at the bottom of the education pyramid: teachers, students, and parents. The classroom is left saddled with the most direct, massive, and cumulative effects of external demands. Systems alignment has meant "teaching to the test," forcing schools and teachers to work in isolation, and competing rather than collaborating. Teacher isolation hinders problem solving, creation of supportive networks, and collective self-reflection (Sleeter, 1992).

This study supports the notion that what appears to be most important is what happens at the school level and how the district can support the school site. Sleeter (1992), among other educational researchers, sees the school, rather than individual teachers, as the center of reform and recommends shifting the focus to the organizational arrangements, conditions, and processes at each building. She suggests turning the lens to the collective, people who work in schools, and the culture/climate they create, within the broader external context in which schools exist.

Further, this study reaffirms that educational reform must be grounded within individual schools and classrooms that need increased autonomy from external domination (Meier, 1995; Snyder et al., 2000), particularly domination based on fear. In the words of Meier (1995), it may be possible to have "schools that work," but that requires abandonment of the "stance of outsiders." The state and districts appear primarily concerned with supervision of FCAT scores rather than the instruction, resources, and personnel required for effective school improvement. It was clearly perceived by the schools that the sustaining variables were not deemed as significant within the state-mandated framework. The emergent framework is grounded in high vertical and horizontal alignment of internal accountability measures within each school. These schools had begun establishing these internal alignments and accountability networks before the state mandates, meaning that strong structural and supportive core values, grounded by a strong culture/climate, orchestrated the organizing and sustaining variables. Rather than focusing initial and immediate attention on the upper parts of the tree, the findings of this study suggest priority development of strong and supportive root systems.

Further, since little vertical alignment was found between these high-performing schools and districts in the area of instruction, one might presume that districts do not want to intervene in a system of instruction that worked well. In fact, it was found that in these high-performing schools, educators had more autonomy, which empowered them to negotiate external intrusion and even "massage" instructional plans to fit their unique needs and reduce massive, regimented student testing. While local autonomy is a requirement for school effectiveness, schools that do not meet externally imposed standards of achievement are indeed the ones most saddled with external domination and little ability to self-organize. Districts tend to reduce the demands placed on high-performing schools, allowing them more freedom to grow internally. Ironically, most high-performing schools tend to represent more affluent and mainstream non-Hispanic White/Caucasian student populations that continue to enjoy greater self-determination and autonomy.

This study supports a holistic approach to school effectiveness and educational reform focusing deeply below the surface on those not-so-apparent structures and processes that hold the sustaining nutrients to keep the entire system moving in responsive directions. Those rushing to control and punish schools, teachers, and children simply do not understand the nature of schools as human energy systems, the significance of power relations in establishing healthy and strong core values, or the notion of schools as learning partnerships. They fail to understand that the nutrients of sustainable school progress are found in positive relationships; sharing of power and information; the valuing of others; and the building of strong, stable, and trusting relationships. They do not understand that there are no fixed recipes for success, only a philosophy that promotes additive schooling, includes professional respect and dedication, supports shared leadership, and the building of collective expertise (Newmann, King, & Rigdon, 1997).

The next section describes and summarizes findings across schools regarding how these schools were able to transform their school cultures from an instructional paradigm to a learning paradigm, where expertise is valued and included. The section highlights the schools' internal locus of control that enabled them to respond to student and community needs in positive ways, suggesting that external mandates only measured what these schools were already doing. The findings depict school cultures deeply rooted in a learning paradigm where relationships are central to the work these professionals engage in, guiding their collective learning together, and resulting in dynamic and robust human energy systems to meet daily challenges as well as state and federal requirements

Findings Across the Schools

What matters most is what happens at the school.

- Establishment of an internal locus of control that empowers the organization to decide what it needs to sustain student achievement and negotiate external mandates.
- Development of internal accountability systems that include continuous sharing of student achievement data.
- Expectation for success originated from within the organization rather than from external pressure.

Power relationships are based on sharing, collaboration, and building consensus.

- Relationships between parents and schools based on mutual respect, trust, and access.
- Power vested in expertise to solve problems and work with students.

Transformation moves from an instructional paradigm to a learning paradigm. The entire organization becomes a learning organization.

- Ongoing professional development related to students' needs.
- Using data for self-assessment beyond what is provided and/or mandated by the state.
- Core values and beliefs that support learning and success for all students.
- Selection of teachers that match the organizational core values and work collaboratively to self-reflect and problem solve.
- Leadership that is distributed across professionals with expertise.
- Recognition of the role of the teacher as being critical to the school's success.

A highly developed culture supports professionalism, an ethic of care and respect, inclusiveness, openness, additive schooling, recognition of achievement, and shared leadership that fosters integration.

- Community of professionalism, ethics, and high standards.
- The community is considered an asset.
- Frequent recognition of achievement.

- Discipline philosophy focused on an ethic of care and a concern for assisting students to solve their problems (i.e., the student has a problem—the student is not the problem).
- Additive schooling that affirms, integrates, and builds on the community's social and cultural capital.
- Multiple communication networks, including bilingual.
- Stable shared leadership with high levels of commitment and joint responsibility for student outcomes.
- Culture that includes all students, regardless of programmatic designations.
- Ongoing open communication with parents about school and student achievement.

Instruction is seen as matching the appropriate level of instruction to the specific needs of students while encouraging students to engage in authentic learning and critical thinking that extends beyond core academic subjects to recognize problem-solving and creating caring students.

- Selection and use of instructional materials and programs that match the interests and needs of the school's unique student population.
- Instructional focus is not on the state-mandated test but on what students need in order to think critically and be effective problem solvers and caring community members.
- Focus on building strong literacy programs that simultaneously support student achievement in all content areas, including math, science, and social studies.
- Instruction beyond the "core" academics.
- Providing additional assistance to students needing it.

Questions for Discussion

1. This chapter looks across the findings and uses the original lenses for the study, the Systems Alignment Model (SAM) that we introduced in Chapter 2 to frame the study. One of the research questions sought to answer what practices lend credibility to the initial conceptual lenses for the study. What can you now say?
2. A second research question asked whether the practices in these high-performing schools confirm or reject the SAM. How would you respond to this question. Support your response with evidence.

3. What can you now say generally about the organizing variables? The sustaining variables? The importance of culture and the climate?
4. How did the reconceptualization of the SAM to the LPT shift away from testing to learning? What and how does the leadership play a role in this shift?

The next chapter answers more fully the remaining research question we posed at the beginning of the book. "What theories-in-practice seem to sustain school progress over time?" Although we concluded in this chapter that dynamic systems theory, partnership power, and additive schooling are theories-in-practice across these schools, this next chapter grounds the LPT in a broader theory-in-practice that shows how these schools were able to sustain their school improvement efforts over time. Therefore, this last question is more fully answered in Chapter 11.

Note

1. This chapter was adapted from Acker-Hocevar et al. (2005/2006).

11

Grounding a Theory

Sustainable School Improvement

The journey into the seven schools taught us much about how these leaders, teachers, and community members work collaboratively to build and sustain school improvement over time. Leadership from the ground up, therefore, is a compelling tale of seven schools able to make continuous progress in spite of the odds being stacked against them. How could they do this? The seven cases demonstrated how school improvement is possible with high populations of students from low-SES backgrounds, students of color, and students who are ELLs. When we began this study, we had no idea that these seven schools would continue to sustain school improvement for a decade under the ever-increasing and watchful eyes of state and federal mandates of accountability. We just continued to observe these schools' progress, wondering how they would fare.

Although there is no prescription, no definitive set of absolutes for how school improvement might be sustained, we have found some evidence to present in our theory-in-practice of Sustainable School Improvement (SSI)

Leadership from the Ground Up, pages 191–220
Copyright © 2012 by Information Age Publishing

that describes, explains, and interprets what we have learned from these educators about their journeys and what we think might be important for others to pay heed to as they strategize school development plans that lead to sustainable school improvement. Findings suggest that strong relationships with one another and within the communities served by these schools built a collective energy system for school improvement through their core values and beliefs.

There are two phases to this study. In the first phase of the study, we illustrated how the initial findings, depicted in the Learning Partnership Tree (LPT), fostered cultures and climates of strong connections internally. These connections extended outward to the community and built capacities for educators to respond ably to demands placed on them externally. These schools practiced additive schooling and partnership power that defined their relationships and sustained their emphasis on the human side of schooling (see Chapter 10). Partnership power spanned across key players and encouraged school cultures of shared and collaborative decision making for purposeful actions aligned with core values and beliefs we would identify in the second phase of this study.

In the second phase of the study, which grounds the LPT, we returned to three of the original sites and learned more about the actual tasks, knowledge, and skills related to the 10 variables in the LPT model. We validated the LPT and deepened our understanding of how these educators built cultures that enabled their continued success. During this process, the SSI theory emerged from our interviews and focus-group data. We identified values and beliefs that underpinned the work in these schools—a virtual turning point for us; a major breakthrough in how this theory-in-practice planted the LPT in fertile soil. We learned that accountability was connected to leadership and that the standards-based reform organizational variables were morphing into new conceptions of how this leadership and accountability were fused.

The SSI theory raises fresh questions for us, however, about the role of school reform literature in assisting educators in school improvement efforts over time. Because the SSI theory is deeply rooted within the core values and beliefs exhibited within these school cultures and climates, it is not a program educators can purchase; it is a way of being and working together often invisible to outsiders whose gaze is usually fixed exclusively outward on test scores. To a large extent, this theory-in-practice suggests more attention be paid to the inner workings of the school, and that the gaze be fixed on the core values and beliefs that act as a gigantic filter for how educators collectively decide, interpret, and enact policies; determine who is involved in decision making; and conceptualize how to use human and material resources to sustain their human energy system within an overarching philosophy.

Because we did the kind of follow-up work we did in the second phase of this study, we could ground the LPT in this theory-in-practice and make connections we would have missed otherwise. Importantly, the impact of the core values and beliefs on the leadership choices made in these schools spread leadership over and out by involving others in school improvement efforts, integral to how this theory-in-practice marries best practices to the culture and climate in which these practices support school development and sustain school improvement. Without the gaze turned inward for a deeper understanding of what is occurring, results usually document meeting external measures, and lack the profound understanding of how sustaining school improvement—in its totality instead of piecemeal—is rooted in core values and beliefs that guide the actions of members in the school like electricity as invisible currency that lights the bulb.

If truth be told, our research suggests that school reform cannot ignore how organizational values and beliefs sculpt how people work together to use their human and intellectual capital resources that will inevitably affect and sustain their school improvement efforts over time, build knowledge capital within a caring and respectful culture, and inform educators' day-to-day practices to impact sustainable school improvement. The SSI theory lays bare principles of how strong relationships guide decision making, influence choices, and underpin behaviors and actions in these schools, which contribute to their sustained improvement and success both internally and externally in meeting accountability requirements.

What We Did

Remarkably, after a couple of years of watching these seven schools' performance indicators, two of the three researchers went back to three of the schools to conduct follow-up interviews with the principals and hold focus-group meetings with the teachers. Our initial goal, to gain a better understanding of the LPT model variables presented in Chapter 10, led to the emergence of the SSI theory-in-practice from our coding of the transcribed interview data. We identified beliefs and values central to the culture and climate around five themes. We asked ourselves if we coded phase one of the study with these new themes, what we would find. Would the new themes hold? Did this emerging theory-in-practice help explain why these schools sustained school improvement over time?

As we looked anew at the data from the first phase of the study, and we tried our emerging theory on for fit across the cases, much to our amazement, the SSI provided an overall fit across the seven cases. We had success-fully been able to re-sift and re-sort the original data through this new lens, gleaning fresh insights into how this theory could help us explain more fully why these schools were successful. By returning to three of the seven school sites to learn more about the actual work in these schools, we were able to validate the LPT model and uncover core values and beliefs through the knowledge, skills, and tasks these educators elaborated to ground the LPT model in a theory-in-practice.

The SSI theory rests on a set of assumptions about the types of schools initially included in the study. As stated earlier, these schools had to meet four criteria:

1. That 65% of students sustained achievement in reading or math for 2 consecutive years on the state achievement test,
2. That 50% of students sustained competence in both these disciplines for at least 2 consecutive years,
3. That 50% or greater students were from low-SES backgrounds, and
4. That 10% or greater students were ELLs.

In other words, the schools selected for this study were already demonstrating that they met school improvement demands for 2 consecutive years prior to being selected for the study. However, 2 years of data does not by itself guarantee that these schools would or could be able to sustain school improvement over a decade's time of looking at school improvement on state and national accountability measures that were changing. But in fact, that is exactly what these seven schools did—successfully met external demands through demonstrated continuous attainment of high-performance criteria.

Expressively, because of our interest in studying schools centered on serving a disproportionate number of students from low-SES backgrounds, students of color, and students who are ELLs, we were most interested in how these subgroups demonstrated progress in these schools—progress that seemed elusive to other educators. Thus, the theory of SSI must be understood within the context of these particular schools. These schools were able to respond to increasing external mandates of accountability because of what went on inside of their schools and while serving students many other educators were struggling with in order to demonstrate significant academic measures of progress. Critically, because we had access to all the state data for every elementary school, the net had been cast broadly, but in the end, we could find only nine schools that met the original criteria for the study. Later, however, we would determine that two of the schools originally included in the initial study had been borderline and included because of the low numbers of schools identified—and to represent other geographical regions of the state. These two schools were dropped, leaving only the seven school cases reported in this book. Not surprisingly these two schools were unable to sustain school improvement over time. The fact remains, there was only a handful of schools that met these original criteria in a very large state. This fact alone would haunt us and remind us over and over again about how unique these seven schools were; these schools were not the norm and neither were their practices.

Grounding the Theory

This chapter lays the groundwork for the themes and subthemes that foster the SSI development. Grounded theory emanates from the bottom up or from the data (Glaser & Strauss, 1967). Charmaz (2003) expands on grounded theory to describe how researchers' analysis of data is colored by collective knowledge from prior learning and work. Researchers do not come into a setting without some working theory or theories that serve as lenses for their interpretation of data. In fact, as scholars, they bring with them their knowledge of past theories and prior experiences that can influence their work-in-progress. Thus, when a team of four researchers assembled to analyze the data, it became particularly critical that two members of the team had no preconceived knowledge of earlier findings or the original conceptual lenses for the study. The research team, composed of two senior and two new members, met over a year to make sense of the collected data. The two new researchers represented two different areas, with little knowledge of research on schools. Therefore, the two senior researchers often asked these two new research members to code data initially, in an attempt to minimize bias in their coding and interpreting data.

The fact the second phase of the study might have been a narrow framework to describe the tasks, knowledge, and skills within the organizing and sustaining variables is a limitation. What we found, however, was that the knowledge and skills required to complete the tasks associated with the 10 organizing and sustaining variables of the LPT were heavily influenced by core values and beliefs held by the educators, elucidating a deeper philosophical grounding for all actions taken across the five themes that emerged from the second phase of the study. These five themes are additive schooling, humanistic philosophy, shared leadership and accountability, resourcefulness, and organizational efficacy.

As stated in Chapter 10, the organizing variables of the Systems Alignment Model (SAM) are represented by the branches of the tree, or standards-based reform variables such as accountability, instruction, personnel, resources, and information management. The sustaining variables represented by the expansive root system such as leadership, parent and community involvement, decision making, culture and climate, and communication. The embedded/sustaining variables were less focused on in the literature at the time of this study. However, we knew from our previous work and research that the embedded/sustaining variables could not be discounted. In fact, much of the school reform literature almost exclusively looks at the systems alignment of the organizing variables, paying scant attention to the embedded/sustaining variables, let alone to the core values and beliefs that underpin the choices and activities of educators' work in a school. Unfortunately, standards-based reform translates into standardization in many schools with cookie-cutter-like practices, ignoring building a positive culture and climate for all members—internal and external to the school through the lens of the embedded/sustaining variables.

Data Analysis

To begin the initial work of coding the transcripts from principal interviews and teacher focus groups in phase two of the study, the research team used the following process. Initially, each researcher read through the transcripts and developed a set of codes. Through this process of open coding, the researchers came back and agreed on a common set of codes that included everyone's input. Descriptors of the open codes were written and the researchers recoded the principals' and teachers' transcripts. QSR N6 software was used by all four researchers to manage the data and coding.

In follow-up meetings, the researchers shared their initial coding schemas with one another. During this time, the researchers agreed to collapse the codes into categories for recoding the tasks and skills. They also separated codes for the values and beliefs (dispositions) across the 10 variables of the LPT model and agreed to separate these codes from the knowledge and skills. Categories were applied to two transcripts to recode them and to see how the new coding schema worked. After the researchers discussed the coded texts, they identified emerging themes across the categories for grouping the knowledge and skills to complete the tasks that made the educators successful. This is where the researchers collapsed categories going back and forth across each transcript to recode principal and teacher focus-group data by one of the five themes. After a series of several meetings and discussions, where each researcher reported the percentages of their transcript coded by each of the five themes, we established a coding schema that yielded strong reliability across the transcripts. We calculated percentages by the amount that each theme explained the overall theory-in-practice. Important for purposes of the five themes, we concluded that the majority of the interview data from principals and teachers fit one of these themes and explained most of the interview data in the transcriptions. Interestingly, across the three schools, the theme of organizational efficacy ranked the highest overall in explaining school improvement work within the schools, while within the three schools, leadership and accountability was either ranked the highest or second highest theme by teachers and principals, and resourcefulness was usually ranked either fourth or fifth. From the five themes, we identified subthemes under each theme which we discussed across all the schools. The subthemes were the common elements across all the schools that each researcher had identified through their own coding and then across the four researchers coming to agreement on what they had coded for each theme. Findings report core values across the schools and then discuss each of the five themes of the SSI theory- in-practice in relation to the literature, highlighting where appropriate, examples of quotes from the data.

Findings: A Theory-in-Practice Emerges

Core Values Across Schools

After we identified tasks and skills from the data under the five themes, we then identified core values across all the themes. Initially, the two senior researchers met to identify these values common to the principals and teachers for one school. Then each researcher was required to recode the remaining transcripts using 13 values for the principals and 13 comparable values for the teachers; 8 values were common to both role groups and consistently held across the two role groups. The final list reports core values across the schools in Table 11.1. The findings show leadership that is authentic, caring, ethical, and creates the conditions for risk taking, with a positive orientation about work implying that the work environment is both motivating and stimulating. The values woven throughout the theory-in-practice in the five themes are important to understanding what drives the educators in these schools to make decisions.

From these five themes, the necessary knowledge and skills required for school improvement, with comparable demographics and settings, shows how the schools, as unified human systems, adapt their work environment to the current climate of high-stakes accountability and standards. The theory-in-practice also explains how these schools gained increased autonomy from external domination to sustain school improvement over time. The next section describes each theme in light of the literature, high-

---

TABLE 11.1 Core Values Identified by Principals and Teachers

Principals	Teachers
Authenticity	Authenticity
Caring	Caring
Commitment	
Cooperation	
Empathy	
Honesty/Transparency	Fairness
	Honesty
	Humility
	Noncomplacency
Respect (mutual)	Respect (mutual)
	Risk Taking
Openness/Open Door	Openness/Open Door
Persistence/Determination	
Positive Orientation	Positive Orientation
Pragmatism	
Pride	Pride
Trust	Trust
	Sharing

---

lighting quotes to illustrate aspects of the theme. The first theme is organizational efficacy.

Organizational Efficacy

At the core of this emergent theory is organizational efficacy. Organizational efficacy transforms the "I" to "We." When organizations are seen from this perspective, they are viewed in their totality, not as isolated pieces on a one-dimensional surface. What is seen is the fluidity and constant movement of the organizational grounding themes and subthemes among and within each other, releasing strength synergistically toward the core of the organization—teaching and learning. Table 11.2 presents the findings from the second phase of the study around organizational efficacy. The culture of professionalism supports confidence in one's own and others' competence. The principal's high expectations, coupled with teachers' trust in the leadership enables teachers to self-identify strengths, volunteer their expertise, or ask for needed support to bolster weaknesses and demonstrates the culture of learning with and from one another. Moreover, educators learn through reflection, introspection, and hands-on experi-

TABLE 11.2   Subthemes for Organizational Efficacy by Principals and Teachers

Principals	Teachers
Professionalism	Professionalism
With-it-ness/Alertness	With-it-ness/Alertness
Confidence in own and others' competence	Cofidence in own and others' competence
Competence/Build and sustain a highly competent workforce	Competence/Build and sustain a highly competent workforce
High expectations/Performance (teachers and students)	Self-presentation
	Self-identity (strengths and weaknesses)
	Critical self-reflection and introspection
Trust in teacher professionalism	Trust in teacher professionalism
Self-directed/Self-confidence	Hands-on/experiential knowledge acquisition and development
	Being successful

ences, and over time, these practices resulted in a culture of increased organizational efficacy.

To illustrate organizational efficacy, studies on religious efficacy and self-efficacy have appeared in the literature since the early 18th century. The concept of self-efficacy (Bandura, 1977) was extended to collective efficacy (Bandura, 1982, 1986). While self-efficacy focuses on personal or individual competency, collective efficacy is about judgments people make about a group's level of competency (Parker, 1994; Zellars, Hochwarter, Perrewe, Miles, & Kiewitz, 2001). Prior to the mid-1990s, the emphasis on teacher education was neither about outcomes nor about the impact of teacher preparation on performance, retention, or students' learning (Cochran-Smith, 2006); then everything changed with the educational accountability movement. Studies on teacher efficacy (Collins, 2005; Emmer & Hickman, 1991; Isiksal & Cakiroglu, 2005), vocational-efficacy, social efficacy (Hochwarter, Kiewitz, Gundlach, & Stoner, 2004), and the efficacy-based change model (Ohlhausen, Myerson, & Sexton, 1992) validate instruments like the Science Teaching Efficacy Belief Instrument (STEBI) (Czerniak & Haney, 1998; Mulholland, Dorman, & Odgers, 2004) and the General Self-Efficacy Scale (GSE) (Schwarzer & Jerusalem, 1993). Although sports scientists have verified an existing relationship between collective efficacy and performance (Greenlees, 1999; Greenlees, Graydon, & Maynard, 2000), few researchers are making the connection with the organization or appear to be concerned about organizational efficacy as a construct. The search for evidence on factors that drive school improvement took us to review the literature on what contributes to the identification, development, analysis, and relevance of organizational efficacy as a construct.

Efficacy is perceived as an important component of motivation and a strong predictor of performance (Bandura, 1977, 1982, 1986, 1997; Porter, Bigley, & Steers, 2003). Organizational efficacy is considered to be the group's shared belief in its joint capabilities to perform courses of action to successfully achieve a certain level of performance (Bandura, 2000; Bohn, 2002; Greenlees, 1999; Stajkovi & Lee, 2001, cited in Porter et al., 2003).

> In its most basic form, organizational efficacy is a sense of "can do." Organizational efficacy is the generative capacity within an organization to cope effectively with the demands, challenges, stressors, and opportunities it encounters with the business environment. It exists as an aggregated judgment of an organization's individual members about their: (1) sense of collective capacities; (2) sense of mission and purpose; and, (3) sense of resilience. (Bohn, 2002, p. 66)

Throughout this chapter, collective efficacy will be used interchangeably with organizational efficacy. Although Parker (1994) found that the socioeconomic composition of a school's student body was a strong predictor of teachers' collective efficacy, and that teacher's collective efficacy was associated with school-level achievement, it was observed that the relationship was no longer significant when prior achievement levels were controlled. Parker's recommendation for an examination of mediators between efficacy and performance is fulfilled by at least two other studies: *The Impact of Vocational and Social Efficacy on Job Performance and Career Satisfaction* (Hochwarter, Kiewitz, Gundlach, & Stoner, 2004) and *Self-Leadership and Performance Outcomes* (Prussia, Anderson, & Manz, 1998).

This research identifies the key ingredients of organizational efficacy as (a) group's shared belief, (b) joint capabilities, (c) generative capacity within an organization, and (d) aggregated judgment. The shift from self and collective to organization clearly emphasizes "We" instead of "I." Consequently, we suggest that educators consider organizational efficacy as the resourcefulness, the accomplishments, and achievements of the school community or a team of teachers working together with the principal. School principals build organizational efficacy by providing direction and encouragement to stay the course, by allocating resources to meet expectations and by setting goals. There is compelling evidence in this study that organizational efficacy is essential to high-performing schools. All principals in this study were found to be instrumental in sustaining competent workforces by building teachers' capabilities. As a consequence, organizational efficacy became the area where the other themes converge, such as humanistic philosophy, shared leadership and accountability, additive schooling, and resourcefulness in this model. Because teachers and other personnel have developed capabilities for sustaining high student performance, students' abilities and socioeconomic standing did not prevent them from achieving their goals.

The professionalism and collective efficacy of all educators at these schools was simply dazzling. All the participants exuded competence and confidence in themselves and each other as a learning partnership. Efficacy represents belief in one's own empowerment to act effectively and move decisively in selected directions, including the ability to move others and be moved by others in the organization as a collective whole. As such, it is belief in one's own and others' competence and readiness. Being efficacious entails holding high expectations and a reflective critical mirror on one's self and others in the organization; it is trust in the collective competence of the team with the ability to critically analyze both strengths and weaknesses. A significant component of this efficacy is that everyone in the system, including noninstructional staff and parents, hold human capital to be brought into the fold for the benefit of everyone, and particularly the students. Both principals and teachers referred to themselves and each other as professionals. A significant aspect of their professionalism was awareness that their preservice preparation programs provided only a foundation, a beginning from which to spring forward. They realized that many things cannot be taught formally, but must be learned on the job, hands-on and/or experientially: "you need that real experience in the trenches." This means that preservice programs must prepare educators to be self-directed learners, ready to learn from each other. This requires highly developed communication and interpersonal skills, the ability to work collaboratively with others, and the readiness to share and learn from team members. Educators coming out of preparation programs, particularly those entering schools with high populations of students from low-SES backgrounds, students of color, and students classified as ELLs must be prepared to "hit the ground running." They must be prepared to share their newly acquired knowledge and skills as well as quickly learn from more experienced colleagues. The next theme is humanistic philosophy.

Humanistic Philosophy

> My whole goal is that I want teachers to wake up in the morning happy to come to work. Because if you are dealing with pupils and you have a headache, you are not happy—you cannot do the work; shove it today. You have 30 children in front of you, you need to be happy. That's why I make sure—I walk around and give you a little gift today, or when you have a problem, teachers can come in and say, "Oh, I had a problem with my son yesterday." And I'll say, "Take time—I'll cover your class. You go on and rest because you need sleep." You know, we are human. The humanistic approach we have to be—is it Maslow? (X2 Principal)

Often associated with fields purportedly aiming to increase our understanding of humanity and the "human condition" through ethics, character education, values clarification, and the humanities (i.e., ancient and modern languages, literature, law, history, philosophy, religion, and the arts), a humanistic philosophy has also come under criticism, been misrepresented as religious secularism, with demands for separation of church and state. Table 11.3 represents the findings from the study aligned to the Humanistic Philosophy. In this table, the values of human development, motivation theory, creating nonthreatening environments of learning, principal's acting as good listeners through an open-door policy create social cohesion and the freedom for teachers to choose and experiment in their classrooms. This in turn creates openness for teachers to respond to the needs of students. Teachers are flexible and adaptive not only to what

TABLE 11.3 Subthemes for Humanistic Philosophy by Principals and Teachers

Principals	Teachers
Culture of caring for students, teachers, and parents (student welfare)	Culture of caring for students, teachers, and parents (student welfare)
Human Development	Human Development
Motivation Theory	Motivation Theory
Perceptiveness	Social cohesiveness
Nonthreatening	Happy family
Good Listener	Freedom (to experiment)
Freedom (teachers have freedom to choose)	Flexibility
Relevance/sense of purpose (people have to have meaning in what they do)	Open to the needs of students
	Concern for children's well-being

students need but also to varied abilities within classroom settings, because each child is a unique individual.

Yet, as an educational paradigm that emerged in the 1960s, a humanistic approach or philosophy to education is more focused on human freedom, dignity, and potential. It considers informal as well as formal curricula. It considers the whole child rather than just behavior and/or cognition. The arts, health, and humanities are considered as equally valuable as science and math (Ornstein & Hunkins, 2009). It evolved from increased interest in and understanding of child psychology and humanistic psychology, especially a greater understanding of the "interdependence of cognition and affect" (p. 9). It emerged in contrast to behaviorist operant conditioning, which minimized learning as externally driven by rewards and punishments, and cognitive learning theories emphasizing that the construction of meaning is essential to learning. As well, it represented a move away from the perception of cognition as divorced from affect. Instead, humanistic philosophy views motivation and achievement as basic human needs; learning is a personal act aimed at fulfilling one's potential. It further contends that it is necessary to study the person as a whole, especially as the individual develops over the life span, as learning cannot be divorced from a person's full life experiences and contexts. Affective and cognitive needs are central, and the goal is to develop self-actualized people in a cooperative and supportive environment. As such, understanding of the self, motivation, and goals are of significant interest.

Beyond the classroom and instructional curricular programs and activities, humanistic psychology also deals with the individuals involved; from students, teachers, parents, and administrators to other members of the school community as a collective unit that impacts teaching and learning—everyone involved in the process of education. Humanists "emphasize socialization and adjustment of students, stronger family ties and school-community ties" (Ornstein & Hunkins, 2009, p. 9). Humanism views persons as individuals and as members of groups focusing on the personal, intrapersonal, and interpersonal. It sees human interactions from the perspectives of human caring, human values, and human concerns for self (identity, individuality, self-esteem, self-concept, etc.), health, hope, love, creativity, nature, being and becoming, and seeking meaning.

That is, a humanistic philosophy to education is a broader and more encompassing understanding of the total human existence. This is referred to as the whole person, wholesomeness, or person-centeredness, and emanates from within each person on out to the person's reciprocal reactions to/from and influences on/from others. This means looking at persons not only as individuals but through their significant interrelated, interconnected, and interdependent associations—or connections with others in various settings wherein individuals are valued and cared for. Further, humanism is strongly grounded on notions of trust—that individuals are fundamentally trustworthy—with incumbent confidence in their human capacity. "Humanism emphasizes that perceptions are centered in experience as well as the freedom and responsibility to become what one is capable of becoming" (Merriam & Caffarella, 1999, pp. 256–257).

As a guiding philosophy, humanism provides direction, ideals, and goals in pursuit of "the good life." Of significant concern is a focus on the development of critical consciousness that uncovers and reduces oppressive human interactions, which limit both individual and collective human potential. While it has its origins in philosophical humanism, phenomenology, and existentialism, today, humanism is considered strongly grounded in Maslow's (1968, 1970) theories of motivation and self-actualization, personal responsibility, and human potential; Rogers' (1969, 1977, 1980) person-centered approach to understanding individuals and human relationships; and May's (1994, 1996) existentialist need to find beauty and purpose in life.

Schools that adhere to a humanistic philosophy and approach integrate teachers more in curricular decisions. Professionalism and professional collegiality with networking, sharing, and mentoring systems are more prevalent. "Curriculum committees are bottom up instead of top down" (Ornstein & Hunkins, 2009, p. 9). From the humanistic perspective, the teacher is only one member of the learning community and not the source and gatekeeper of all classroom activities. Learning is student-centered and personalized, and the teacher's role is as facilitator of and participant in learning. In this sense, teaching and learning are inseparable as teacher and students become partners in the process of understanding and knowledge construction. Humanists emphasize the agency (decision and choice) and freedom of children and adults in developing and guiding their own learning interests in the classroom. The humanistic approach implies that schools are living workshops for developing and practicing the skills and dispositions required for members of the school community to enhance their capacity for effective moral and productive social and democratic involvement.

Within the seven schools in our study, the culture is clearly one of caring for teachers, parents, and students. This caring cannot be understood as separate from leadership and accountability, because the leadership invites "others" to participate, embrace the development of self and group, and acknowledge individual strengths. Principals have created highly motivating work environments for teachers, parents, and students wherein they feel respected and valued, affording opportunities to choose ways of expressing and enacting how to be successful. The three principals in the follow-up study shared their perspectives:

> I don't feel that because of the position that I have that I expect respect this way only. I have to give that respect in order to get the respect. And many times with different departments... when they see that respect is two ways, they step up and that creates the culture and climate of our school. (X5 Principal)

> Having an agenda, establishing guidelines for those meetings so that everyone is valued, everyone can contribute, there is no fault, and the meetings are timed, because we have to respect people's time. (X1 Principal).

> I am very sympathetic—I cover a class. They call and say, I'm going to be late, can you cover my class? I think I make it [so] that they don't feel intimidated by me. (X2 Principal)

The overall result is a culture of relevance and strong internal connections to the real world, with freedom to experiment, strong cohesion among all members, and an overall concern for the well-being of everyone in the organization, especially the children. Caring, concern for each others' welfare, and the corresponding values that go hand-in-hand with a humanistic philosophy are foundational in these schools. Authenticity, respect, mutual trust, and a positive and strong feeling that everyone is a leader working in unison to make a difference becomes the natural outcome. The next theme is shared leadership and accountability.

Shared Leadership and Accountability

Shared leadership and accountability promotes a collective sense of responsibility that enhances a *power through* paradigm, as opposed to *power over* (Acker-Hocevar et al., 2005/2006; Snyder et al., 2000). *Power through* creates the freedom and trust to foster a collective sense of purpose that encourages the sharing of expertise to attain the vision of the bigger community. The first step in moving to *power through* is to move away from *power over.* Shared leadership and accountability thwarts heroic leadership and coercive *power over* decision making in the hands of the principal as the savior and all-knowing expert. In schools where coercive power is used over people to garner compliance, members are not risk takers, because no one wants to be seen as noncompliant with the principal for fear of punishment. In schools where there is *power over,* no one would think of carrying out something without asking permission from the principal (French

& Raven, 1959). This stymies collective action and nullifies any sense of shared accountability and responsibility because facilitative power to move the school forward is vested only in the hands of the principal (Dunlap & Goldman, 1991). Further, it places expertise outside of the realm of the individual and in the hands of an "other," namely the principal.

The *power through* paradigm requires that power be enacted through every member of the system, and this necessitates that district and state administrative units recognize how a school's success depends on every organizational member working collaboratively with and through each other. States must resist top-down mandates and reject holding individuals and subgroups hostage through fear, intimidation, and punishment. Table 11.4 shows the areas that emerged in the second phase of the study, where shared leadership and accountability support expertise, team building, shared decision making, and participatory practices in day-to-day work through leading different activities. When schools share expertise and hold teams accountable for making decisions around common goals, the school reflects a different organizational form of distributed leadership, which is more fluid and emergent, less centered on individuals, and more dispersed across the whole school (Elmore, 2000; Gronn, 2002; Spillane, 2005).

In other words, it is impossible to think of shared leadership and accountability without first understanding that the structure and culture of the school will mirror how leadership is enacted. With increased state and

TABLE 11.4 Subthemes for Leadership and Accountability by Principals and Teachers

Principals	Teachers
Shared Expertise	Shared Expertise
Team Building/Collaboration	Team Building/Collaboration
Shared decision making with principal at the helm	Shared decision making with principal at the helm
Connectedness/System	Collective sense of responsibility
Power to give teachers voices and choices	Empowerment (strong sense of empowerment to make decisions)
Importance of student learning/Focus on student learning	Continuous Improvement
	Openness to learning
	Importance of student learning/Focus on student learning
Collegiality	Share Children

federal accountability, some school leaders feel they have to exert more control over the school to meet external mandates of accountability rather than build capacity and identify areas of individual and collective expertise. This raises questions about the motivation of the leader delegating tasks (Snyder, Acker-Hocevar, & Snyder, 2008), particularly if delegation is billed as distributing leadership under a guise of giving teachers more responsibility with no say in how decision making or accountability is shared. This is both duplicitous and manipulative. Because without the autonomy to direct one's work and make decisions about that work, it is not ethical to hold someone accountable.

Importantly, educators in the study had developed a sense of shared identity deeply embedded in their teams, where each member is interdependent, interrelated, and interconnected to their other team members, but not at the expense of the school vision and/or meeting the needs of the community-at-large. Teachers and principals addressed the requirement to learn more about systems theory (see Kast & Rosenzweig, 1979; Senge, 1990; Snyder et al., 2000; Snyder & Anderson, 1986; Wheately, 1992), including the identification and development of the processes required to solve underlying systemwide problems (Deming, 1986). They recognize that that no one within the system stands alone. Issues and/or concerns in one part of the system are not separate from other parts; what affects one aspect of the system ultimately affects other aspects. In one of the schools, the Comer Philosophy of "no fault" represents this idea well. That is, teams work together to study the data as information to help them achieve their goals systemically and to identify problems holistically. No one person is at fault. Shared leadership goes hand-in-hand with accountability. Accountability is about the whole school working with each other on their teams, across their teams, and within the larger community to encourage collaboration and collegiality, with openness to ongoing learning. Accountability directs the leadership action of individuals, the team, and the school toward student learning. Keeping parents informed, using benchmark assessments, analyzing data to assess progress, relying on team dialogue within and across the teams to make decisions to positively impact students' success links these two areas together inextricably.

In systems theory, no one believes in holding back; on the contrary, each member believes in his/her ability to make their collective assets much larger and much more powerful than they are alone. Participants at the schools talked with pride about their own and each other's expertise. They acknowledged how they relied on each other to successfully address problems, and how they augmented each others' knowledge with what they could contribute, while simultaneously moving in unison to build and sustain a highly competent workforce. Collectively, teachers indicated,

> We are on district leadership where we can speak comfortably about the problems we have at our school, the solutions we are using, and a definition of the problem as we see it. This is what we do at our school; it's open. So we've each taken some sort of leadership role in the school, and I think that's also trickle down, because we are allowed to. We are told or we are asked if you want to do this or want to do that. It helps out a lot too. We all have a say in the climate, the actual culture of the school, because we all can direct it—we have that freedom because of our principal.... Teachers share...ideas with each other and go and observe other teachers' classrooms.... We mentor each other a lot. I think [this is] because of the openness between teachers and the administration and the teachers within themselves. (X3Teachers)

Although much has been written about distributed leadership, distributed leadership augments what we know about participatory leadership theories (Argyris, 1964), relational leadership (Uhl-Bien, 2006), and shared leadership across team members (Day, Gronn, & Salas, 2004). Both shared leadership and distributed leadership are spread over its members to work collectively to achieve goals within the organization (Brown & Gioia, 2002). Although the schools do not claim to be using distributed leadership, they were in fact distributing leadership broadly to their members through their teams with open invitations to individuals to participate in areas in which they had expertise or wanted to grow. Shared and distributed leadership are different from the leader delegating what needs to be done. Rather, shared and distributed leadership are organizational in nature and may be viewed as additive, if the person wants to exercise leadership without taking into account the activities of others, and/or holistic, when the person takes into account the "synergistic relationships" of others in the organization practicing leadership (Leithwood et al., 2007, p. 39). The following quote illustrates this:

> We have a professional environment in this school.... We have leaders on our faculty; ... without the leaders on our faculty we probably couldn't get off square one. They are willing to do it. They are willing to go the extra mile; they believe in what we are trying to accomplish. They are the heart and soul of this school. We have surrounded ourselves with the most high quality human beings and the nicest people that you would do anything as an administrator because you just know they are doing the right thing by the children. (X5 Principal)

Resourcefulness

Historically, funding for public schools has come from a variety of sources. As early as the 1830s, public schools were funded through parental contributions, local taxation, and money from the state (Hacsi, 2002). Since these early days of public schools, it has been necessary for principals and teachers to know how to use resources wisely (Hacsi, 2002). Resourcefulness in this theory-in-practice is the ability to use resources wisely, as well as the ability to solicit resource support from others. In the early 20th century, local taxation provided 80% of the funding for education. Today, public schools rely on 37% from local funding and 46% from state funding for support (U.S. Department of Education, 2006). Only 8% of funding comes from the federal government. Federal funding for education rose during the 1960s and 1970s to support the war on poverty and civil rights; however, it has been limited for the most part since that time (Hacsi, 2002).

In order to reduce the dependence on local money, foundation funding became popular in the 1920s. Foundation funding is the charitable giving of resources in the form of a grant by an unrelated private or public organization or institution. These days, individual states provide basic resources through foundation funding (Hacsi, 2002). Resourcefulness, according to the SSI theory-in-practice, is the ability to use monetary, human, and community resources wisely, as well as the ability to solicit resource support from others to address deficit funding. In order to raise resources for basic school needs, principals use the practice of creatively soliciting support for education from community businesses, called an entrepreneurial strategy and entrepreneurial leadership (Jones, 2000). Table 11.5 presents the findings concerning resourcefulness.

The role of the principal that was developed in the mid-19th century shows how principals once had numerous responsibilities in the community; however, managing the schools eventually became the primary respon-

TABLE 11.5   Subthemes for Resourcefulness by Principals and Teachers

Principals	Teachers
Deficit Funding	Deficit Funding
Entrepreneurship	Entrepreneurship
Go-getter	Go-getter
	Business Orientation
	Confidence in resource allocation
	Transparency in the budget

sibility of the principal (Goldman, 1966). Today, principals and teachers find it necessary to procure additional funding for programs needed to assist students in academic achievement. Effective principals use business strategies to manage funding for their school and engage others in identifying and seeking creative funding solutions (Ward, 2004). These strategies include programs and resources necessary to meet achievement objectives for the school year such as technology upgrades and other materials for students (Ward, 2004). Effective principals and teachers build intellectual capital in order to achieve high-performing schools (Lockwood-Zisa, 2002). Intellectual capital is knowledge or skills that a company or business has that can be used for making money or other useful purposes critical to the success of the company or business. School leaders have begun to use this form of business strategy to provide resources to close the achievement gap, build on their knowledge capital, and close funding gaps. This strategy of maximizing human capital through human resources is a strategy principals rely upon for ongoing school improvement.

In 1965, the Title I Program began providing federal aid to assist children from impoverished urban and rural areas. However, Title I funding does not provide sufficient resources to the programs necessary to fulfill the demands of the NCLB Act. This Act was designed to close the achievement gap by offering states and school districts more flexibility in the use of federal education funds. States are held accountable by detailing how they will close the achievement gap for all students and are required to demonstrate progress is being made. School districts are allowed the flexibility of transferring up to 50% of federal grant funds for supplemental programs (such as after-school tutoring) as a means to close achievement gaps. In many schools, resources were allocated to before- and after-school tutorials, Parent Outreach Centers, and paraprofessionals to assist teachers in their classrooms.

Effective principals were found to have the ability to use resources wisely through skills in money management, budgeting, supplementing budgets, relying on enterprising teachers, and spending money wisely. These principals sought resources for their schools and saw everyone in their school as a resource. Further, they were able to allocate resources in ways that helped them get the biggest bang for the buck. Principals must have an understanding of how to "allocate monies and resources to each of those objectives and the programs [you] have in the school to meet those objectives" (X1 Principal). The needs and priorities of the school and teachers are also taken into consideration when there is extra money in the budget. Opportunities to supplement the budget through grants are an additional source of funding to public schools (Herman & Herman, 1998). Effective principals were found to actively identify and seek outside resources in the business community by providing an opportunity for them to contribute in a meaningful way. "If you don't have that vision and you don't have that plan, the money can really get away from you" (X5 Principal).

Effective teachers were found to have a special ability to form relationships with the community and the parents in order to meet the needs of the students and school. This reveals a relationship between resourcefulness and community. Effective schools continuously build on the concept of social capital, which allows principals and teachers to trust, depend on, and learn from others (Lockwood-Zisa, 2002). Teachers in high-performing schools indicated skills that included networking, public relations, budgeting, fundraising, and grant writing. "You have to promote your school in a way that will encourage people to participate in your school and provide help either financial[ly] or [with] their expertise. You have to have public relations skills" (X1 Teacher).

Despite the low-income areas of these high-performing schools in the study, the parents and community support included volunteering. Strategies for soliciting funding included forming partnerships with parents, community organizations, and local businesses (Ward, 2004). School-business partnerships, volunteer programs, and newsletters mailed to community members (Herman & Herman, 1998) were all effective strategies utilized by principals. The Adopt-a-School Program also increases the resources available to schools (Herman & Herman, 1998), and many of the principals actively sought out community resources. "Using our resources of parent and community involvement, what we do for that, I would say that we tap into our PTA" (X1 Principal). Resourcefulness in this theory-in-practice provides both monetary and community support to low-income high-performing schools. Principals and teachers are effective in their entrepreneurial strategies to solicit resources for the schools and build support for teachers writing grants and seeking external funding. A strong relationship between resourceful principals and teachers and the community supports helping students achieve. The principals were all "go-getters." They were out in the community, connected to a number of different groups, networking, and publicly telling success stories of their schools. Although parents could not often contribute financially, they did agree that they were willing to give of their time because of how well these schools were doing in educating their students.

The best analogy for why these schools were able to attract resources is this: If you were given money to invest in a company, would you choose a company with a record of success or one with failure? These schools were attractors for additional resources and support because they had a history of sustainable success. They had built strong ties within their communities. If the local communities could not provide fiscal resources, they would provide in-kind resources such as donations of materials for instruction or rewards for students. Significantly, they provided resources through community networks and organizations. The communities looked to these schools with pride and were willing to provide human resources as an investment of time and energy back into these schools. The schools built on the human capital of the teachers, the community, and the district. Although these schools operated from a "deficit funding" perspective, in reality they never came from a place of lack. What they lacked fiscally, they made up for through their wealth of human capital. Instead, they built on their strengths and strong linkages within existing networks, working to attract new resources. Everyone in the school was committed to presenting the school's image positively. Teachers were confident resources and were used wisely within the schools. The internal locus of control drove an entrepreneurial and business orientation to seek additional revenues aggressively through local, state, and national grants; business partnerships; school district monies; professional development for school growth; partnering with national organizations; and applying and winning recognition, such as the Florida Sterling Award for continuous quality improvement.

Additive Schooling

This theme represents the school as a human system encompassing everyone from principal to teachers, students, parents, support and maintenance staff, and even community members and organizations. Everyone in the system is acknowledged as having human capital pulled together to build community through multidirectional/multifaceted communication and networks that promote inclusion and a supportive teaching and learning culture. Unlike quantitative or fiscal resources, human capital signifies other valuable community assets such as cultural values and perspectives, family and social networks, including extended families, formal and informal organizations, and regular and irregular schedules. In short, additive schooling is everything a community can contribute, whether tangible or intangible, that supports the school. Table 11.6 presents the findings from this theme.

In this light, additive schooling is the opposite of subtractive schooling (Valenzuela, 1999); the school community works to add to the human capital of everyone in the system. For example, second and first language development becomes additive and developmental rather than transitional and thus, subtractive. Additive schooling is grounded in the notion of synergy; the whole becomes greater than the sum of the parts. This necessarily

TABLE 11.6 Subthemes for Additive Schooling by Principals and Teachers

Principals	Teachers
Building Community	Building Community
Multidirectional/multifaceted communication	Multidirectional/multifaceted communication
Supportive teaching and learning culture	Supportive teaching and learning culture
Building rapport with the parents	Culture of trust
Culture that promotes the inclusion of all students	

means that educators and community members are engaged in ongoing capacity building.

The schools demonstrated a strong internal culture focused on their community's culture(s) and language(s). This new lens of analysis is termed additive schooling (Acker-Hocevar et al., 2005/2006), that drew on the work of Valenzuela (1999). Notably, the assumptions underpinning subtractive schooling and its converse, additive schooling, were examined in this study. Several well-established notions drive subtractive schooling, particularly assimilationist policies and practices designed to divest diverse students of their cultures and languages. Instead, Valenzuela writes that education must be viewed as a "foundational cultural construct" that prepares us for successful participatory membership in the human community, both within our individual microcultures and the larger national macroculture. Valenzuela's 3-year ethnographic study in a predominantly Mexican American school uncovered how many students lament how adults at their schools, including teachers, do not care about them or their families and communities. This inevitably leads the researcher to question what happens when students are not taught at school to care for themselves, each other, their parents, or their communities. Furthermore, and significantly, what happens when students are, instead, taught at school to devalue themselves, each other, their parents, and their communities?

What happens when schools and communities disagree on the goals and values of a formal education? In many cultures, particularly Latino ones, the concept of *educación* is not the same one of *education* applied within the dominant mainstream U.S. culture. Rather than the focus on reading, writing, mathematics, and formal book knowledge attained within a classroom setting, *educación* entails preparing citizens as integral individuals who are caring, moral, and collaborative members of their extended families and communities. As such, a person could be very educated—in the formal school sense—yet lack *educación* and real worth within some communities. Without formal schooling, a person can be very *educado* and a much valued, contributing member of their family and community. As a former principal, this author/researcher recalls Latino/Hispanic parents voicing their frustrations with the U.S. educational system:

> I send my children to school to be educated. Instead you teach them to be selfish and self-centered; to think that they are better than anyone else, including their brothers and sisters and parents. You teach them not to help each other because that is cheating. You teach them to be embarrassed and disrespect their parents and elders. They make fun of us and say we don't fit in. You teach them to feel ashamed of their culture and language. You teach them to push everyone else aside so they can step up individually. That is not what I send my children to your school for.

In fact, sometimes Latino parents feel that formal U.S. education is a detriment, rather than an asset, to their families and communities because it slowly splits families and communities by moving children away; first, emotionally and eventually, physically as they leave their communities to seek "appropriate" employment and lives within the dominant mainstream society. Rather than adding, or enriching, the community, formal U.S. education is perceived as impoverishing the community by depleting it of its greatest assets and potential: its youth.

To the contrary, additive schooling is based on (a) affirming the community's definition of education and schooling, (b) maintaining and promoting students' cultures and languages, (c) additive acculturation rather than subtractive assimilation, and (d) reciprocal respect and trust between schools and the communities they serve (Espinoza-Herold, 2003; Gibson, 1995; Nieto, 2001b; Valdés, 1996; Valenzuela, 1999). This perception shifts the analytical focus from communities, families, students, and a deficit paradigm (e.g., What is wrong with them? What do they lack? How can we fix them?) to the schools themselves (e.g., What are we doing wrong? What do we lack? How can we improve our services?). This model shifts from one of cultural assimilation to one of cultural pluralism, multiple acculturation (Banks, 2001; Gibson, 1995), and accommodation without assimilation (Espinoza-Herold, 2003).

This paradigm shift further entails that the schools' curriculum be perceived not only as what is taught but what is not taught, including the hidden curriculum, how it is taught, and how it is influenced by other significant variables including the self-perceptions of teachers, students, and parents; perceptions of each other; and perceptions of the educational process, its purposes, and their roles within it. It is well-understood that what is taught teaches what is valued, while what is not taught teaches what is not. Slowly, across the curriculum and educational experiences, some students get the subliminal, yet cumulative message that they do not count in schools and the larger society.

Additive schooling shifts the analytical question from "How can schools transform students' cultural and language deficiencies to convert them into assimilated persons who can function within the norms of the dominant mainstream culture and language?" to a focus on what schools can do to embrace communities' values and social assets in order to prepare persons who can remain sustaining components of their communities and who can contribute their unique values and assets as productive members of the broader, mainstream society. In order for this analytical shift to occur, the schools must also assume that students and their community possess empowering social capital. Social capital is defined as the network of community systems—social, political, and economic—that sustains and empowers all members (Valenzuela, 1999; Valenzuela & Dornbusch, 1994). Extended families composed of biological and nonbiological members are common in many communities of color. Families may include members of the nuclear family (parents and siblings) along with extended family members (grandparents, cousins, and others who may be immediate and/or several generations removed, i.e., second and third cousins, aunts, etc.). Extended community networks, may even be part of the immediate family unit, including members of the community. Latino families, for example, may be further extended through *compadrazgo*, or oaths of allegiance to mutual lifelong support between individuals and families, whether they are related through family bloodlines or not. Once that bond is established, the parties consider themselves members of the same family. Our schools do not understand and/or accept this social structure. When one of the author's sisters asked her to keep her children for a few months, she ran into a real brick wall—the local school would not accept the children because "You are not the real parent. Your sister must obtain a legal affidavit relinquishing the children to your custody." They could not understand or accept that the thought of legally ceding the children, although to a family member, was unacceptable and extremely inappropriate—in fact, offensive—culturally.

As such, additive schooling assumes community organizations and groups, including churches and clubs, neighbors, women's and men's circles, and even students' friends and peers as components of a community's social capital. When second and subsequent generations of Latino students accept their first-generation, Spanish-dominant, parents, peers, and friends as role models and resources; when students who are ELLs view their English-proficient peers and friends as role models and resources; and similarly, when students of color see their parents and other members of their family and community as appropriate role models and resources, the community is effectively accessing its social capital. When communities value cultural renewal brought by the influx of recent immigrants, it is accessing its social capital. Clearly, this extensive network serves as social capital to support all members. On the other hand, Valenzuela (1999) posits that today's schools work to fracture community's social capital. Students who are ELLs are mocked and rejected by same-group English-speaking peers. First-generation students' culture is disdained by more assimilated members of the community. The pressure is for persons to shed their cultures and languages and become "like everyone else." The tragic result of this is often families that cannot communicate with each other, breaking the cultural thread of passing beliefs and values from generation to generation. This leaves families, and particularly children, perilously vulnerable. Parents, either unable to speak or deficient in the language of the schools become increasingly lost in their inability to communicate with their children who are, in turn, increasingly losing the home language and embracing the schools' language. The pressure to shed the home language is strong and perceived early. This author/researcher shares an anecdote below from overhearing a conversation:

> I was at the supermarket waiting at the cashier's line. A family in front consisted of a mother, grandmother, a young girl of approximately six to seven years, another of nine to ten years—both of school age—and a toddler sitting strapped in the cart. The mother and grandmother spoke to each other in Spanish. They also spoke to the toddler in Spanish. The two older girls spoke to each other in English. Soon, I noticed on repeated occasions that when the grandmother addressed the older child in Spanish, the child would not respond and sometimes looked away. Suddenly, the mother reprimands the child in Spanish: "Why aren't you talking to grandma? Why are you ignoring her? Why are you being so rude to her?" The child shrugged her shoulders and responded in English, "I don't understand." The mother quickly replied, "Of course you understand. You understand very well. You speak Spanish to grandma at home. Why can't you speak it here? Why do you hurt grandma like that?" The middle child quipped, "She tells everyone in school that she doesn't speak Spanish anymore, that she forgot." The older child rolled her eyes down and remained silent.

This child has apparently already learned that the use of the home language in public places is not viewed favorably and must be avoided. She has also learned to be ashamed of her heritage and language, including her own family. By embracing students' cultures and languages, the schools hold students' social capital as integral components of the schools' network and vice versa. Schools access the community's social capital in a joint effort to educate all children and community members. The school commits to educating itself about the community. In turn, community members access the school not only to educate their children, but also to educate themselves and increase their network of sustaining assets (Valenzuela, 1999).

Uppermost, additive schooling is deeply predicated on trust as the glue that binds communities and schools (Espinoza-Herold, 2003; Valenzuela, 1999). Mutual trust is essential to school improvement and is guided by the belief that schools and parents are both doing the best for children; that both have a genuine interest in children's educational and social competency. Teachers must sincerely believe that all children can learn. They must hold robust expectations for student achievement and support those expectations. Teachers must trust that students and their communities have assets and contributions to give to the educational enterprise. Students and parents must trust the schools to be safe places where students are educated primarily as wholesome individuals and community members who value themselves and their communities, and who value others in the world beyond (Espinoza-Herold, 2003; Valenzuela, 1999).

Bringing it Together in a Theory-in-Practice

School improvement within the LPT model looks different in each of the seven schools. The SSI's five themes, however, identify the theory-in-practice that sustains each of these schools' improvement efforts over time and unifies what each of the schools is doing in practice. This theory suggests that each of these themes is important and linked to the other themes. In fact, in illustrating this theory, we depict it as a spiral that weaves in on itself and reflects the core of organizational efficacy radiating out to the other themes (see Figure 11.1). We found that leadership and accountability kick-start the organization to promote learning, but the evidence of how effective this leadership is viewed is understood by the extent to which organizational efficacy is present within the school. Critically, the core values and beliefs that shape the humanistic philosophy, additive schooling, and resourcefulness are also evident in leadership and accountability and seem to have a bidirectional relationship. Leadership and accountability free up the human energy system to build collective efficacy for sustaining school improvement and unleashing the energy within the other three themes. Organizational efficacy is not an end in itself, therefore, but the result of the other themes working synergistically within the overall belief that in-

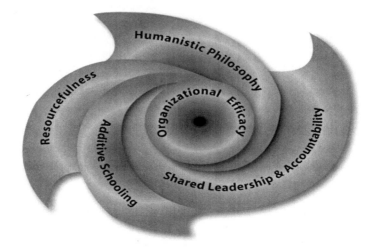

Figure 11.1 Sustainable School Improvement (SSI). The SSI theory-in-practice emerged from the follow-up study. It represents the five common themes found across all the schools. It is "depicted as a spiral that weaves in on itself and reflects the core of organizational efficacy radiating out to the other themes." These five themes served as guiding principles for the theory-in-practice that took shape in the schools in this study. They represent the philosophical grounding for all actions taken within the school community

dividuals are capable and can learn from one another in their learning partnerships.

It seems that much of what we purported to sustain these schools' improvement over time is grounded in some basic ideas about how you treat others, how you value them, how you recognize each person's potential contributions, and how you add value to the school, instead of subtracting resources away. How is it that we have become so focused on the goal of raising test scores that we have forgotten about and negated the human side of our enterprise? We are working with real people who are students, teachers, principals, and parents, and hopefully we are creating caring schools that support learning partnerships where people want to come and work together.

Recently, there has been a movement in psychology called positive psychology (Snyder & Lopez, 2007), which provides us with an alternative narrative to most of what we hear about schools that are failing. In this narrative, resiliency factors enable positive and healthy responses instead of focusing on dysfunctional and deficit behavior models. Our theory-in-practice seems to be in tandem with this narrative and movement in psychology to identify strengths within each individual and school to build upon, instead of focusing on a deficit perspective and behaviors. We learned that in these schools, the role of the principal is one of a human developer of the talents, skills, and knowledge that promotes individual and group learning by pulling together with others for the good of the school. This creates an energy system that expands human capital exponentially instead of subtracting from it, an energy system where other teachers and the community model what the principal does.

The study began with the identification of schools meeting external criteria but shifted thereafter to look inward. Strong connections internally extended to the community externally. Core values and beliefs connected human needs with organizational goals for ongoing improvement. In other words, the group's shared values and beliefs to accomplish things together shifted the "Me" to "We," the piecemeal approach to the collective whole, and to what matters most to the individual school's core values and beliefs that enable individuals to make decisions directed toward the common good. These schools, exemplary learning partnerships, place teaching and learning as inseparable and at the core of their work. Decision making promotes agency for acting, choice, and ongoing improvement, where power is shared within the school, and people are treated as professionals, with the autonomy and freedom to do what they need to do for students. We asked ourselves, "What if struggling schools we see today grounded their learning partnership in the principles of SSI? What might happen if schools trying so desperately to turn around their low performance built on their human capital and looked at what we found in this study as a starting place for re-culturing their schools as learning partnerships?"

The schools in this study were not narrowing their gaze to focus exclusively on improving test scores but were in fact broadening their lens to embrace the full range of human experiences within dynamic and motivating places to work. Similarly, this was at the same time when so many other schools were narrowing their focus and "teaching to the test." We have learned that leadership from the ground up shares leadership and accountability, embraces values and beliefs within the SSI theory-in-practice to promote a safe place to work, which encourages practices that reinforce the idea that people are valued; the most important resource within the school. Any one of us would feel proud to work at one of these schools that ground their LPT in values of learning together in partnership with one another and their communities to promote the health and well-being of competent individuals who care for one another.

Questions for Discussion

1. This chapter grounds the theory-in-practice and answers the research question about what theories enabled the success of educators in these schools. What can you now say about what makes these schools successful from this theory-in-practice?

2. How does additive schooling and humanistic philosophy mutually reinforce these schools as caring places to work and attend school?

3. Why is the finding of leadership and accountability so critical? What are the implications of this finding for how leaders share their leadership and involve others? Where and how does expertise contribute to the leader's confidence to charge others with key tasks?

4. How does building a sense of collective and/or organizational efficacy add to building sustainability? In what ways do the other aspects of the SSI contribute to this organizational efficacy?

5. What does the SSI add to your understanding of the LPT? Why is it important to keep this learning partnership focus?

12[1]

The Journey Continues

What We Learned to Improve Preparation Programs

> You need to develop the knowledge and the skills of the people around you, because the school is going to be as good as the people who are in that place. When I am talking about that, I am talking about everybody from the teachers, the custodians, the cafeteria, everybody in the school—and especially our volunteer people, because they are here for part of the day only, and they provide a very important part and provide a very important service to the school. (X4 Principal)

Findings from our previous research raised questions about preparation programs for teachers and principals. These questions focused, particularly, on seven high-performing schools that served primarily students from low SES backgrounds, students of color, and students classified as ELLs. These schools consistently described their daily realities and routines in ways glaringly absent from current teacher and principal preparation programs. We sought to find out what distinguished these schools as high-performing when others with similar student demographics are still seeking answers to their persistent underachievement. This work undoubtedly raises questions about how current preservice programs may or may not

Leadership from the Ground Up, pages 221–237

be adequately preparing educators for today's schools and has import for preparation programs with future teachers and principals. If we are going to close the achievement gap, schools such as these hold value for researchers wishing to study whether current pre- and in-service programs are preparing teachers and principals to be successful. This research fills a void, not only in the current literature but also in studies critical of preparation programs (e.g., Levine, 2005). The focus continues to be on preparation of teachers and principals in separate tracks with a one-size-fits-all mentality shaped by traditional mainstream, non-Hispanic White/Caucasian, middle-class norms (Larson & Olvando, 2001). Preparation programs continue to define the roles of teachers and principals through traditional theoretical constructs rather than the realities of today's schools, particularly those that fit the profile of these seven high-performing schools.

As reported in Chapter 11, a follow-up study was conducted during summer 2005 to validate the findings of the initial study and to further understand what teachers and principals self-report as they see themselves and others perform the tasks in which they actually engage. Furthermore, the follow-up study sought to identify needed reforms in teacher and principal preparation programs based on the actual work educators performed and attributed to their successes in these schools. Three schools agreed to participate in the follow-up study. Two focus groups with a total of 12 teachers and three individual principal interviews were conducted. This chapter identifies the tasks, knowledge, and skills principals and teachers at these schools identified as enabling them to establish and sustain high performance across the years. The knowledge gained from these schools suggests a mismatch between external demands and the daily realities of schools, including a mismatch between the subject matter taught in preparation programs and what the administrators and teachers at these schools felt were strongly needed to sustain their school's organizational development and effectiveness.

Purpose and Research Questions

This follow-up study was guided by the following research questions:

1. What are the actual tasks performed by teachers and principals at these schools and what are the skills and knowledge they identify as required to perform these tasks?
2. How do these tasks correspond to the skills and knowledge garnered from their preservice university preparation programs?
3. What are the recommendations made by these teachers and principals for preparation programs?

Method

A total of 3 principals and 12 teachers from the three follow-up schools were asked to describe the real work they do in terms of actual tasks performed. They were then asked to identify the skills that assisted them in their work; how skills connected to the needed knowledge to be successful; and where and how they had acquired these skills and knowledge. Initially, the researchers were looking at deconstructing teacher and principal role definitions by moving from the theoretical to the practical, or from how these roles are defined and taught in preparation programs. Instead, the study uncovered the need to shift to how these roles are actually enacted at these schools. Effective practices at these schools must help guide the development of new theory and thus role definitions for schools with similar demographics. The schools have stepped outside of the traditional mold and are successful at what most other schools with similar demographics are unable to achieve; we need to be studying and learning from them.

The two principal investigators gathered data through individual interviews with principals and focus groups with teachers. An interview protocol was developed using the 10 variables identified in the previous study known to impact school effectiveness (Wilson et al., 2005/2006). These variables are divided into two major categories: organizing and embedded/sustaining variables. The organizing variables are accountability, information management, personnel, instruction, and resources. The embedded/sustaining variables include leadership, decision making, communication, parent and community involvement, and school culture and climate. Questions were developed to elicit the actual tasks performed under each organizing and embedded/sustaining variable. Additionally, the participants were asked to identify the skills and knowledge needed to perform each task and where they obtained those. Principals were asked to self-report on their tasks, skills, and knowledge, then on their perception of teachers' tasks, skills, and knowledge. Teachers were equally asked to self-report and then report on the principal. The participants were instructed to focus on actual tasks rather than roles. For this, the operating terms were defined as

Role: broad (sometimes theoretical) definition and characterization of a function, or office.
Task: (actual) versus role (theoretical) work, function, or labor undertaken.
Skills: aptitude, ability, dexterity, knowledge, expertness, and proficiency.

The questioning cycle was ordered by each organizing and embedded/ sustaining variable. In addition, each variable and operating term was defined at the beginning of each questioning cycle. The interviews were audiotaped and transcribed. The transcripts were mailed to each participant for verification. Two additional researchers joined in data analysis. Using QSR Nudist software, each researcher developed their own list of codes for each one of the teacher and principal datasets. During initial meetings, each researcher shared their coding system. Through consensus, a common list of codes was identified and the research team then went back to the data to identify the actual tasks, skills, and knowledge that teachers and principals related.

Findings

It is significant to begin by stating that the current study validates the finding of previous work that led to the LPT model (see Chapter 10; Acker-Hocevar et al., 2005/2006). Participants agreed that the LPT model most accurately described them; that a strong tree requires a very strong root system. The entire system must be grounded through a school culture and climate, with sustaining core values that support and nurture the health of the entire system. Each teacher and principal interviewed agreed that the LPT model accurately represented their organizational functioning that enabled their success. This model represents schools as dynamic positive energy systems that are nonlinear and self-organizing around their core values. It helps to better understand the internal dynamics of schools that are able to become high performing with large populations of students from low SES backgrounds, students of color, and students classified as ELLs. The LPT model

> supports a holistic approach to school effectiveness and educational reform focusing deeply below the surface, on those not-so-apparent structures and processes, which hold the sustaining nutrients to keep the entire system moving in responsive directions. Those rushing to control and punish schools, teachers, and children simply do not understand the nature of schools as human energy systems, the significance of power relations in establishing healthy and strong core values, or the notion of schools as learning partnerships. They fail to understand that the nutrients of sustainable school progress are found in positive relationships, sharing of power and information, the valuing of others, and the building of strong, stable, and trusting relationships. (Acker-Hocevar et al., 2005/2006, p. 265)

A significant finding, often ignored by current school reform policies and practices, is that what matters most in making these schools successful—against the odds—is what happens at the schools (Acker-Hocevar et al., 2005/2006). The school, as a dynamic human system, is grounded and guided by the roots, composed of the taproot or school culture and climate, and the branching roots of leadership, communication, decision making, and parent and community involvement. The embedded/sustaining variables, through the school culture and climate, forge the core values, or trunk of the organization that align with the organizing variables. The core values uphold the entire system and connect the organizing and embedded/sustaining variables and sustain the healthy system. As such, the core values orchestrate a fluid relationship and beneficial balance between all the variables as needed by the organization, ensuring the well-being of the entire system and sustaining organizational efficacy (Acker-Hocevar et al., 2005/2006).

It is noteworthy that the participants talked with more ease and in greater detail when questioned about the sustaining variables. Responses to questions related to the organizing variables were often expanded through descriptions of how each of the embedded/sustaining variables supported decisions that impacted the organizing variables. Participants were able to explain how the embedded/sustaining variables, through the core values, guided their actions "from the ground up." For example, personnel decisions were guided by how candidates, be they teachers, secretaries, or volunteers, fit within the school culture and climate and added to the human capital, or human assets, of the school community as a whole. The school community was defined as everyone involved in the education of children at the school, including teachers and all support staff (even bus drivers and cafeteria workers), to parents and community members.

Teacher candidates were carefully selected for their contributions and fit within the system and quickly folded into the school culture and values through careful mentoring. They were also assessed on their ability and willingness to become part of a professional learning community and enhance the entire school's resources and efficacy. Succinctly, decisions about accountability, information management, resources, instruction, and personnel are not strictly guided by external mandates, including standardized high-stakes testing. Instead, these schools have become self-empowered, self-managed, and able to "massage" the mandates in ways that suit their beliefs and needs. New principals often found a well-established, very effective system already in place and learned it carefully before making alterations. In this way, new principals were able to make enhancements that moved school efficacy further ahead. From this, it became apparent that two significant elements present in these schools, yet lacking in low-performing schools with similar demographics and settings, are continuity and longevity. Teacher and principal turnover was very low, allowing everyone within the organization to develop over time, forging together a deep understanding of the system and their collective fit within it.

For more accurate data analysis, the language used by teachers and principals is used as precisely as possible throughout this chapter. For example, teachers repeatedly talked about the need for a "business orientation." Although teachers and principals talked about related tasks such as being risk takers and innovators, having initiative, fundraising through grants and money-making programs, such as before- and after-school childcare and soliciting business sponsors, principals never used the word "business orientation" in their dialogue. To teachers, business orientation specifically meant added understanding of public relations and marketing to "advertise" and "sell your school" in various ways commonly used in the private sector. One teacher stated, "You have to do public relations of your school. You have to promote your school in a way that will encourage people to participate in your school and provide help either financial[ly] or [with] their expertise or any way that they can come back and provide you with something—you have to have public relations skills, how do you market your school?" Another teacher added,

> When we went to college, we had no business orientation whatsoever. That's exactly what we were lacking, and that's what we have been learning for the last five years...And we are learning more and more that you have to have business skills to be in education. There are many business acts that we are realizing in education; we need to bring this in. We are not an isolated little building anymore. We belong to a community; the community has to participate. The community just doesn't participate; there is a give and take. The teachers need to learn.

Part of that business orientation is knowing how to work with private businesses so they benefit as they support the school. From yet another teacher,

> Every year, every teacher in the school gives their kids supply lists for red pens and...etc., etc. And one of the most frustrating things is you set a deadline for those materials coming in and they don't come in, or you find out the parents can't afford them,...and it is so hard to get the year started when you are waiting so long for the kids to bring in whatever you've asked the kids to bring in...for them to go out and pay thirty bucks for a supply list and have to run all over town to get it is a real burden. So I was talking with this Office Depot guy and I said, well, this is a problem I've got. So I said, if I e-mailed you my supply list, would you be willing to put it all together in a bag, discount it, label it for [school name], Mr. G's class, would you be ready for pick up by my parents? And he said, "Oh yeah, oh yeah, you've

got that, right away. Furthermore, we'll send an e-mail to every teacher in the school so they can do the same thing." Now, if you don't think they are going to be awfully supportive in the future and do whatever we want them to do. It's your hand-in-glove kind of thing.

A business orientation also includes knowledge of data analysis and statistics in order to examine and track student progress on an ongoing basis. A teacher equated this to following the stock market: "Who is making gains and by how much? Who is falling behind?" She goes on to say we need to understand "Data analysis and statistics. Unfortunately, I didn't see them until my master's program. And I was able to understand actual quantitative research and qualitative research and action research—we took it together—but it opened our eyes more towards the classroom than I think the undergraduate." Another teacher explained, "Being able to see the data. When the scores came in, I sat down to find out who our lowest twenty-five percent were . . . who were the students who need to make learning gains . . . get all this data, quantitative data, and break it down."

Decisions at these schools are not random. Educators carefully scrutinize the data "to interpret and extrapolate" and analyze ideas before making final decisions. They are very data driven and look at numerical information to ensure "it's not something like out of the hat. I'm going to try this out just because I want to" (Teacher). There's a process involved before "jumping into an idea" that emphasizes collection and analysis of data to make appropriate decisions. They strongly recommended that all educators be prepared to understand and use test scores. In addition, they agreed that educators coming out of preparation programs must be skilled in action research, ready to use the classroom as a learning laboratory to "diagnose and adapt curriculum and instruction" through a combination of quantitative and qualitative data. Action research must also enable educators to evaluate their own strengths and weaknesses. As described by one teacher,

> If you study it, you figure out why it doesn't [work], what you need to change about it, and then you start the cycle all over again. It's the DaVinci cycle of invention, analysis, and re-creation over and over again—action research. It's data driven. You observe, it's the scientific process, it's a management skill, it's an inventor's skill. It's all those things wrapped up in one, and it's a great management decision-making skill; a tool to be used all the time.

Data analysis and action research were linked to technology skills. Teachers and principals agreed that new technologies, including computers, opened unlimited doors to essential information, especially related to teaching and learning reform. They explained how technology leads them to endless resources, including grants, activities, information, organizations, and many opportunities to enhance their school programs. Through technology, they learn about new educational research and innovations. Technology links the school to the students' homes, the community, and beyond. All the participants agreed that today's educators must acquire and keep up with emergent and constantly changing technology. One of the teachers proudly acknowledged that they are often mentored by new teachers coming in with the latest technology skills. A principal spoke of not being very computer "savvy" but surrounding herself with very skilled teachers who help analyze the data while making data-based decisions together. Teachers expressing a desire to know more about how to successfully market their school to attain additional resources, using action research to see their classrooms as learning laboratories, and employing technology to connect to broader-based networks for additional resources and making better decisions led us to represent the various related ideas presented through the term "entrepreneurship." For all the teachers, a significant aspect of entrepreneurship was risk taking. Risk taking was described as follows:

> It means that if I implement something in my classroom, I'm doing something because I'm motivated to do it and it doesn't work out, my principal is not going to come up to me and ... blame me, because I'm doing it for the best interests of the kids. And when you are doing something for the students, you try new things ... and it doesn't mean that one-hundred percent are going to work out, but no one is going to finger point and no one is going to say, hey, it's your fault this is not working. (Teacher)

At other times, principals specifically talked about "building rapport with parents." While teachers did not directly use the same terminology, it was surmised that, holistically, "building community" encompasses the same notion for both principals and teachers. Building community was seen as a process necessitated within the entire learning community, in and out of the school. An essential element to building community requires knowing the community. Participants strongly recommended not only knowing the languages of the community but the cultures: "Learning about other cultures so that you are able to understand them when they come here. Being open to different cultures" (Teachers). Effectively working with various cultures entails affirming all cultures and valuing the wealth of human assets they bring. Yet all participants agreed educators must start by becoming cognizant of their own socialization and identity development to realize how they belong in various overlapping groups according to gender, race, ethnicity, age, and other forms of human attributes that constitute human diversity. They must also comprehend how such identity and in-group membership molds their perceptions of out-groups and/or persons unlike themselves.

It was quickly realized that many subthemes were common to both principals and teachers. Both agreed that the skills and knowledge needed to create a culture of mutual caring, respect, and inclusiveness must also be taught formally. Educators must have knowledge of developmental psychology and various humanistic philosophies, including motivational theories. Furthermore, teachers and principals focused heavily on communication and agreed that it is an absolute necessity that must be taught formally. They stated that many educators do not know how to communicate effectively with each other or with parents and community members. As a result, much meaning is lost, often leading to distancing between the parties. Some participants stated that they had taken formal communication courses and/or workshops when they realized that communication goes well beyond mere talking, listening, reading and writing; it must include deep affective listening and critical comprehension. Educators must be able to "hear" and comprehend more than what is actually stated verbally or written. They need the "skills of listening and really hearing what somebody is saying and communicating back" (Principal). Educators must be able to "read" the hidden emotions and motives of those they communicate with in their daily work. Often, effective communication requires more listening and little talking on the part of teachers and principals. "I use that [listening] all the time, whether it is with kids or with parents. It's also something that can be taught—it's really one of the language arts, one of the arts of listening that can be taught to the kids. There again, I think you have to know how to do it in order to teach it" (Teacher).

It was agreed that programs must further prepare educators for effective communication across diverse audiences and settings. The researchers called this multidirectional/multifaceted communication. A principal described it as, "communication that is across the board, vertical and horizontal, across grade levels, from the school to the parents, from the administration to the teachers; it just goes in every direction and it is very available to all." Communication includes the ability to work collaboratively. Preservice programs still prepare teachers to function as individuals encapsulated within their own classrooms. That causes teachers to be unprepared for collaborative teamwork and pits teachers against teachers, and teachers and principals against each other to work for what benefits oneself instead of a broader community. New teachers entering the schools often shy away from sharing fresh knowledge and take years to develop the needed presentation skills. In today's environment of decreasing funding, resources, and support services, educators cannot afford to work within exclusive psychological barriers. Budgetary deficits were alleviated through collective human capital and entrepreneurship. Pulling individual skills and resources, they were able to put together successful grant proposals in a week or less. Along with this, educators coming out of preparation programs with fresh ideas, skills, and knowledge, must be ready to provide a boost of energy and invigorate the schools. Every member of the learning partnership must have the skills to share their own human capital. In addition, the organization must develop team-building leadership to help identify, develop, and bring the human capital of all players into the pool. "I think it's very important. Teachers can't be afraid that if they have something that works in the classroom that it should be passed on and shared between them and not kept to themselves" (Principal). The organization in these schools was not around power hierarchy, but around skills and knowledge, and sharing what they knew. Teachers and principals must become strongly networked within their schools, communities, external businesses and organizations, their district, and other state and national agencies. Although existing within organizational bureaucracies, schools must develop internal control to act more like networks that promote fluidity and initiative, and connect them to experts in other high-performing professional learning communities.

Teachers need to be able to identify their own and each others' expertise. They must pool their individual skills and knowledge to support one another in the classroom. They must not hesitate to volunteer their leadership in areas of expertise as needed; as participants stated, to "roll up their sleeves and do whatever needs to be done" (Teacher). It should not be uncommon for new teachers to mentor veteran teachers in emergent theories and skills. Veteran teachers can help new teachers hone skills usually improved over time. Rather than the current system, wherein many veteran teachers resent, devalue, and undermine new teachers, and new teachers fear their veteran colleagues, a paradigm must be created where everyone recognizes the benefits of fresh ideas and pulling all resources together. Teachers must be comfortable observing each other's practices and giving constructive feedback. Everyone in the learning partnership holds a piece of the puzzle—a piece of the total skill and knowledge pool, which coherently empowers the organization: "How to co-teach with another teacher; how do you do this? How do you take your knowledge if you are better in one subject than in another; how do you back each other up and do that?" (Teacher).

In order for this sharing and collaboration to occur, an educator must be a communicator: "You have to know how to work with a group of people, how to express yourself, how to listen to somebody else, how to exchange ideas without getting overheated because you're not saying what I'm saying. You need communication skills, how to work in a group, how to do a collaborative group with other people, because this is how these things happen" (Teacher).

Another teacher added,"You have to be flexible. You need to listen to what the other ones were saying and if you don't agree with that, be able to see what is the reason you are not agreeing with that, and maybe engaging to what they are saying." Communication must also include highly developed speaking, writing, and presentation skills to share ideas with parents, colleagues, and businesses as well as market the school. Teachers must be excellent writers. "I'd say that college education these days—maybe some of the preparatory college courses don't teach new teachers how to write. There's a lot of emphasis right now on writing instruction throughout the K–12 system; there's going to be more . . . if you're going to teach writing, you have to know how to write" (Teacher). Within a business orientation context, educators must become adept at canvassing a target audience that is constantly on the move with umpteen personal and career demands, to create relevant presentations and announcements (newsletters, brochures, posters, etc.) that are "catchy"—that quickly attract attention and bring essential information to the forefront, etc. These are skills taught in business marketing programs, but not in teacher preparation programs.

Content knowledge was deemed extremely essential, but beyond that, educators must also learn how to make their subjects relevant to students' lives. Content knowledge must include "More of a life-skills preparation—technical application. Teaching college kids how to present curriculum in a way that makes whatever they are teaching . . . something the students are going to use the rest of their lives. Why is it important to learn this? Learning must prepare students for success in the real world" (Teacher). Another teacher adds, "Real world . . . applying real-world skills to the classroom, so the children make a connection between what they are learning . . . not just an abstract, not just to give them an open book; but what application am I going to have once I learn this? And I think we are seeing more and more that the outside world is requiring that of schools." To do this, teachers and principals must be very knowledgeable and well-versed in public affairs outside of their classrooms and schools, within their communities, state, nation, and world. They must understand the historical and current sociopolitical realities of their students and families; if they are from immigrant families, which countries they come from, what the sociopolitical realities in their countries of origin are, reasons for migration, etc. This study made it apparent that what strongly impacted effectiveness at these schools was a seamless system in which role definitions were not discrete. Teachers and principals saw common tasks, skills, and knowledge combined within their organization's readiness and willingness to step across defined role boundaries as contributing to its success. Teachers and principals called this "multitasking with the ability to wear multiple hats and play different roles. You are not only in front of the classroom with children teaching on the board. Your presence may be required elsewhere to do a different kind of task."

Conclusion

This follow-up study suggests reform of teacher and principal preparation programs at a time when these programs are under increased local and national scrutiny and condemnation for failure to adequately prepare educators for the job realities they face today, particularly with student populations that are underperforming. It is becoming apparent that principal and teacher preparation programs must be charged "from the ground up" through the realities of those in the trenches; away from traditional theoretical role definitions and better connections to the actual tasks performed in these schools as well as the skills and knowledge that enable them to be successful. Both teacher and principal interns express concern that they are not being properly prepared to work in such schools and with such students. When the research on these seven schools is presented in our own teacher and principal preparation courses, students first do not believe that such schools exist. Then they ask with dismay why, if these schools seem to hold answers, are they kept so hidden? Why isn't everyone, including the media, exhorting their accomplishments? Why aren't preparation programs teaching what these schools have come to know? They also want to know how these schools accomplished such achievements in today's standards-based accountability environment, saddled with increasing external mandates and sanctions.

Present studies and preparation programs are not making clear connections to the tasks, skills, and knowledge that teachers and principals at these particular schools report as essential to their success. Before examining preparation programs and making recommendations, researchers must talk to teachers and principals to find out what they in fact "do" and "need" to be successful. Many current studies appear to be theoretically based instead of actually linked to the practices of educators (making a difference). The theory seems to drive practice with a tendency to apply theory to practice and/or justify practice according to established theory. As a result, teachers and principals often describe their preparation programs as "jumping through (theoretical) hoops," disconnected from the real work they will be required to do once they are on the job. Teachers and principals often state that once they complete the preparation program, they must unlearn some of what was learned because it does not apply to their work realities, and must in fact, learn the real work they are going to do. Most of the learning in preparation for the real demands at their schools happens on-site, on-the-job, through self-directed learning, trial and error, and from each other.

Clearly, as we move the research and instructional paradigm from what teachers and principals should be doing to what teachers and principals are actually doing, we need to rethink schools; in fact, reinvent schools. Research needs to be "bottom-up" rather than "top-down"; "internal" rather than "external" to the schools. Of particular interest must be theories and practices in use at effective, high-performing schools with students who have been historically and persistently low achieving. While it is accurately debated that practice alone should not drive theory and vice versa, it must be accepted that theory and practice are inseparable and must hold a mutually dynamic, constantly evolving relationship. It cannot be denied that practices long discredited by sound theory such as top-down, hierarchical leadership, and lack of involvement of parents and the community in shared decision making are still very prevalent in far too many schools. Equally alarming, many unsound theories are still guiding pedagogy, while sound, often emergent, theories such as building collaborative learning communities continue to be ignored. Preparation programs and schools need to work in seamless collaboration, yet led by the voices of those who are in fact successfully engaged in current practice.

Implications for reform further suggest that both teacher and principal preparation programs need to assist educators in school/organization development with the appropriate acquisition of knowledge and skills to support such competencies as advertising and marketing, prospecting and fundraising, including grant writing, community development, shared leadership, mentoring, entrepreneurship, finely honed interpersonal and communication skills, and the ability to successfully work on various fluid teams. It must be recognized that not every member of an organization has or can acquire all the skills and competencies necessary for success. It must be equally recognized that the success of an organization does not hinge on one or a few persons but on collaborative teamwork. This truth runs counter to the continuing practice of preparing teachers to work alone and in isolation from each other. Members of the learning community within schools hold varying identified expertise that must be pooled together and enlisted on an as-needed basis.

Questions raised and suggestions made frequently through current research appear to be around the theoretical construct of teacher and principal roles instead of actual tasks that are comprised in the real day-to-day work of educators. When students in teacher and principal preparation programs are asked to describe the role of principals and teachers, then asked to compare that with what teachers and principals actually do, they see a disconnect between theoretical role definitions and actual work requirements. Principals often share concerns about being told by their supervisors that their jobs are "on the line" regarding increasing student achievement at their schools, particularly, and because of mandated standardized test scores to assess school effectiveness. What is alarming about this trend is that principals are told that they are ultimately the only person accountable for raising student achievement, even when the research makes it clear that it takes a whole school and community to make a difference. At a time when effective schools have come to the realization that leadership roles and accountability must be shared with everyone in the school community, teachers are not prepared for these leadership roles.

Teacher and principal preparation programs continue to operate separately from each other when there is a need for some coursework to be taught jointly. Although principals are taught—theoretically—to be collaborative leaders, they are socialized within the profession to be top-down managers, overseers whose role "keeps teachers in line" and "holds their feet to the fire." According to a *power over* paradigm, principals must control what goes on in their school rather than work to build the human capital, or assets, (cultural, linguistic, intellectual, social, etc.) that promote a *power with* and *power through* culture of shared ideas and mutually agreed-upon values (Acker-Hocevar et al., 2005/2006; Snyder et al., 2000; Wilson et al., 2005/2006).

Thus, the crucial question coming from both preservice and practicing teachers and principals is why are preparation programs not keeping up with the changing realities of today's schools and empowering educators for the schools that are here today (or are becoming), rather than the schools of the past or those that exist someplace else? Instead of preparing teachers and principals with a one-size-fits-all model based on mainstream White/Caucasian middle-class norms, preparation programs need to shift gears to acknowledge the need for different models. Research must ground theory and practice on these new models. The crux of education today is the urgency to think outside the box; allowing for new, even unknown, models to emerge. Educator preparation programs must unstrap their thinking and allow voices from the classroom to guide them. One such model must prepare teachers and principals—specifically—to work in seamless collaboration within urban schools that often serve students from low SES backgrounds, students of color, and students who are ELLs.

Pressing education within an industrial model of standardized assembly lines has outlived its time. Each school community is unique and must adopt, adapt, and/or develop effective strategies and models that meet its own needs. We must move away from preparing teachers and principals apart from each other, within isolated assembly lines, with separate sets of skills and perceptions of schools and each other. This paradigm has resulted in a disconnection between teachers and principals: teachers who are much too fearful of principals and do not see them as their instructional leaders and partners; principals who are conditioned to be "the boss" and "shape" teachers into compliance with external mandates and their wishes. We end up with principals who have been "promoted" out, up, and away from classrooms. We end up with principals who have not been able to keep up with instructional innovations, especially emergent theories. Too often new teachers are met with resistance from fellow teachers and even principals, then forced to do things "our way."

Reforms entail moving away from perceptions of principals as "keepers" (managers) of schools and controllers of the decision makers, while representing teachers as obedient "receivers" and "doers" of orders. Teachers must be prepared as decision makers and leaders within "true" learning communities. It must be acknowledged that leadership and accountability are not separate but inextricably intertwined; not mandated externally, but grown within the culture of the school where relationships are forged, not to meet externally imposed criteria and controls, but merely because these relationships benefit everyone within the school.

To add to the disconnect, on each line of the factory model, individuals work on their part of a product to be assembled much later without a clear vision of what the end product, as a whole, looks like or how it operates; without seeing the other lines' processes; without making many connections with other parties as they proceed; without understanding how each step contributes to the end product; and/or without comprehending how operation of the final product is influenced by each particular part and step along the way. Teachers must have a clearer understanding of what the school, as a unitary system, looks like or how it functions. Teachers and principals must be prepared to see and understand how each part influences the whole; to be fluid and move back and forth, up and down, and in every direction with ease and as needed. This is crucial for low-achieving schools with similar demographics and settings, where teacher and principal turnover tends to be high. Such schools need teachers and principals who come in with a developed understanding of how schools represent human systems and how all members must overlap and hold each other together and accountable. Such schools need teachers and principals accustomed to learning and working in unison—to talk to each other in open and collegial ways, problem solve, share ideas and resources, step in and out of each other's spheres, etc.—who fully understand what it means to be on the same team. The smooth flow and operation of everyone to move together and respond to things quickly was immediately apparent. From the moment we set foot in the schools, we were met with secretaries, teachers, custodians, parents, etc., who clearly knew who other members were, how they functioned, how they connected to each other, and were often able to step in and out of each other's roles.

We need to stop offering courses á la carte, with little articulation and/ or coherence among each other. We must halt the increasing numbers of persons stepping into teaching and the principalship through perfunctory "quick-fix" alternate certification programs, and those entering the principalship with less and less, and even worse, no classroom experience. We must prepare teachers and principals through models that allow them to see the theory-in-practice in successful schools as they learn rather than through completion of a brief clinical experience—student teaching or principal internship—toward their program completion. They must see how all skills and knowledge in their preparation programs are connected and cumulative. Rather than placed across various disconnected settings, far too often to learn "what not to do" in their own classrooms and schools, they need to learn within authentic learning communities that have demonstrated their effectiveness. Furthermore, we must prepare teachers and principals to use their classrooms and schools as learning laboratories to reflect upon and improve their practices. This must be done in connection with ongoing learning of instructional innovations and emergent theories. Teachers and principals must become true models of lifelong learning, to welcome new skills and knowledge to be quickly shared and implemented.

It is often the invisible, unquantifiable, and ungeneralizable variables that are most overlooked by the current standards-based accountability models. It must be understood that skills and knowledge alone will not sustain high performance in these or similar schools without acknowledging that the driving force is the shared, enabling core values within the organization. Preparation programs need a clearer understanding of how to help schools develop strong core values. We simply do not understand how to do that. Andy Hargreaves called for a shifting of the present focus on standards-based accountability models to a better understanding of the developmental processes and pathways for creating authentic learning communities at the International Conference of School Effectiveness and Improvement (ICSEI). Preparation programs need to move away from the technical and mechanical aspects of standards-based accountability and more toward processes that assist schools in developing their core values as the nexus to learning.

In these times of global compression, bringing forth greater awareness of escalating national and international human diversity and changing social demands requires increased local freedom and flexibility. Beyond our national boundaries, members of the international community are investigating similar issues and concerns in preparing teachers and principals for historically low-performing schools. The conversation in other parts of the world has begun to shift toward examining internal school cultures with the recognition that "one size" does not fit all; what works in one school may not be applied to another school *carte blanche*. Significantly, it requires that the international community come together to share, rather than reinvent, ideas. In the words of scholars like Hargreaves, there is an urgent need for "deep change" in school leaders' and teachers' work cultures.

Questions for Discussion

1. What can we learn from how these teachers saw their classrooms as learning laboratories?
2. Do you agree or disagree that educators should know how to market their schools and seek additional resources?
3. Why do you think that teamwork and team-building skills are so important in today's schools?
4. As you think about your preparation for either teaching and/or leadership, what were you prepared to do well? What challenges did you face?
5. Why is technology competence so important today in schools?

Note

1. This chapter was adapted from Acker-Hocevar & Cruz-Janzen (2007).

EPILOGUE

Too Many Eggs in the FCAT Basket

The state of Florida has unwittingly placed too many of its "school accountability eggs" in the FCAT basket. The grades that schools receive annually as part of the state accountability system are largely determined by how students perform on the FCAT in select grades within the school. In fact, at the elementary level, the FCAT scores are the sole factors considered in the grade that schools receive on their report cards from the state. As confirmed so succinctly by one of the senators from the largest school districts in the state "who has been a vocal critic of the FCAT," it appears, "We [the state of Florida] have handed public education over to the testing companies'" (McGrory & Teproff, 2010). Circumstances in the 2009–2010 academic year provide examples of the consequence of what can happen when a state indeed turns over its public education to a testing company. During that academic year, Florida found itself in quite a quandary when the company (NCS Pearson) it contracted for scoring the assessments informed them that the reporting of that year's FCAT assessment data would be delayed due to "computer glitches that mismatched test results with each child's demographic information" (Florida earns, 2010). In

Leadership from the Ground Up, pages 239–243
Copyright © 2012 by Information Age Publishing
All rights of reproduction in any form reserved.

one local newspaper, it was reported that "Company president Doug Kubach told the State Board of Education on June 15 that he 'deeply regrets' the holdup. He said the results would be accurate and valid when they are released. The company has also promised to reimburse school districts for any expenses incurred as a result of the late release" (Travis, 2010). The delay in reporting FCAT results had a devastating and "domino effect" on the FDOE, school administrators, and teachers, and ultimately, parents and students. For example, school grades calculated by the FDOE could not be done without FCAT scores. As a result, "the federal school choice program, which allows parents to pull their children out of schools that fail to meet 'Adequate Yearly Progress' for three years in a row," was in limbo (Travis, 2010). According to Travis, "Districts say the delays make it hard for districts to comply with state and federal law. State law requires parents be given two weeks to select their first-choice school, and then two weeks to make a final decision once the district assigns them. Federal law prohibits parents from being notified of their assignments after the school year begins, although the state is asking for an exemption." (p. 12B).

The deputy superintendent from the second-largest school district in the state had this to say about what the delay meant for their district: "We had this great plan until we were told the test scores were coming in later...We may be balancing more than we ever had because of the lateness." Additionally, "school officials say they may have to shuffle student schedules on into the school year" (Travis, 2010). The delay in receiving the scores would also have an economic impact as school districts expected to "have to pay hundreds of assistant principals, guidance counselors, and office workers to come in over the summer and revamp student schedules." Estimated costs to the two largest districts in the state were $2.3 million and $1.8 million (Sampson & McGrory, 2010). Such costs were expected to be reimbursed by the testing company.

In addition to the effect on school districts, individual schools also found themselves in a decision-making "holding pattern" about scheduling and staffing until they were informed about the FCAT test results, without which,

> Schools say they don't know how many intensive reading or math classes to offer. If the scores are worse than expected, they might need to cut electives and add more academic classes. If the scores are surprisingly good, they may end up with more reading teachers than they need...You can take educated guesses, but every year you'll have those that do extremely well, and then you have those that you counted on to do well, but for whatever reason didn't. (Travis, 2010, p. 12B)

Since some Florida schools use FCAT data to determine whether electives such as music, art, and physical education will be offered, teacher jobs were affected. Many left their positions at the close of the 2009–2010 academic year not sure if they would have their same jobs the next year or not knowing if they would be in the same schools. This is because some administrators cut out elective offerings when FCAT scores do not meet certain predetermined minimum requirements. Additional consequences for teachers and principals often include being moved out of schools based in part on students' poor FCAT performances. Furthermore, decisions affecting schools also include the fact that "schools with top or improved grades can earn extra money from the state, while those with poor or failing marks can face state-dictated improvement plans" (Postal, 2010).

Finally, parents and students were affected by the delayed FCAT reports as school districts could not offer options about school choice to parents until progress reports from the FDOE came out. When parents called schools looking for answers; they were told things were on hold until the schools got the FCAT results. "'It's crazy, and unfortunately, there's not much we can do. Our hands are tied,' said one principal" (Travis, 2010, p. 12B). Regarding students, delayed FCAT scores could result in students being "misidentified as needing remedial help when they don't or getting passed along when they do need help" (Florida earns, 2010). Further, state law requires that FCAT scores be used as a factor in determining if third graders get promoted, and some school districts use the scores in their decisions regarding promotion for students to the fourth and fifth grades as well.

Following the public exposure of the delay, newspaper articles decried the predicament the state was in because of its reliance on FCAT scores for so many of its most important educational decisions. The following are headlines from the local papers: "FCAT Delay Creates Chaos" (Travis, 2010); "State Postpones School Grades Until 2 FCAT Audits Are Done" (McGrory, 2010); "Florida Earns F For Accountability" (2010); and "Superintendents Blast FCAT Audits" (Postal, 2010).

It cannot go without saying that the saga did not end, even when the scores were finally available from the testing company. There was not much faith and trust in the accuracy of the scores. In fact, after a preliminary review of the data, superintendents from five of the largest school districts in the state, which are also some of the largest school districts in the country, questioned their accuracy. The superintendent of one school district stated, "After a preliminary analysis, we detected some statistical anomalies . . . particularly in the highest-achieving elementary schools that were disturbing enough for us to demand some answers" (McGrory & Teproff, 2010, pp. 1A, 2A). Another superintendent said, "Something is clearly amiss here that we don't understand. We are pleading with the commissioner to help us make sense of this" (p. 2A). Clearly, the superintendents believed there were "widespread irregularities." Notably, more than half (36 of 67) of the school districts in the state expressed concerns with the scores (McGrory, 2010). The source of the superintendents' concerns were with the learning gains, which express the amount of improvement an individual student makes from one academic year to the next. The accuracy of measuring learning gains is significant, because these account for 50% of a school's letter grade and are factors in determining if schools make adequate yearly progress (Florida earns, 2010). In three of the largest school districts in the state, the reported 2009–2010 FCAT results revealed an average decline in learning gains of 69% of elementary schools. "Statistics expect a 20 percent swing in any given year on test scores, but the percentage of this year's declines is simply alarming. 'It was quite a shock when we started analyzing the numbers,' said the individual who is in charge of testing for the largest school district in the state" (Florida earns, 2010; McGrory & Teproff, 2010). The deputy superintendent in the second largest school district put it this way, "There are obvious concerns." Even the governor of the state was compelled to comment and expressed concerns that "the anomalies" were "unbelievable." The governor supported the superintendents' call for an audit of the scores before they were released to the public (McGrory & Teproff, 2010).

Though the commissioner of education stated, "The department remains confident in the accuracy and reliability of this year's [2009–2010] FCAT results" (McGrory, 2010), he agreed to conduct a review of the scores. This would of course result in yet another delay in the release of the scores! Nevertheless, two private firms were hired by the state to conduct the audit. "The state hired two companies—at a potential cost of more than $37,000—to audit the FCAT" (Postal & Johnson, 2010). Both companies concluded that the results were accurate. The report stated, "While there might be room for improvements in coming years, 'parents and teachers should have no concern [beyond the usual] about using and interpreting these FCAT results'" (Postal & Johnson, 2010). Finally, all the FCAT results could be released to the public.

Unfortunately, the saga does not end there, as all still was not well. While the commissioner of education expressed "complete faith" in the scores, the superintendents were not persuaded. So strong was their doubt, that they composed a "strongly worded" letter to the commissioner. "We all need to have confidence in an assessment system that has so many consequences and at this point 'WE DO NOT,' the Florida Association of District School Superintendents wrote" (Postal, 2010). The superintendent's association said it was "deeply concerned about this year's FCAT results and did not think the Florida Department of Education's 'hastily prepared analyses' adequately addressed their concerns" (Postal, 2010).

These events in Florida did not escape national attention as Robert Schaffer of the National Center for Fair and Open Testing, a nonprofit that works to expose the flaws of standardized testing, raised questions about the results: "'The [FDOE] commissioner is asking school leaders and the public to accept on faith that this company which has screwed up so much in the past got it right this time,' said Schaeffer. 'How do we know? Where's the outside check and balances? Where's the accountability?'" (Teproff, McGrory, & Sampson, 2010). Apparently, the accountability is all in the FCAT basket; therefore, the FDOE has to believe in the FCAT scores as reported by the testing company. In conclusion, the FDOE, numerous school administrators, and educators throughout the state have permitted the FCAT to drive their educational decision making, putting all their accountability eggs in one basket—the FCAT basket. However, this was not the case concerning the schools that we feature in this book. The featured administrators, educators, and parents made conscious decisions that they would not focus on the FCAT; they would not teach to the FCAT. So while there was chaos and panic throughout the state and school districts in the 2009–2010 academic year, there were at least seven schools in the state that were not so affected. These schools likely took some solace in the knowledge that they had not been driven in their educational decision making by the FCAT. Rather, they had relied upon the human capital that came from the educators, parents, and community that make up their schools. Alas, they would be rewarded; for these seven schools sustained their high performance yet another year. Each of them achieved a letter grade of "A" in the tumultuous 2009–2010 academic year!

Florida Schools' Practices Interview Instrument

Accountability

Equity

1. How do you ensure that all students have equal access to the knowledge and skills they need?
2. How have you shown continual growth toward higher standards of learning for all students?
3. How do you demonstrate a commitment to cultural sensitivity?
4. How do you socialize new personnel, parents, and students to the school?
5. How do you ensure that school improvement teams are demographically represented?
6. How do you involve parents and teachers in the decision-making process?

Assessment and Evaluation

7a. What type of assessments do you administer other than those that are mandated?

7b. Are teachers involved in the development of any assessments (school classroom)?

8. How do you ensure that assessments measure higher-order thinking? To what extent are these assessment tools research based?

9. What is the policy regarding administering the FCAT to ESE and ESOL students (district, school)? How do you accommodate ESE and ESOL students with regard to the FCAT testing (school, classroom)?

Monitoring

10. To what extent is there consistent curriculum across schools, grades, and academic subjects?

11. What systems are in place for the monitoring of student performance?

12. How do you assist parents in the monitoring of student performance?

13. What do you do to hold personnel accountable for achievement goals and objectives? (district, school)

    How are you held accountable for achievement goals and objectives? (classroom)

14. Which key stakeholders are involved in the development of a district behavior management plan? (district, school) How?

    To your knowledge, who are the key stakeholders involved in the development of a district behavior management plan? (classroom)

15. How do you involve key stakeholders in the development of school behavior management plan? (district, school)

    To your knowledge, who are the key stakeholders involved in the development of the school's behavior management plan? (classroom)

16. Which personnel are involved in leadership and how?

17. How would you describe your leadership? (district, school)

    How would you describe the school leadership? (classroom)

Resources

Budgetary

18. How are budget and decision making linked to academic goals and student achievement? To instructional planning and professional improvement plans (school)?
19. To what extent are principals, teachers, and parents involved in budget-making decisions?
20. Where and how are budget decisions made?
21. How is budget decision making related to student diversity and special needs?
22. What are other sources of funding beyond the state allocation?
23. How are these external sources of funding identified and allocated?

Support

24. How is the budget linked to professional development and improvement?
25. How are areas of professional development and improvement identified?
26. What professional development improvement activities do you engage in beyond what is provided at the local level (e.g., school and district professional development provided)?
27. How is the budget linked to recognition of students, personnel, and programs?
28. How are areas of recognition identified?
29. How are FCAT merit monies (A+) dispersed?
30. How are community resources identified and allocated?
31. In what ways does the budget reflect allocation for student interventions, including enrichment and remediation?
32. How does the system provide time to fulfill your professional responsibilities? (district, school)

    How does the school administration provide time to fulfill your professional responsibilities? (classroom)

Technology

33. How are technology needs identified? How are technology needs linked to academic goals and objectives?
34. How is the budget linked to technology needs?

Information Management

Access

35. Describe the information systems you have in place to access data?
36. What types of data do you have access to for strategic planning purposes?
37. Who has access to the school improvement plans (i.e., parents, faculty, district personnel)?
38. How is this access achieved?
39. Who has access to student assessment data?
40. How are assessment data used?

Use

41. Generally, what types of decisions do you make using data collected?
42. What additional data have you found you need?
43. How have you gotten these data?
44. How do you use data to make evaluations (e.g., student, teacher, and administrator performance)? To determine goal attainment?
45. What types of evaluations are made?

Personnel

Selection

46. What is the process in place to hire personnel at all levels and to match them to particular sites (e.g., principal, teachers, staff)?
47. How is the selection and placement of personnel linked to students' needs?
48. What characteristics make an educator successful in this district? (district)

    What characteristics make an educator successful in this school? (school, classroom)
49. How much autonomy do principals have in the hiring process?
50. How do you work with the union contract?

Recruitment and Retention

51. What is the process in place for recruitment at all levels (e.g., principal, teacher, and staff)?

52. What is the process for mentoring at all levels (e.g., principal, teacher, and staff)?
53. How do you minimize personnel turnover?

Professional Development

54. What standard professional development opportunities are provided at the district and school levels for such things as
    - Developing new and veteran leaders
    - Teaming at grade levels and across grade and subject areas
    - Curriculum articulation
    - Classroom management
    - Behavior management
    - Student achievement?
55. How is professional development tailored to meet specific needs?
56. What types of training does the school improvement team receive, if any?
57. What, if any, professional development has made a difference?
58. What else would you like to share about professional development?

Instruction

Coherence

59. How do principals, teachers, and parents participate in the development of a district mission and strategic plan?
60. How do you ensure familiarity and understanding of the district mission and strategic plan? (district)

    What efforts are made to ensure familiarity and understanding of the district mission and strategic plan? (school, classroom)

61. How do you ensure the district mission and strategic plan are aligned? (district)

    What efforts are made to assure the district mission and strategic plan are aligned? (schoo, classroom)

62. How do you assess progress toward meeting the district mission and strategic plan? (district)

    What efforts are made to assess progress toward meeting the district mission and strategic plan? (school, classroom)

    Is there a link between district goals and the school improvement plan? (school, classroom)

63. How do principals, teachers, and parents participate in the development of a school mission and school improvement plan?

64. How do you ensure familiarity of the school mission and the school improvement plan? (district, school)

    How is familiarity with the school mission and the school improvement plan ensured? (classroom)

65. How do you ensure that the school mission and school improvement plan are aligned? (district, school)

    What efforts are made to ensure that the school mission and school improvement plan are aligned? (classroom)

66. How do you assess progress toward meeting the school mission and school improvement plan? (district, school)

    What efforts are made to assess progress toward meeting the school mission and school improvement plan? (classroom)

67. How is the (district and/or school) curriculum established?

68. How is the curriculum connected to a sequenced learning plan for all students?

69a. How do you ensure that the curriculum extends beyond required FCAT academic goals and objectives?

69b. How are FCAT-based documents used to form the basis for what students are to learn?

69c. Is there a link between goals and objectives and student learning?

70. How are instructional materials and methods established?

71. On what basis do you determine instructional groupings? Are groupings flexible?

72. Who is involved in making these instructional decisions?

73. What role does research play in making instructional decisions?

74. If articulation exists across grade levels, subject areas, and feeder schools, how does it function?

75. How are student-learning objectives established? How is student learning linked to Sunshine State Standards?

76. What systems are in place to support the ongoing assessment of programs?

77. How is a classroom-management plan developed and administered?

78. How is instruction adjusted according to student needs?
    - Students performing at and above expectations
    - Students performing below expectations.

79. How is relevance of the curriculum for the learner assessed?

80. Which, if any, math and/or reading instructional programs, or specific practices, have contributed to your success?
81. Are there other factors that you feel have contributed to your success?

Florida Schools' Practices Parent Interview Instrument

Accountability

Equity

1. How are new parents, teachers, and students socialized to the school?
2. How is the school improvement team demographically representative?
3. How are parents and teachers involved in the decision-making process?

Assessment

4. What are some of the ways students' progress is assessed?

Monitoring

5. To what extent is there consistent curriculum across schools, grades, and academic subjects?

Leadership from the Ground Up, pages 253–254
253

6. How are parents assisted in monitoring student performance?
7. To your knowledge, who is involved in the development of the school's behavior management plan?

Resources

Budgetary

8. How is budget decision making linked to academic goals and student achievement?
9. To what extent are principals, teachers, and parents involved in budget decision making?

Support

10. If your school has been given FCAT merit monies, how has it been dispersed?
11. How are community resources identified and allocated?

Information Management

Access

12. Who has access to the school improvement plan?
13. How is this access achieved?

Personnel

Selection

14. To your knowledge, how are principals and teachers selected for a school?
15. What characteristics make an educator successful in this school?

Recruitment and Retention

16. How is personnel turnover at this school minimized?

About the Authors

Michele A. Acker-Hocevar is associate professor at Washington State University in the Educational Leadership and Counseling Psychology Department. She was recently named the co-editor of the *Journal of Research in Leadership Education*. Her interdisciplinary background and PhD in organization studies and administrative experience emphasize the importance of individual (personal) and school (organization) development. She views behavioral and organizational constructs of power, culture, and change as interdependent and mutually reinforcing paradigms that potentially influence individual behavior and choices of educators within an organization. She is a scholar of how organizational development within schools as living, dynamic, and adaptive systems requires educators to choose to do the right things for students and their communities, while simultaneously addressing and meeting increasing federal and state accountability demands and mandates that require compliance. These two areas of development and compliance are not mutually exclusive. Dr. Acker-Hocevar teaches in the master's and certification programs for school leadership and the statewide doctoral program of the Educational Leadership Program. She applies her background and expertise in courses such as leadership studies, instructional leadership, and leadership behavior.

Marta I. Cruz-Janzen is a professor at Florida Atlantic University (FAU) in the Department of Teaching and Learning. She has over 30 years experience in the field of education, from elementary school through postsecondary education. She also has an extensive background in private industry. Her background encompasses elementary bilingual/ESOL classroom teaching in New York City and Denver, bilingual/ESOL curriculum and

Leadership from the Ground Up, pages 255–256
255

staff development, race and gender equity technical support to urban and rural school districts with the Colorado Department of Education, elementary principalship, and teacher preparation with the Department of Secondary Education of Metropolitan State College of Denver. Currently, Dr. Cruz-Janzen teaches Developmental and Educational Psychology, TESOL/ESOL, and multicultural education classes at FAU. Throughout her career, Dr. Cruz-Janzen has also been involved with gender equity and women's studies. Her research centers on (a) the role of teachers, schools, and society on schools' curricula and subsequent impact on student achievement, particularly low-SES students, students of color, and ELL students; (b) educational policy and reform: teacher and principal preparation programs; (c) effective/high-performing schools with high populations of low-SES students, students of color, and ELL students; and (d) multicultural education program reform.

Cynthia L. Wilson is a professor in the Department of Exceptional Student Education at Florida Atlantic University (FAU) on the Davie campus. Her professional experience includes teaching in classrooms for students with disabilities, serving as a consultant to local school districts, working in the Bureau of Education for Exceptional Students in the Florida Department of Education, and a university faculty position at the University of Miami, encompassing 30 years of experience as a special educator. Her research and instructional focus emphasizes the preparation of educators to implement research-based, effective practices to improve educational opportunities for students with disabilities and students at risk for academic failure. In her tenure at FAU, Dr. Wilson has been the department chair and the director of a teacher education project. She has also been the recipient of the FAU Award for Excellence in Undergraduate Teaching, College of Education Award for Excellence and Innovation in Undergraduate Teaching, and Research Faculty Incentive Program Award. She has significant experience in grantsmanship and has been principal/co-principal investigator and project manager of several research and teacher preparation grants.

References

Acker-Hocevar, M., & Cruz-Janzen, M. I. (2007). Teacher and principal preparation programs: Reforms that sustain high performance and learning in high poverty and diverse schools. *International Journal of Learning, 14*(10), 87–95.

Acker-Hocevar, M., Cruz-Janzen, M. I., Wilson, C. L., Schoon, P., & Walker, D. (2005/2006). The need to reestablish schools as dynamic positive human energy systems that are non-linear and self-organizing: The learning partnership tree. *International Journal of Learning, 12*(10), 255–266.

Acker-Hocevar, M., & Touchton, D. (2002). How principals level the playing field of accountability in Florida's high poverty/low-performing schools: Part I: The intersection of high-stakes testing and effects of poverty on teaching and learning. *International Journal of Educational Reform, 11*(2), 106–24.

Argyris, C. (1964). *Integrating the individual and the organization.* New York: John Wiley.

Bali, S. J., Demo, D. H., & Wedman, J. F. (1998). Family involvement with children's homework: An intervention in the middle grades. *Family Relations, 47,* 149–157.

Bandura, A. (1977). Self-efficacy: Toward a unifying theory of behavioral change. *Psychological Review, 84,* 191–215.

Bandura, A. (1982). Self-efficacy mechanism in human agency. *American Psychologist, 37,* 122–147.

Bandura, A. (1986). *Social foundations of thought and action: A social cognitive theory.* Englewood Cliffs, NJ: Prentice-Hall.

Bandura, A. (1997). *Self-efficacy: The exercise of control.* New York: Freeman.

Bandura, A. (2000). Exercise of human agency through collective efficacy. *Current Directions in Psychological Science, 9*(3), 75–78.

Leadership from the Ground Up, pages 257–265

Banks, J. A. (2001). *Cultural diversity and education: Foundations, curriculum, and teaching.* Boston: Allyn and Bacon.

Beck, L. (1994). *Reclaiming educational administration as a caring profession.* New York: Teachers College Press.

Bohn, J. G. (2002, Sept). The relationship of perceived leadership behaviors to organizational efficacy. *Journal of Leadership & Organizational Studies, 9*(2), 65–79.

Brown, M. W., & Gioia, D. A. (2002). Making things click: Distributive leadership in an online division of an offline organization. *Leadership Quarterly, 13,* 397–419.

Brown, R. J., & Cornwall, J. R. (2000). *The entrepreneurial educator.* Lanham, MD: Scarecrow Press.

Brunner, J. (1977). *The process of education.* Cambridge, MA: Harvard University Press.

Carter, S. C. (1999). *No excuses: Seven principals of low-income schools who set the standard for high achievement.* Washington, DC: Heritage Foundation.

Carter, S. C. (2000). *No excuses: Lesson from 21 high-performing, high poverty schools.* Washington, DC: Heritage Foundation.

Charles A. Dana Center, University of Texas at Austin. (1999). *Hope for urban education: A study of nine high-performing, high-poverty, urban elementary schools.* Washington, DC: U.S. Department of Education, Planning, and Evaluation Service.

Charmaz, K. (2003). Grounded theory: Objectivist and constructivist methods. In N. K. Denzin & Y. Lincoln (Eds.), *Strategies of qualitative inquiry* (pp. 249–291). Thousand Oaks, CA: Sage.

Chenoweth, K. (2007). *"It's being done:" Academic success in unexpected schools.* Cambridge, MA: Harvard Education Press.

Cochran-Smith, M. (2006). Evidence, efficacy, and effectiveness: Introduction to the double issue. *Journal of Teacher Education, 57*(1), 3–6.

Coleman, J. S. (1990). *Foundations of social theory.* Cambridge, MA: Harvard University Press.

Collins, K. M. T. (2005). Preservice teacher efficacy: Cross-national study. *Academic Exchange Journal, 9*(2), 295–300.

Coyle, L. M., & Witcher, A. E. (1992). Transforming the idea into action: Policies and practices to enhance school effectiveness. *Urban Education, 26*(4), 390–400.

Cummins, J. (1996). *Negotiating identities: Education for empowerment in a diverse society.* Ontario, CA: California Association for Bilingual Education.

Czerniak, C. M., & Haney, J. J. (1998). The effect of collaborative concept mapping on elementary preservice teachers' anxiety, efficacy and achievement in physical science. *Journal of Science Teacher Education, 9*(4), 303–320.

Darling-Hammond, L. (1995). Policy for restructuring. In A. Lieberman (Ed.), *The work of restructuring schools: Building from the ground up* (pp. 157–175). New York: Teachers College Press.

Darling-Hammond, L. (2000). Teacher quality and student achievement: A review of state policy evidence. *Education Policy Analysis Archives, 8*(1), 1–49.

Davis, S., Darling-Hammond, L., Meyerson, D., & LaPointe, M. (2005). *Review of research. School leadership study: Developing successful principals.* Palo Alto, CA: Stanford University, Stanford Educational Leadership Institute.

Day, D. V., Gronn, P., & Salas, F. (2004). Leadership capacity in teams. *Leadership Quarterly, 15,* 857–880.

Decker, L., & Decker, V. A. (2000). *Engaging families and communities: Pathways to educational success.* Fairfax, VA: National Community Education Association.

Deming, E. W. (1986). *Out of crisis.* Cambridge, MA: Institute of Technology.

Design-Based Research Collective. (2003, January-February). Theme issue: The role of design in educational research. *Educational Researcher, 32*(1).

Dunlap, D., & Goldman, P. (1991). Rethinking power in schools. *Educational Administration Quarterly, 27*(1), 5–29.

Edmonds, R. R. (1979). Some schools work and more can. *Social Policy, 9*(2), 28–32.

Elmore, R. F. (2000). *Building a new structure for school leadership.* Washington, DC: Albert Shanker Institute.

Espinoza-Herold, M. (2003). *Issues in Latino education: Race, school culture and the politics of academic success.* Boston: Allyn and Bacon.

Emmer, E. T., & Hickman, J. (1991). Teacher efficacy in classroom management and discipline. *Educational and Psychological Measurement, 51*(3), 755–766.

Florida earns F for accountability. (2010, July 15). Editorial. *The Miami Herald,* p. 20A.

Gibson, M. (1995). Additive acculturation as a strategy for school improvement. In R. Rambaut & W. Cornelius (Eds.), *California's immigrant children: Theory, research, and implications for educational policy.* La Jolla, CA: University of California, San Diego, Center for U.S./Mexican Studies.

French, J., & Raven, B. H. (1959). The bases of social power. In D. Cartwright (Ed.), *Studies of social power* (pp. 150–167). Ann Arbor, MI: Institute for Social Research.

Glaser, B., & Strauss, A. (1967). *The discovery of grounded theory: Strategies for qualitative research.* Chicago: Aldine.

Glickman, C. D. (2002). *Leadership for learning: How to help teachers succeed.* Alexandria, VA: Association for Supervision and Curriculum Development.

Glidden, H. G. (1999). Breakthrough schools: Characteristics of low-income schools that perform as though they were high-income schools. *ERS Spectrum, 17*(2), 21–26.

Goldman (1966). The school principal. *The Center for Applied Research.* Retrieved April 26, 2006, from http://www.nd.edu/~rbarger/www7/roleprin.html

Greenlees, I. A. (1999). The impact of collective efficacy beliefs on effort and persistence in a group task. *Journal of Sports Science, 17*(2), 151–158.

Greenlees, I. A., Graydon, J., & Maynard, I. (2000). The impact of individual efficacy beliefs on group goal selection and group goal commitment. *Journal of Sports Sciences, 18*(6), 451–459.

Gronn, P. (2002). Distributed leadership as a unit of analysis. *The Leadership Quarterly, 13,* 423–451.

Hacsi, T. (2002). *Children as pawns: The politics of educational reform.* Cambridge, MA: Harvard University Press.

Herman, J. J., & Herman, J. L. (1998). *Effective decision-making.* Lancaster, PA: Technomic Publishing.

Hochwarter, W. A., Kiewitz, C., Gundlach, M. J., & Stoner, J. (2004). The impact of vocational and social efficacy on job performance and career satisfaction. *Journal of Leadership & Organizational Studies, 10*(30), 27–41.

Holloway, J. H. (2003). Sustaining experienced teachers. *Educational Leadership, 60*(8), 87–89.

Isiksal, M., & Cakiroglu, E. (2005). Teacher efficacy and academic performance. *Academic Exchange Quarterly, 9*(4), 28–32.

Jones, B. (Ed.). (2000). *Educational leadership policy dimensions in the 21st century.* Stamford, CT: Ablex.

Kast, F. E., & Rosensweig, J. E. (1979). *Organizations and management: A systems and contingency approach* (3rd ed.). New York: McGraw Hill.

Kozol, J. (1992). *Savage inequalities: Children in America's schools.* New York: Harper Perennial.

Larson, C., & Olvando, C. (2001). *The color of bureaucracy: The politics of equity in multicultural school communities.* Florernce, KY: Wadsworth/Thomson Learning.

Leithwood, K., Seashore-Louis, K. S., Anderson, S., & Wahlstrom, K. (2004). *Review of research. How leadership influences student learning.* Paper commissioned by the Wallace Foundation. Minneapolis: University of Minnesota.

Leithwood, K., Mascall, B., Strauss, R., Sacks, N., Memon, N., & Yashkina, A. (2007). Distributing leadership to make schools smarter: Taking the ego out of the system. *Leadership and Policy in Schools, 6,* 37–67.

Levine, A. (2005). *Educating school leaders.* Washington, DC: The Education Schools Project.

Lockwood-Zisa, V. (2002). *Implementing, sustaining and inspiring the work of the writer's workshop in our schools.* Retrieved May 5, 2006, from http://www.noycefdn.org/literacy/documents/VLZisaHandouts11-14-02.pdf

Marks, H. M., & Printy, S. M. (2003). Principal leadership and school performance: An integration of transformational and instructional leadership. *Educational Administration Quarterly, 39*(3), 370–397.

Maslow, A. H. (1968). *Toward a psychology of being* (2nd ed.). New York: Van Nostrand.

Maslow, A. H. (1970). *Motivation and personality.* New York: Harper and Row.

May, R. (1994). *The courage to create.* New York: W. W. Norton & Company.

May, R. (1996). *Psychology and the human dilemma.* New York: W. W. Norton & Company.

McGrory, K. (2010, July 15). State postpones school grades until 2 FCAT audits are done. *SunSentinel,* p. 3B.

McGrory, K. (2010, July 20). Minnesota finds flawed test scores. *SunSentinel,* p. 4B.

McGrory, K., & Teproff, C. (2010, July 13). Delay sought on grades for schools. *The Miami Herald,* pp. 1A, 2A.

Meier, D. (1995). *The power of their ideas: Lessons for America from a small school in Harlem.* Boston, MA: Beacon Press.

Meier, D. (2002). Educating a democracy. *Boston Review, 24*(6).

Merriam, S. B. (2001). *Qualitative research and case study applications in education.* San Francisco: Jossey-Bass.

Merriam, S. B., & Caffarella, R. S. (1999). *Learning in adulthood. A comprehensive guide.* San Francisco: Jossey-Bass.

Mulholland, J., Dorman, J. P., & Odgers, B. M. (2004). Assessment of science teaching efficacy of preservice teachers in an Australian university. *Journal of Science Teacher Education, 15*(4), 313–331.

Newmann, F. M., King, M. B., & Rigdon, M. (1997). Accountability and school performance: Implications from restructuring schools. *Harvard Educational Review, 67*(1), 41–74.

Newmann, F. M., Secada, W. G., & Wehlage, G. G. (1995). *A guide to authentic instruction and assessment: Vision, standards and scoring.* Madison: Wisconsin Center for Educational Research.

Nieto, S. (2001a). *Affirming diversity* (3rd ed.). New York: Longman

Nieto, S. (2001b). *Language, culture, and teaching: Critical perspectives.* New York: Routledge.

Noddings, N. (2006). *The challenge to care in schools: An alternative approach to education* (2nd ed.). New York: Teachers College Press.

No Child Left Behind. (2001). Retrieved April 13, 2003, from http://www2.ed.gov/policy/elsec/leg/esea02/index.html

Northwest Regional Educational Laboratory. (2003). *School improvement through teacher decision-making.* Retrieved October 1, 2003, from http://www.nwrel.org/scpd/sirs/8/s030.html

Ohlhausen, M. M., Meyerson, M. J., & Sexton, P. (1992). Viewing innovations through the efficacy-based change model: A whole language application. *Journal of Reading, 35*(7), 536–542.

Parker, L. E. (1994). Working together: Perceived self- and collective-efficacy at the workplace. *Journal of Applied Psychology, 24*(1), 43–60.

Peterson, W. (1996). Filling the communication gap. *Thrust for Educational Leadership, 25,* 38–40.

Patton, M. Q. (1990). *Qualitative evaluation and research methods* (2nd ed.). Newbury Park, CA: Sage.

Porter, L. W., Bigley, G. A., & Steers, R. M. (2003). *Motivation and work behavior* (7th ed.). Boston: McGraw-Hill.

Posner, G. F. (1998). Models of curriculum planning. In L. E. Beyer, & M. W. Apple (Eds.), *The curriculum: Problems, politics, and possibilities* (pp. 79–100). New York: State University of New York Press.

Postal, L. (2010, August 6). Superintendents blast FCAT audits. *SunSentinel,* p. 1B.

Postal, L., & Johnson, A. (2010, August 5). Audits show FCAT results are accurate state says. *SunSentinel,* pp. 1A, 10A.

Prussia, G. E., Anderson, J. S., & Manz, C. C. (1998). Self-leadership and performance outcomes: The mediating influence of self-efficacy. *Journal of Organizational Behavior, 19*(5), 523–539.

Purkey, S. C., & Smith, M. S. (1993). Effective schools: A review. *Elementary School Journal, 83,* 427–452.

Reyes-Guerra, D. (2009). *The relationship between principal leadership actions and business and social justice cultures in schools.* Unpublished doctoral dissertation, Florida Atlantic University.

Roderick, M., Jacob, B. A., & Bryk, A. S. (2002). The impact of high-stakes testing in Chicago on student achievement in promotional gate grades. *Educational Evaluation and Policy Analysis, 24*(4), 333–357.

Rogers, C. (1969). *Freedom to learn: A view of what education might become.* Columbus, OH: Charles Merrill.

Rogers, C. (1977). *Carl Rogers on personal power: Inner strength and its revolutionary impact.* New York: Delacorte Press.

Rogers, C. (1980). *A way of being.* Boston: Houghton Mifflin

Sampson, H., & McGrory, K. (2010, June 25). Tardy FCAT scores ready for release. *The Miami Herald,* pp. 1A, 11A.

Sanders, W. L. & Horn, S. P. (1995). The Tennessee value-added assessment system (TVAAS): Mixed model methodology in educational assessment. In A. J. Shrinkfield & D. Stufflebeam (Eds.), *Teacher evaluation: Guide to effective practice* (pp. 337–350). Boston: Kluwer.

Sargent, B. (2003). Finding good teachers and keeping them. *Educational Leadership, 60,* 44–47.

Scheurich, J. J. (1998). Highly successful and loving public elementary schools populated mainly by low-SES children of color: Core beliefs and cultural characteristics. *Urban Education, 33*(4), 451–491.

Scheurich, J. J., & Skrla, L. (2003). *Leadership for equity and excellence: Creating high-achievement classrooms, schools, and districts.* Thousand Oaks, CA: Corwin Press.

Schwarzer, R., & Jerusalem, M. (1993). *Generalized self-efficacy scale.* Retrieved February 2, 2006, from http://userpage.fu-berlin.de/~health/engscal.htm

Scribner, J. D., Young, M. D., & Pedroza, A. (1999). Building collaborative relationships with parents. In P. Reyes, J. D. Scribner, & A. P. Scribner (Eds.),

Lessons from high-performing Hispanic schools: Creating learning communities (pp. 36–60). New York: Teachers College Press.

Senge, P. M. (1990). *The fifth discipline: The art and practice of the learning organizations.* New York: Doubleday.

Sergiovanni, T. J. (1994). *Building community in schools.* San Francisco: Jossey-Bass.

Siegel, D. (2003). *Performance-driven budgeting: The example of New York City's schools* (Report No. EDO-EA-03-05). East Lansing, MI: National Center for Research on Teacher Learning. (ERIC Document Reproduction Service No. ED474305)

Sleeter, C. (1992). *Keepers of the American dream: A study of staff development and multicultural education.* Washington, DC: Falmer Press.

Snyder, K. J., Acker-Hocevar, M., & Snyder, K. M. (2000). *Living on the edge of chaos: Leading schools into the global age.* Milwaukee, WI: ASQ Quality Press.

Snyder, K. J., Acker-Hocevar, M. & Snyder, K. M. (2008). *Living on the edge of chaos:Leading schools into the global age* (2nd ed.). Milwaukee, WI: American Society for Quality (ASQ).

Snyder, K. J., & Anderson, R. H. (1986). *Managing productive schools: Toward an ecology.* San Diego, CA: Harcourt, Brace, and Jovanovich.

Snyder, C. R., & Lopez, S. J. (2007). *Positive psychology: The scientific and practical explorations of human strengths.* Thousand Oaks, CA: Sage.

Southern Regional Education Board (SREB). (2007). *Schools need good leaders now: State progress in creating a learning-centered school leadership system.* Atlanta, GA: Author.

Spillane, J. P. (2005, Winter). Distributed leadership. *The Educational Forum, 69,* 143–150.

Spillane, J. P., Halverson, R., & Diamond, J. B. (2001). Investigating school leadership practice: A distributed perspective. *Educational Researcher, 30*(3), 23–38.

Spillane, J. P., & Seashore-Louis, K. (2002). School improvement processes and practices: Professional learning for building instructional capacity. In J. Murphy (Ed.), *The educational leadership challenge: Redefining leadership for the 21st century* (pp. 83–104). Chicago: University of Chicago Press.

Steinberg, L. D. (1996). *Beyond the classroom: Why school reform has failed and what parents need to do.* New York: Simon & Schuster.

Supovitz, J. A., & Poglinco, S. M. (2001). *Instructional leadership in a standards-based reform.* Philadelphia: University of Pennsylvania, Consortium for Policy Research in Education.

Swanson, C. B, & Stevenson, D. L. (2002). Standards-based reform in practice: Evidence on state policy and classroom instruction from the NAEP state assessments. *Educational Evaluation and Policy Analysis, 24*(1), 1–27.

Teddlie, C., & Reynolds, D. (2000). *The international handbook of school effectiveness research.* New York: Falmer.

Teproff, C., McGrory, K., & Sampson, H. (2010, June 30). Broward FCATs: "Glass half full." *The Miami Herald,* pp. 1A, 5A.

Thacker, J. L., & McInerney, W. D. (1992). Changing academic culture to improve student achievement in the elementary schools. *ERS Spectrum, 10*(4), 18–23.

Travis, M. P. (2001). Looking under the bushels: Schools still applying local solutions to national teacher recruitment problems. *Momentum, 32*(2), 43–45.

Travis, S. (2010, June 28). FCAT delay creates chaos. *SunSentinel,* pp. 1B, 12B.

Tyler, R. W. (1949). *Basic principles of curriculum and instruction.* Chicago: University of Chicago Press.

Uhl-Bien, M. (2006). Relational leadership theory: Exploring the social processes of leadership and organizing. *Leadership Quarterly, 17*(6), 654–676.

U. S. Department of Education. (2006). *The federal role of education.* Retrieved April 26, 2006, from http://www.ed.gov/about/overview/fed/role.html?src=ln

Valdés, G. (1996). *Con respeto: Bridging the distance between culturally diverse families and schools.* New York: Teachers College Press.

Valenzuela, A. (1999). *Subtractive schooling: U.S.-Mexican youth and the politics of caring.* Albany: State University of New York Press.

Valenzuela, A. & Dornbusch, M. (1994). Familism and social capital in the academic achievement of Mexican origin and Anglo adolescents. *Social Science Quarterly, 75*(1), 18–36.

Van Der Linde, C. (2000). The teacher's stress and its implications for the school as an organization: How can TQM help? *Education, 121,* 375–382.

Ward, R. (2004). *Improving achievement in low-performing schools.* Thousand Oaks, CA: Corwin Press.

Waters, T., Marzano, R. J., & McNulty, B. (2003). *Balanced leadership: What 30 years of research tells us about the effect of leadership on student achievement.* Aurora, CO: Mid-continent Research for Education and Learning. Retrieved from www.mcrel.org

Weick, K. (June, 1982). Administering education in loosely coupled schools. *Phi Delta Kappan, 63*(10), 673–675.

Weiss, I. R., Knapp, M. S., Hollwag, K., & Burrell, G. (2001). *Investigating the influence of standards: A framework for research in mathematics, science, and technology education.* Washington, DC: National Academy Press.

Wentz, P. (1998). Successful communications for school leaders. *NASSP Bulletin, 82,*112–115.

Wheatley, M. (1992). Leadership and the new science: Learning about organization from an orderly universe. San Francisco: Berrett-Koelhler.

Wiggins, G. P., & McTighe, J. (1998). *Understanding by design.* Alexandria, VA: ASCD.

Wilson, C. L., Walker, D., Cruz-Janzen, M. I., Acker-Hocevar, M., & Schoon, P. (2005/2006). A systems alignment model for examining school practices: A standards-based alignment model. *International Journal of Learning, 12*(7), 303–310.

Wilson, S. M., Darling-Hammond, L., & Berry, B. (2001). *A case of successful teaching policy: Connecticut's long-term efforts to improve teaching and learning.* Seattle, WA: University of Washington, Center for the Study of Teaching and Policy.

Yan, J. (1999). *What affects test scores?* Miami, FL: Applied Sciences and Technology.

Yukl, G., & Lepsinger, R. (1991). An integrating taxonomy of managerial behavior: Implications for improving managerial effectiveness. In J. W. Jones, B. D. Steffy, & D. W. Bray (Eds.), *Applying psychology in business: The manager's handbook* (pp. 563–572). Lexington, MA: Lexington Press.

Zellars, K. L., Hochwarter, W. A., Perrewe, P. L., Miles, A. K., & Kiewitz, C. (2001). Beyond self-efficacy: Interactive effects of role conflict and perceived collective efficacy. *Journal of Managerial Issues, 13*(4), 483–500.

Index

Leadership from the Ground Up, pages 267–274
Copyright © 2012 by Information Age Publishing
267

CPSIA information can be obtained at www.ICGtesting.com
Printed in the USA
BVOW030713220212

283524BV00002B/35/P